Counselling Skills For Dummies®

D1382464

Using a Holistic Approach

Remember that each person is a whole individual who has many different aspects and experiences. Each person has his or her unique history and social experience, and these have helped form who and where he or she is today. Use the *BEST-I BEST-R* model to remind yourself of this:

- ✔ Body
- ✔ Emotion
- ✔ Sensation
- ✔ Thinking
- ✔ Imagery
- ✔ Behaviour
- ✔ Environment
- ✔ Spirit
- ✔ Time
- ✔ Relationships

Chapter 12 and Appendix A have lots more about the *BEST-I BEST-R* model.

The Three-Stage Framework

Use the three-stage model to manage each helping encounter. Be clear about the time you have available and structure the time into three sections:

- ✔ **Stage 1: Exploration.** This stage takes at least a quarter of the time in single or early sessions of a series because it includes getting-to-know-you time and time to establish trust. Exploration may take less time later in the helping relationship.
- ✔ **Stage 2: Understanding.** This usually takes half of the time of the encounter.
- ✔ **Stage 3: Action.** Around a quarter of the time is given over to deciding what action to take after the session.

Chapters 9, 10, and 11 have more about the three stages.

Knowing Your Responsibilities

As a listening helper, you need to be clear about your role.

- ✔ If you're in an organisation, make sure you know what your company expects of you in your listening-helper role, what the limits are, and what supports are available.
- ✔ Be clear with yourself about what you can manage in terms of your time, offering support, taking action, and containing emotion, and remember the help-seeker's own responsibility for him- or herself.
- ✔ In the helping relationship, be clear with the help-seeker about what you can offer and its limits.

All these can help you avoid getting overinvolved and overwhelmed. Head to Chapter 4 for more about your responsibilities and how to deal with them.

For Dummies: Bestselling Book Series for Beginners

Counselling Skills For Dummies®

Taking Care of Yourself

When faced with a tricky situation when using counselling skills, remember to take:

- A deep breath.
- Your time. Pauses and silences are always shorter than you think.
- A different tack from questions. Questions give *you* the agenda and responsibility – try giving the agenda and responsibility back to the help-seeker.
- Note of emotion words and reflect them back with more weight.
- Note of *feelings*, *thinking*, and *behaviour* and summarise them.
- Courage to be honest (as long as it's in the help-seeker's best interest). Admit you don't know what to do, don't know what to say, feel muddled, and so on.
- Summaries seriously. Don't underestimate the usefulness of summarising. (Chapter 9 explains summarising in more detail.)
- Time to consult others and to reflect on the situation.

Remembering That We Are Responsible for Our Feelings

We are each responsible for our own feelings. People react in different ways to the same events, so our reactions are not inevitable – they are the result of our history and *tendencies*. Other people do not *make* us feel particular emotions (although they may intend or try to).

Think of a recent emotional reaction that you didn't like and reflect on it:

- If you had a different reaction, what kind of person would you be?
- If you had a different reaction (think of one or two), how would the other person react to you and then what would happen?
- Trace your original emotional reaction back to the earliest experience of it that you can remember and write about that event and ask yourself the previous two questions again.

Managing Endings

Many listening helpers struggle to end helping conversations. Try these tactics:

- Make sure you mention the time you have available at the beginning of the conversation or as soon as you can during it.
- Keep a clock in view.
- At *least* five minutes before the time runs out, mention that the session is coming to an end.
- Stop asking any open questions that invite elaboration.
- Don't open up any 'big' issues. If the help-seeker seems to be launching on a big issue anyway, be firm and say, 'I'm sorry we're out of time because that sounds important. Perhaps we can pick up on that when we next meet, when we have time to do it justice.' Bear in mind that the speaker may have raised the big issue at the last minute so that it *can't* be discussed – the speaker may want to broach the subject and gauge your reaction.

For Dummies: Bestselling Book Series for Beginners

Counselling Skills FOR DUMMIES®

by Gail Evans

BICENTENNIAL
1807
WILEY
2007
BICENTENNIAL

John Wiley & Sons, Ltd

Counselling Skills For Dummies®

Published by
John Wiley & Sons, Ltd
The Atrium
Southern Gate
Chichester
West Sussex
PO19 8SQ
England

E-mail (for orders and customer service enquires): cs-books@wiley.co.uk

Visit our Home Page on www.wiley.com

Wiley also publishes its books in a variety of electronic formats. Some content that appears in print may not be available in electronic books.

British Library Cataloguing in Publication Data: A catalogue record for this book is available from the British Library.

ISBN: 978-0-470-51190-9

Printed and bound in Great Britain by Bell and Bain Ltd, Glasgow

10 9 8 7 6 5 4 3 2 1

WILEY

About the Author

Gail Evans is Head of the Counselling Studies Unit at Sheffield Hallam University where she is course leader for the Diploma in Counselling. She is also in partnership as co-owner of a private Counselling and Therapy Centre. Gail has been involved in social work and counselling for over 30 years, working in private practice and a variety of settings. She worked for more than 20 years with Relate as a couple counsellor, sexual therapist, GP surgery counsellor, telephone counsellor, supervisor, and trainer, also representing Relate in some television and radio programmes. Gail also worked for several years with SAIL (Sexual Abuse and Incest Line) as supervisor, consultant, and researcher.

Dedication

Jean, thank you for your loving support and especially for doing so much ironing and household stuff while I've been beavering away on the computer.

David, thank you for always believing in me and for encouraging me to pursue whatever would develop me. You mean more to me than words can express.

Author's Acknowledgements

I hate acknowledgements that list great swathes of names; I find it excluding and boring. But I know now why authors do it! So many people contribute to the success of a piece of writing and its dissemination. So I'll go light on individual names but I do want to do some thanking.

This book wouldn't have been written but for encouragement and interest from family, colleagues, students, and friends. I particularly want to thank my colleague Colin Feltham for suggesting me to his publisher. He has been gently prodding me to write for some time. Thanks too to the staff at Wiley who have been enthusiastic and encouraging all the way.

I've learned my craft from more people than I can possibly list. Amongst the most important are the clients who've passed through my hands over the years. Despite sincere intentions to help, I've made many mistakes along the way and probably learned more from them than they from me. I hope I was mostly 'good enough' for mistakes to be forgiven. If any of my clients are reading this, thank you for trusting me and letting me into your inner world.

I'm lucky to have had excellent supervisors and colleagues to learn from and support me from the start of my career into the present. They pushed me to extend myself in directions I wouldn't have had courage to take and I owe them a huge debt of gratitude. My students and supervisees deserve a mention because they've taught me so much – more, I'm sure, than they realise. One in particular, now my business partner, has shouldered more responsibility while I was preoccupied with writing: to Sue Campbell a big thank you.

I've been inspired and learned a great deal from other writers and thinkers, especially from authors who drew on their own experiences of life and therapy. I hope some of their inspiration and collective wisdom is passed on through my own efforts to teach and write.

Publisher's Acknowledgements

We're proud of this book; please send us your comments through our Dummies online registration form located at www.dummies.com/register/.

Some of the people who helped bring this book to market include the following:

Acquisitions, Editorial, and Media Development

Project Editor: Rachael Chilvers

Development Editor: Kelly Ewing

Content Editor: Steve Edwards

Commissioning Editor: Alison Yates

Copy Editor: Martin Key

Proofreader: David Price

Technical Editor: Cathy Ingram

Executive Editor: Jason Dunne

Executive Project Editor: Martin Tribe

Cover Photo: © Getty Images/ Elizabeth Knox

Cartoons: Rich Tennant, www.the5thwave.com

Special Help: Zoë Wykes

Composition Services

Project Coordinators: Erin Smith, Jennifer Theriot

Layout and Graphics: Carl Byers, Joyce Haughey, Stephanie D. Jumper Alicia B. South

Proofreader: Susan Moritz

Indexer: Rebecca Salerno

Publishing and Editorial for Consumer Dummies

Diane Graves Steele, Vice President and Publisher, Consumer Dummies

Joyce Pepple, Acquisitions Director, Consumer Dummies

Kristin A. Cocks, Product Development Director, Consumer Dummies

Michael Spring, Vice President and Publisher, Travel

Kelly Regan, Editorial Director, Travel

Publishing for Technology Dummies

Andy Cummings, Vice President and Publisher, Dummies Technology/General User

Composition Services

Gerry Fahey, Vice President of Production Services

Debbie Stailey, Director of Composition Services

Contents at a Glance

Table of Contents

Introduction

●●●

Counselling skills are often referred to as 'active listening skills', which makes them sound simple – after all, everyone knows how to listen, don't they? In reality, though, the following is true:

- ✔ Listening isn't so simple after all.

- ✔ Truly listening is a very powerful tool.

- ✔ Finding out how to truly listen is intriguing, worthwhile, and exciting.

- ✔ You can discover a lot about yourself in the process.

- ✔ Active listening skills improve helping (and other) conversations and your relationships as a result.

Active listening skills are usually associated with a helping role but they are the foundation for helping conversations in many different contexts where interpersonal skills are important.

About This Book

For most of my adult life, and even earlier, I have been fascinated by human beings and found great personal satisfaction and a sense of achievement from helping people when they're distressed or anxious. My goal in this book is to impart my enthusiasm and enduring interest for helping people with their concerns through the medium of the listening relationship. My own experience has been that discovering how to help people with their difficulties is a life-long process, because people and their situations are complex. This stretched me and kept me hooked even when the going got tough. What I didn't expect at the outset was how much I would find out about myself, and how much I needed to discover about myself to be a better listener. What you will notice in this book is the emphasis on growing your self-awareness as well as increasing your knowledge and developing your skills.

Of course I hope that this book is going to help make you a brilliant listening helper, but there are some things it cannot achieve. This book can't

- ✔ **Provide you with direct practice.** You need to find people to practise on, which poses an ethical dilemma (this is only the beginning of the ethical dilemmas in this area of work!). Counselling skills can be very powerful tools for opening people's emotions. You need to be aware of this and decide whether the other person is a willing participant and whether using your developing skills is likely to help.

✔ **Give you feedback, which is vital for your progress.** I do encourage you, however, to practise and find ways of getting feedback from others about how you're doing with your listening skills.

✔ **Tell you absolutely everything you need to know.** I've had to be selective because this fascinating activity contains so much information.

✔ **Make you a counsellor.** Listening skills are an important part of counselling (sometimes called psychotherapy, or just therapy). This book isn't about being a counsellor. You may have ambitions to become a counsellor and if so, I hope this book helps you along the way to deciding whether this is a rewarding career for you. Counsellor training courses usually require you to have grounding in the theory and *practice* of counselling skills in an environment where you can practise and get feedback on your developing skills from willing (well mostly!) participants. You can find many counselling skills courses in Further and Higher Education colleges around the country.

Conventions Used in This Book

Throughout the book I use the terms *listening helper* or *helper* to refer to you (and me) and *help-seeker* or *speaker* to refer to the person who needs to talk. The phrases *counselling skills*, *listening skills*, and *active listening skills* are used interchangeably to mean the set of skills that contribute to effective listening help. I have tried to use everyday terms but whenever doing so isn't possible, I explain what the technical terms mean. Web addresses are set in monofont. Even-numbered chapters use female pronouns and odd-numbered chapters are male, to be fair to both genders!

Foolish Assumptions

In writing this book, I assume a few things about you, the reader. I assume that:

✔ You're not a counsellor, but you're in a position at work or elsewhere where people talk to you about issues and problems. Or perhaps you are a counsellor and want to hone your active listening skills.

✔ You're willing to be an explorer, a detective, and a reflector. The process of developing understanding is like a journey of discovery.

✔ You're a person who's interested in other human beings. You can acquire each individual counselling skill, and 'do' it passably. But being an effective listening helper is more than being a skilled technician – you need to base the skills in positive, personal qualities.

✔ You're probably reading this book because you're interested in other people, and maybe in how you yourself tick. However, even if you're reading this book because someone told you that you need to learn how to listen, or to get some counselling skills training, you can gain something valuable if you're willing to reflect on yourself.

✔ You have some listening skills already, even though some things may seem basic to you. You're an individual with different experiences and skills than the next person who picks up this book. Certain parts of the book probably appeal more to you than other parts, depending on your personal interests.

✔ You and I and the people you want to help are essentially the same. Most people are prone to being vulnerable, erratic, under-confident, helpless, defensive, and so on – even if you're lucky enough for this to be only some of the time.

Given that you've picked up this book, you're likely to find that some of these statements apply to you:

✔ You're interested in and intrigued by people in a general way.

✔ People seem to turn to you for advice.

✔ You gain satisfaction from helping someone who talks to you about being distressed, vulnerable, or worried.

✔ You sometimes feel distressed or worried, or are puzzled by your own reactions.

✔ You are in a role that brings you into contact with distressed people.

✔ You sometimes have frustrating conversations.

✔ You're in a role where understanding people through listening to them can help them and you.

If any of these statements is true for you, then you'll find that acquiring and developing counselling skills is helpful.

How This Book Is Organised

This book is made up of six parts and two Appendixes, each focusing on a different topic. Here is an overview of the different parts of the book and what they focus on.

Part I: Focusing on Yourself First

Imagine a doorway set in an arch. Above the arch are the words 'Know Yourself All You Who Enter Here.' On the door is a notice saying, 'Take Care of Yourself.' Both of these statements are very important to opening the door to effective work as a listening helper and contribute to being a safe and ethical practitioner. These concepts are the main focus of this part. Ethics can seem dry and remote. In this part, you see how they become alive and relevant.

Part II: The Listening Helper

You may be wondering whether, and how, being a listening helper will fit with you as a person, with your life, and work. I look at all these aspects of counselling in this part. This part also considers how your own defences may block you from listening. Here, I explore why listening is so valuable, whether it can be harmful, and some common concerns about being a listening helper. I also introduce you to the three-stage model, which you can use as a structure to guide you as you develop counselling skills.

Part III: Structuring a Helping Conversation

Because the journey of helping others is complex and sometimes overwhelming, it helps to have a map. In this part, you find a structure, or map, of the three-stage model to help you manage the endeavour, along with skills and scene-setting to help you get started. This section covers the middle and ending stages of the helping relationship and describes the various skills and how to use them productively.

Part IV: Understanding People and Problems

Although Part III is a map of the journey of helping, Part IV gives you some understanding of the terrain using the BEST-I BEST-R model, along with two chapters on how social and psychological impacts on people's experiences shape their lives. Understanding the whole person – and the context of their lives – by using the BEST-I BEST-R model as a guide, is helpful to the helping process and the helping relationship.

Part V: Handling Challenges

This part looks at different types of helping conversation; for example, what working on the telephone as a listening helper is like and how to cope with the unexpected.

Part VI: The Part of Tens

Here you find a quick reference to ten key counselling skills, each with a description, its purpose, and where in the book to find out more. I also provide ten resources to fuel your continued discovery.

Part VII: Appendixes

Appendix A provides some case studies and discussion to help you hone your counselling skills. Having developed your listening skills you may be interested in going further, to train as a counsellor. Appendix B gives you information about taking this step.

Icons Used in This Book

Throughout the margins of this book, you see icons that highlight particular types of information:

This icon marks stories from my own experience.

This icon draws attention to important points you want to remember.

This book is full of detailed suggestions and ideas for dealing with different situations. The Tip icon highlights particular suggestions that can help your development as a listening helper.

These exercises help you think about the topic at hand. Often I ask you to remember or imagine a situation so that you can put yourself in the position of a help-seeker. Sometimes I ask you to rehearse a situation in your imagination.

 This icon alerts you to potential dangers in the listening endeavour as a whole and in using particular skills. By being aware of these pitfalls you're better equipped to avoid them.

Where to Go from Here

You can start at the beginning of this book and read it from cover to cover – the chapters are organised in a logical sequence – but few people read reference books in this way. What may work best from the perspective of your individual development as a listening helper is to start in a section that interests you, or that you have a pressing need to understand. Within each chapter, you find links to other chapters that can contribute to understanding the topic that interests you.

For example, if you're a person who likes a structure to guide you, start out with the three-stage model (see Chapters 6 and 9), which I use as one framework in this book, and also the BEST-I BEST-R model (see Chapters 12 and Appendix A), which is another framework I use.

Alternatively, you may be more interested in reading case examples, so you may want to start with Appendix A. Perhaps you're struggling with some helping conversations right now and want some practical guidance. If so, Chapters 9, 10, and 11 are for you.

Maybe you wonder what it is about you that keeps getting you involved in helping situations, or why you have difficulty listening sometimes. Flip to Chapter 2.

You can also look at the Table of Contents to get an idea of where to find what you need, or you can look up a particular topic of interest in the Index.

Part I

Focusing on Yourself First

The 5th Wave   By Rich Tennant

"The reason I think stress might be a factor in your life is because of research, statistics, and the fact that you've straightened out an entire box of paper clips during our conversation."

In this part . . .

Welcome to the world of counselling skills. Before you start using listening skills to help other people, you need to be comfortable with yourself, and know your strengths and limitations. In this part you find out why knowing yourself is important, ways to know yourself better, how to take care of yourself, and how to be a safe practitioner.

Chapter 1

Introducing Counselling Skills

· ·

· ·

*1*n all sorts of work and personal situations, you come across people (family, friends, work colleagues, employees, and others) who are experiencing some kind of personal difficulty or dilemma, or simply need to review an aspect of their life. The task of listening to and helping such a person is made easier and more productive by using counselling skills within a supporting framework. These skills can even help in other situations, such as when the other person is your boss or with an annoying neighbour. By developing your capacity to use these skills, you can:

✔ Have fewer frustrating conversations.

✔ Understand better where the other person is coming from.

✔ Understand your own reactions better.

✔ Manage the listening process more effectively.

Using counselling skills in a helping relationship enables help-seekers to become less distressed and to lead more constructive, satisfying lives.

Developing as a listening helper and going through the helping process are often depicted as journeys because people can feel transformed, as if they've travelled a significant distance. Like all journeys, you'll face frustrations and you may wonder why you ever set off in the first place but, because human beings are complex and using counselling skills is challenging, you have a fascinating and rewarding journey ahead. In this chapter I walk you through this journey.

Knowing Yourself to Understand Others

The saying goes that to understand another person you have to walk a long way in his shoes. Although this is a neat way to say you need to *feel* what being the other person is like, you need to have a good look at your own feet first – walking a few miles in someone else's shoes may damage his shoes and hurt your own feet into the bargain.

You bring your life experiences, attributes, and ways of thinking and feeling to the helping relationship and have a significant impact on it, both positive and negative. For this reason I frequently explore thoughts about personal development and self-understanding in this book.

Chapter 2 focuses on self-development and ways of taking it further, and Chapter 7 puts the spotlight on your defences, but I refer to your self-understanding throughout. In Chapters 8 and 9, I explain the Core Conditions which are fundamental to the approach of this book. These conditions are key qualities expressed in terms of skills but they're more than just a skills checklist. Being able to demonstrate the Core Conditions to a help-seeker means developing your self-knowledge and self-awareness.

Working Safely and Ethically

Although working as a listening helper is rewarding, it can pose some challenges and dilemmas and drain you of energy at times. In Chapter 3, I talk about the importance of making sure you take care of yourself and get support for your work. Self-care contributes to being a safe helper.

Another part of working safely is reflecting on what makes for good practice. Helping situations routinely throw up ethical dilemmas. Chapter 4 gets you thinking about your practice, risks, and protective measures, including an ethical decision-making model.

Appendix A considers some case studies and ethical dilemmas, while some of the things that can go wrong are explored in Chapter 16. Chapter 15 looks at the influence of your role and setting and prepares you for different types of helping conversation, such as by telephone.

Being a Listening Helper

Think of your development and work as a listening helper as a journey: travelling with a companion in the helping relationship. The vehicle for the trip is the helping relationship – a safe environment which contains, supports, and conveys the help-seeker to his destination.

Some things you read and hear may trigger uncomfortable thoughts and feelings, so take care of yourself.

Counselling skills are the nuts and bolts, the engine, of the helping relationship, while the fuel is the motivation and energy of both parties in the process. In the helping relationship, you assist the help-seeker to get somewhere by helping him to work out the final destination and how to get there, using your growing understanding of the him, of yourself as map-reader and guide, and of the process of the journey. These tasks involve certain skills and knowledge, but most importantly require particular attributes and qualities. You are encouraged to reflect on these in Chapter 6. Reflection is a key part of being a listening helper. You also need to know your role and how being a listening helper may affect you; I explore both these aspects in Chapter 5.

Counselling skills are also referred to as *active listening skills*. 'Active' denotes that the helping relationship is not just about listening, but is concerned with demonstrating that you are listening carefully and attentively.

Your journey as a listening helper

The journey, whether as help-seeker or as aspiring or practising listening helper, can be daunting but it is also life-enhancing. As you explore your development as a listening helper, bear in mind that you'll go through a cyclical process:

- ✔ You start with enthusiasm and excitement and blissful ignorance.
- ✔ As you begin to develop, you hit a depressive, under-confident period of realising how much you don't know.
- ✔ As you continue to grow, your confidence starts to return, but in a self-conscious way.
- ✔ You reach the point where you almost instinctively know what to do without constant checking and self-questioning.
- ✔ The cycle begins again every time you challenge yourself with new developments.

You make more progress in this journey if you develop your reflective skills and maintain a regular journal that records your experiences and associated feelings, thoughts, wonderings, and so on. Look back over your writing at intervals to see how your preoccupations have changed and how you have grown. Some people draw, copy, or write poems, paste in articles and cartoons – whatever captures the imagination and emotions.

Using counselling skills or being a counsellor

Although counsellors use counselling skills, being a counsellor and being a listening helper using counselling skills are different, even though the boundary is blurred in some situations. In this book I focus on the listening helper using counselling skills. The differences are to do with a combination of time, focus, boundaries, role, and depth:

- ✔ Counselling skills are usually used as part of another primary role, such as being a teacher, youth worker, welfare worker, advice worker, or working in human resources, for example.

- ✔ Normally counselling skills sessions are short (typically 20–40 minutes) whereas counselling appointments are typically 50 minutes.

- ✔ Counselling skills sessions are less likely to be at regular intervals than counselling and are usually a short-term relationship (although the counselling skills sessions may be part of a wider relationship).

- ✔ Counselling skills are aimed at either simply listening without offering advice, or possibly focused on a specific issue with an expectation of reaching some kind of outcome by the end of the session. Counselling is usually working on underlying issues and less likely to be interested in an immediate outcome.

- ✔ Counselling has clearer boundaries which define certain limits of the relationship, distinguishing it from other relationships. For example, confidentiality and time boundaries are stricter and the counsellor is unlikely to have another relationship with, or dual role, with his client.

- ✔ Normally when you're in a role in which you use counselling skills but you're not being a counsellor, you work at a relatively superficial level. This statement may seem to denigrate the importance of the counselling skills role, which this book is about. However, I say that only to highlight the fact that when you're in the position of using your counselling skills, you generally function in another primary role, such as the aforementioned teacher, welfare worker, and so on, so you can't afford the time and commitment to delve deeper.

If you are interested in continuing your listening helper development by becoming a counsellor, check out Appendix B for more useful information.

An important feature of all listening help is that the helper doesn't offer advice, in the sense of 'If I were you I'd do this'. Knowledge from your primary role or elsewhere may mean you can inform a help-seeker about choices available to him, but never advise someone what to do.

The key skills you need

Helping conversations involve:

- ✔ Engaging the speaker in being comfortable enough to speak openly.
- ✔ Helping the speaker to deepen exploration of the issues he wants to discuss.
- ✔ Enabling the release of emotions.
- ✔ Making sense of the issues.
- ✔ Moving on to deal with the issues.

In order to embark on and work through this process, you need to develop not only your personal qualities but also a set of skills that have been identified over many years as being most helpful in the listening helper interaction. Chapter 18 gives you a list of some of these skills, with a brief explanation of each skill and its purpose. To gain a more in-depth understanding of the full range of skills you need, have a look at Part III, which covers them in detail.

Common problems that stop you from listening

However willing and keen you are to listen and be helpful, some things can interrupt your listening. On a practical level, the distractions of a busy or unsuitable environment can do so. You don't always get to choose an ideal situation, but you can pay some attention to minimising or avoiding distractions. You'll find discussion of such distractions in Chapter 7.

You can also suffer from practical internal distractions, such as being hungry, thirsty, or needing the toilet.

You can be disrupted from careful listening by worries such as being unsure what to say next, not knowing anything about the specific topic the help-seeker has brought up, or panic about disclosures that have been made.

People tend to carry around prejudices, assumptions, and needs (such as the need to be liked or seen to be competent) that can interfere with their ability to really listen. I talk more on this subject in Chapter 2 and in Chapter 7 I expand on the discussion of defences, which protect people from difficult feelings and may make them miss the help-seeker's emotions.

Increasing your knowledge, skills, and self-awareness through the information in this book can help to improve your confidence and therefore progress your ability to concentrate without distraction. Having a structure to guide you is also helpful.

Beginnings, Middles, and Ends: Structuring the Conversation

This book uses a three-stage model to guide you through the process of the helping conversation. I give you an outline of the model in Chapter 6, and then expand on that model in Part III. In a nutshell the model divides the process into beginning, middle, and end, corresponding to *Exploration*, *Understanding*, and *Action* respectively. Holding this structure in mind can help steer you through the time you have with a help-seeker, both for an individual session and for a series of meetings.

In Chapter 8 you have a section on making a contract with the help-seeker which clarifies your role and responsibilities as a listening helper. You will feel more secure if you have made a contract and have a structure in mind.

Understanding Others

Understanding yourself is a good preparation for understanding others. Although you are a unique individual, you share some very common themes in human experience and share the same gamut of emotions with everyone else. However, everyone arrives in this world with different strengths and vulnerabilities and is subjected to various personal, social, educational, and relationship experiences and events which shape his or her capacities to cope, or not.

Being prepared for common personal problems

In this book I use a model that attempts to capture the range of human experience using an acronym, BEST-I BEST-R. Like all models this one aims to assist your thinking, but is undoubtedly incomplete. Use your own experience and what you know of the experiences of others to compare with the information you find in this book. The initials of the acronym stand for *Body*,

Emotion, *Sensation*, *Thinking*, *Imagery*, *Behaviour*, *Environment*, *Spirituality*, *Time*, and *Relationships* and I encourage you to view people in their context. Check out Chapter 12 for a description of this model.

Other chapters that aim to prepare you for dealing with the everyday problems you may encounter as a listening helper are Chapters 13 and 14, which look at people's social and psychological experiences.

Chapter 11 focuses on the ending phase of the helping – relationship, which means that it considers how to encourage action and also looks at the meaning of endings and transitions, which are intrinsic to many problems people come for help with. Although I can't cover everything in this book, I can tell you that the bounds of human distress are wide. Read, talk to people, and watch television programmes to broaden your knowledge and understanding of what can distress people.

Spotting signs of stress and distress

Many people who seek help from listening helpers, especially counsellors, have identified that they are distressed. Most often people hide the true extent of their distress for various reasons – embarrassment, not wanting to make a fuss, protecting others, and so on. I see people's emotions as being like an iceberg – nine-tenths submerged and hidden from view. Many listening helpers find that they are the first person to notice that someone is struggling or needs to talk. Perhaps you are reading about counselling skills because this happens to you all the time. Being sensitive to signs and symptoms of stress and distress in yourself is one way of developing your sensitivity to others.

Chapter 12 explores signs and symptoms. Chapters 13 and 14 are on social and psychological understanding, and the case studies in Appendix A all help to develop your sensitivity.

Coping with different types of conversation

As a listening helper with another primary role, you may find yourself facing a potentially wide variety of helping conversations, planned and unplanned, sometimes with conscripts rather than volunteers, all influenced by your setting or context. Conversations are mostly face-to-face but they may be mediated by telephone or other electronic means. Chapter 16 explores some of the issues connected with these different situations.

Exploring Counselling Further

You have no end to the information and skills development that will prove helpful to you to develop and grow as a listening helper. Chapter 18 focuses on resources such as the professional bodies where you can obtain general relevant information and guidelines, including how to take your development forward if you want to train as a counsellor. Chapter 19 describes some books, and their authors, that will further your understanding. In Appendix B, I give details about becoming a counsellor, some of the things you need to think about, and how to go about training.

Chapter 2

Understanding Yourself through Personal Development

*B*ecoming an effective listening helper, someone who helps another to explore issues in her life by using active listening skills, involves more than simply identifying and practising the individual skills of active listening. You may be technically correct in using each particular skill and yet be an inadequate listener if your attitude to the speaker is poor, self-awareness absent, or you have unresolved personal issues that you need help with yourself.

An in-depth understanding of what motivates you to help makes you a better listening helper. In this chapter I explore some aspects of personal development which can increase your self-insight.

Identifying Obstacles to a Helping Relationship

Someone seeking help with a problem needs to trust you before she can open up to you. You must pay full attention to her without judging her – let her direct her own path and decisions.

In order for you to be a non-judging, reliable, and attentive listener, you must develop an increasing awareness of yourself and what you're bringing to the helping relationship. Aspects of yourself to bear in mind include:

- ✔ Your values, prejudices, assumptions, and internal 'rules'
- ✔ Your need to be regarded by the speaker in a certain way (for example, to be liked, needed, or viewed as a capable expert)
- ✔ Your own emotional triggers or blind spots
- ✔ Your ways of defending yourself against difficult feelings.

All of the aspects in the preceding list can be a source of internal distractions to you. Do you get distracted by thinking about what to say next? If the other person behaves in a way you find difficult (being aggressive, or needy, for example), does it get under your skin and keep you from listening? If she tells you a disturbing or shocking tale, will it be too hard for you to hear? As a listening helper, you sometimes need to challenge the person who is speaking to you, or you may need to discuss the possibility of breaking confidentiality. All these examples require a level of assertiveness and confidence to carry out actions sensitively without being hung up on your own worries and concerns.

You'll be a better listening helper if you're secure in yourself and have a reasonable level of self-esteem. However, everyone has insecurities and ways of protecting themselves against difficult feelings. These self-protective *defence mechanisms* can sometimes be of help, more often a hindrance, depending on the particular situation. They often (but certainly not always) date back to your upbringing and early experiences and are learned patterns of relating to others. Part of your personal development may be to expose yourself to things that are difficult issues for you and challenge any outdated defences. (I discuss the role of your defences further in Chapter 7.) Undertaking some personal counselling can significantly help with this (see the later section Personal Development Through Personal Therapy).

Assessing your motivations

When starting out as a listening helper, you may only be aware of your surface reasons for becoming one. Perhaps you find that others think you easy to talk to, or maybe they seek you out to ask your advice. Being helpful can be personally rewarding, giving you an internal glow. Below this, however, you may have some other powerful motivations that can distract you from careful listening. The factors that drive you to be a listening helper can be double-edged – positive or negative, dependent on the particular circumstances and also on your own self-awareness.

Take a little time to consider as honestly as you can the following questions to help you start to focus on some of the issues that may get in the way of listening, including what makes you want to take on this role:

- ✔ How did you decide to be a listening helper?
- ✔ Why do you want to be a listening helper?
- ✔ What is it that you want to give?
- ✔ What do you want to receive from people you help?
- ✔ What do you think you'll get from being a listening helper?
- ✔ What are your expectations of anyone you might help?
- ✔ With what emotions are you comfortable?
- ✔ What emotions in yourself or in others give you trouble?
- ✔ How will you deal with the speaker's feelings towards you?
- ✔ How will you handle your feelings towards those you help?

Revisit these questions when you finish this chapter, and later when you've found out more about the processes involved in using counselling skills. One theory about why people want to be listening helpers (and also to engage in intimate relationships) is to heal their own emotional wounds. The eminent American psychologist Carl Rogers suggested that we're all, to a greater or lesser extent, prevented from being fully ourselves by *conditions of worth* that others impose on us: We conform to the expectations of others, rather than being truly ourselves, in order to feel of worth. However, we also have an *actualising tendency*, or drive towards growth. Becoming more able to be yourself through this growth enables you to be a better listener because you're more able to accept others when you're better able to accept yourself. You can find more about some of the issues raised in the previous listed questions in Chapter 5 which focuses on what it means to be a listening helper, and Chapter 7, which looks in more depth at barriers to listening.

Blocked listening

You may be good at problem-solving. This useful skill is potentially of great benefit to others and it gives you a good feeling to help someone by using this skill. If, though, *you* decide what the other person's problem is and rush to solve it, that person could be left feeling useless, learning nothing from the process. What *seems* to be the problem may not be the real issue after all so she ends up not feeling heard. Remember that the help-seeker needs to find her own solutions.

Rushing to offer solutions is a common mistake made by people new to counselling skills. This tendency gets in the way of listening and is a trait you need to overcome.

To illustrate, a person may ask you about a decision she needs to make on whether to change her child's school. You might draw up a list of pros and cons of changing or staying put, suggesting sources of information and other specific advice. All of this could be helpful. However, it could be that the problem in making the decision relates to an underlying issue – the difference between this person and her partner about what's important for their child's future; a clash of expectations and values. If you rush to be helpful with your problem-solving skills, you may never get to this underlying issue.

If you recognise within yourself this tendency to rush in, take time to reflect upon what lies beneath. It could be lack of experience and skill, but it may also be that

- ✔ You lack awareness of the depth of emotion in the other person.
- ✔ You're uncomfortable with probing because of what might emerge.
- ✔ You feel good about your role and yourself when you offer a solution.

Blocked listening manifests itself as a problem in other ways beyond problem-solving. If someone talks to you about her relationship with her sister (or brother, mother, or whoever) and you have a similar problematic relationship, you may assume that her relationship is like your own. You could unconsciously try to influence the person to behave in the way that *you* would like to behave, or manage the situation as *you* do, or would like to. If you're angry or disappointed in yourself because you can't manage your own relationship as well as you want, these feelings may interfere with your capacity to listen or even make you angry and disappointed with the speaker. Maybe you don't have a sister but nevertheless have values about the role of a sister and therefore judgements about how this person *should* behave in the situation. As you can imagine, the help-seeker may notice any of these attitudes even if you try to conceal them.

On a more mundane level, if you're too hot, cold, hungry, remember that you forgot to lock your front door, need the toilet, have an appointment somewhere else, are concerned that your privacy may be invaded, and so on – any of these situations are likely to distract you from the task of attending and listening. You need to be aware of such distractions and be able to do something about them, which often requires confidence and assertiveness (see Chapter 3 for more on assertiveness). Being more self-aware is a step towards developing confidence.

Developing Your Self-Awareness

An important aspect of your qualities and skills as a listening helper is our underpinning self-awareness. The *Johari Window* model of human interaction suggests that we all have an open area, a blind spot, a secret part, and an undiscovered area representing parts of our internal world. (For more detail on the Johari Window, see the next section.) Often our fears and defences get in the way of having a satisfying life and may lead to seeking help. When we block self-knowledge, we tend to make bad decisions for ourselves. When we use energy in maintaining defences, we're distracted from listening well (to ourselves and others).

Being self-aware applies to 'clients' *and* their helpers. For anyone using counselling skills, the aim is to be more aware and less afraid of your internal world, for these three reasons:

- ✔ So that you become free to concentrate on the speaker without your own baggage getting in the way

- ✔ Because the more you understand and accept yourself, the more likely you are to understand and accept others

- ✔ So that you model the ability to be in touch with your inner self, which provides valuable information, known as *emotional intelligence*.

In Chapter 7, you can find more about recognising your barriers to listening. In this chapter I discuss listening obstacles in a general way to start you thinking about the need to understand yourself better, with some ideas about how you can do that.

The Johari Window

The Johari Window, named after the first names of its inventors Joseph Luft and Harry Ingham, explains our inner world by dividing personal awareness into four areas, like four panes of a window:

- ✔ **Open:** Known to yourself and others
- ✔ **Blind:** Known by others but not to yourself
- ✔ **Secret:** Known to yourself but not others
- ✔ **Undiscovered:** Unknown to yourself or others.

As a listening helper, you need to increase your open area by decreasing the other areas and becoming more self-accepting. Always use openness with discretion for the help-seeker's benefit – not to take attention away from them and onto your own concerns. People who have a lot of blind spots lack awareness of how they affect others. Such people are likely to give or receive much feedback or disclose much about themselves. Those who have a big secret area similarly withhold themselves. Beneath both of these behaviours lie fears about being hurt, rejected, or 'found out'. People with large undiscovered areas have little understanding of how they tick. They may not have learned or taken time to reflect on why they think, feel, and behave as they do.

To some extent everyone has elements of each of these characteristics – some blind spots, some unknown parts, and some withheld aspects. Indeed, to survive in the real world, you often have to protect yourself by not opening up these areas and keep defences in place. When helping others, you need to decide if you're willing to take the risk of opening up your self-awareness and make changes in how you relate to others. My own experience is that it is worth it, partly because doing so has made me increasingly comfortable with myself and because it has improved my relationships with others. Self-discovery and self-acceptance are lifelong endeavours.

The way to increase your open area is by one, or all, of the following routes:

✔ Disclose more about yourself so that you keep less of yourself secret. This doesn't mean telling anyone and everyone *all* about yourself, especially when the other person is trying to tell you about her difficulties. It also may not be appropriate to disclose aspects of yourself in certain situations – others *can* make judgements. Self-revelation about an experience or feeling of your own can help the other person to feel more normal in relation to her experiences and model to them the importance of being aware of and expressing emotions. You can practise self-disclosure in everyday life within relationships of trust. Notice what happens both inside yourself and in the other person when you take this risk of showing or describing your feelings and thoughts.

✔ Take time to reflect on experience, to develop self-insight and discover more about yourself. Keeping a diary or journal is a good way to increase self-awareness. You may find it difficult at first, if writing doesn't come naturally to you. Set a time limit of 6 minutes and keeping the pen on the page, keep writing, even if it is gibberish. Doing this, I became better at letting my writing, thoughts and feelings flow. You can take a theme from that 6 minutes of writing and do another 6 minutes focusing on the theme, which can take the exploration deeper. It helps knowing that what you write is personal and for no one else to see. Some people cut and paste poems and pictures, do doodles and sketches in their personal journals. Both the writing itself and reviewing what you've committed to paper straight away, and from time to time, increase your self-knowledge through noticing patterns and repeating reactions.

✔ Seek out feedback wherever you can so that you understand more about how you come over to, and affect, others – challenge your blind spots. The prospect of getting feedback can be very scary, especially if you lack confidence. And yet it isn't usually as bad as you expect and certainly better than your imagination! We are often our own harshest critics. Take time to really listen to any positive feedback – many of us play down the praise we receive, or simply don't hear it – and encourage feedback about how you come over from anyone seeking your help.

Receiving feedback

As a listening helper, you'll rarely receive meaningful feedback on how you come across, for even if you ask for feedback, the other person may not feel able to tell you the truth. However, get into the habit of asking how the other person finds the conversation and encourage her to review and reflect with you.

✔ **Listen carefully all the way through.** Listening properly when you're getting feedback can be hard. If you're like me and my students, you tend to home in on the negative and miss the positives. Even if you 'hear' the positive, you may not give it due weight and take it in. We also sometimes cannot hear negative comments without feeling crushed and criticised. Try to put your defences aside and not take the critical feedback to mean that you're completely useless and might as well give up right now! Always make a note of feedback you have received, as accurately as possible, and go back to it at a later time when you may be able to view it in a more balanced and rational way.

✔ **Ask for clarification if you need it.** From time to time, you may need to ask for feedback to be explained. Perhaps the person giving feedback is not being clear enough – such as not giving you a specific example of what she's highlighting. A common fault in giving feedback is to say something was 'good'. That won't help you to improve. Ask what specifically was good, how it was good, and how it helped the conversation and the helping relationship.

✔ **Try to think of feedback as a gift.** Try to remember that the giver of feedback may be feeling very anxious about telling you what she noticed – many of us are nervous about telling the truth as we see it. For this reason you won't always get the feedback you need to be able to improve and understand yourself better. Sometimes people *are* trying to be cleverer than you, to take a one-up position by giving you criticism. Remember, they do this because it makes them feel less inadequate themselves but they may, nevertheless, be offering something useful, once you strip out their defensive or negative approach. Also, any person you help is likely to be defensive, so dealing with your own and other people's defences is good practice! Finally, remember that a criticism doesn't mean you're a totally worthless person or completely useless – just that you may have something to work on. Thank the giver for the feedback.

✔ **Take time to reflect.** Often it is hard to take in feedback immediately: Perhaps you don't want to hear the feedback; maybe you don't want to believe it; perhaps it was given in an unhelpful manner; what you have heard may not fit with your self-perception. Our defences against hearing 'good' or 'bad' things can be strongly embedded.

✔ **Check it out with others.** Remember that the feedback is just that person's point of view – others may disagree or see things differently. Check with others if you can. Reflect on what you've heard and try to match it to other things you know about yourself to see whether there's a basis for what's been said. Also check with yourself and others about what you could (rather than *should*) do differently.

Giving feedback

Giving constructive feedback is also challenging. Here are some suggestions to help you give feedback. Above all, remember to use all the active listening skills in this book.

Talking about *giving* feedback in a chapter about *your* personal development may seem odd, but in giving feedback to others, you find out things about yourself. When you give feedback, notice your feelings before, during, and after, and the manner in which you deliver it so you discover whether anything blocks you. As a listening helper you need to offer feedback on occasion, so try to get feedback on your feedback skills.

✔ **Use 'I' statements.** Take responsibility for your comments by using 'I'. For example, instead of saying, 'You shouldn't judge people', it's more helpful to say, 'I felt uncomfortable when you told me about giving your brother your opinion.' You can add an explanation, '. . . because it seemed like you were telling him what to do and that you thought he was doing it all wrong – I think I would have felt judged.' Notice that such statements involve realising your own feelings and self-disclosing.

✔ **Give it soon.** Feedback is most meaningful when it is related to what happened recently. If you wait hours, days, or even longer your memories become more vague. If you're reluctant to offer feedback, think what that says about you and the kind of relationship you have (or don't have) with the other person.

✔ **Be specific and concrete.** Imagine that you've acquired a new skill, such as building a space vehicle from instructions. How would you feel if a passing Martian said, 'That was brilliant,' or 'You didn't do so well there'? You might feel good in the first instance and bad in the second, but in both cases you wouldn't have much idea of why you were brilliant or not so good.

Try to identify what specifically made something 'brilliant' so that the other person knows how she can keep on doing brilliantly. For example, you could say 'You were very careful to check every step against the instructions, so that the space vehicle ended up working like it was supposed to.'

Concrete examples help. For example, 'When you screwed part B to part C you followed the instructions and lined them up carefully, but when you assembled the hatch you didn't consult the instructions and the hatch didn't fit properly.'

I often hear students telling each other they did well, saying something like, 'That was really good,' or 'You really listened.' More helpful is to identify *how* the person did well. Perhaps she accurately reflected on what she heard, or she conveyed empathy through her nonverbal communication (looking concerned and interested and maintaining eye contact).

If you find it difficult to be specific and concrete, you can use some simple techniques – which are also a lot of fun – to give you practice. On a course I attended, we were asked to devise instructions for a blind person to open a matchbox and strike a match. When we put our instructions to the test with blindfolded volunteers, the results were hilarious and telling – matches all over the floor. Another exercise in being clear and specific is to draw a diagram using simple geometric figures such as circles, squares, triangles, and so on. Explain your diagram to another person who cannot see it but who has to try to draw it from your instructions. If your family or friends like games, these can be fun to do together.

✔ **Think of the feedback as a gift.** To receive well-thought-out, constructive, and timely feedback that can be used to improve or understand yourself better is rare, so it's a valuable thing for you to offer. Reflect on what stops you from offering your observations.

✔ **Remember not to rush to offer solutions.** You can boost your own self-esteem by seeming to know the answers, but the objective is the other person's understanding. Give her time to think it over and to reach her own conclusions, which is the best way of discovering answers. Reflect on your desire to impress, to rescue, and so on, and what these feelings say about you.

✔ **Don't overwhelm with too much feedback.** In general, limit your feedback so that the other person can readily take it in. Develop the art of picking out themes and/or what seems most important. Be aware of how the other person reacts to what you say so that you can pace giving feedback to her needs. If you find it difficult to concentrate on the other person's reactions, you need to think about what it is that stops you from having enough confidence to forget about yourself.

✔ **Think what the feedback says about you.** In giving feedback what you notice and focus on reflects something about yourself. Two people watching the same piece of interaction will each notice different things, related to their own concerns and preoccupations. One person may notice how empathic a listener is being, or not being, because empathy and being understood is really important to her, whilst another notices how assertive, or lacking in assertiveness, a listener is because she admires or fears assertiveness and challenge.

Avoiding Assumptions and Prejudices

You make judgements and assumptions about other people all the time and you find yourself categorising many aspects of your world in order to manage daily living. You're bombarded with experiences and sensory information throughout the day and you'd probably go mad or be paralysed if you didn't use categories and assumptions to make sense of the world and your experiences. However, some of your assumptions are likely to be based on inaccurate and stereotyped views that get in the way of relating to the real person.

Your views are developed by your whole life experience and influenced by significant people, values, and institutions. Early influences are particularly powerful – when you were small you tended to believe what significant adults in your life told you, or conveyed to you through their attitudes. Beneath prejudice lies fear – of the unknown, of difference, of being overwhelmed, of having power taken away, of being found to be weak or vulnerable. Even now when you're able to challenge assumptions and prejudices, you may find the underlying fear lives on and subtly influences your reactions.

If you've grown up as part of a 'majority', you may be unaware of the impact of oppression. As part of a minority, especially where that minority is subjected to publicly accepted oppression, people live with negative attitudes on a repetitive, daily basis. Individuals and society are often 'blind' to the everyday imbalance of power, and its effects, experienced by oppressed minorities.

As a listening helper, you need to develop your awareness of your own assumptions and prejudices. They can be quite subtle and hard to admit. You can read more about these issues in Chapter 7, which discusses defence mechanisms. *Defence mechanisms* are the behaviours and ways of thinking we develop to protect ourselves from emotional hurt.

ANECDOTE

Illustrating negative stereotypes

As a child I experienced two very obvious forms of negative stereotype from my parents. I relate these stories to illustrate how the fear, which is irrational and often not easy to identify, can remain even when it has been rejected at a conscious level:

- My mother was frightened of people with Down's syndrome (then called Mongolism). She once made me walk back up a downward escalator in order to avoid a 'Mongol' standing near the bottom. This fear definitely communicated itself to me although I don't recall anything being said. Although I rejected this attitude as groundless when I became an adult, I retained a nervousness until I worked with some young people with Down's.

- I have memories from around the age of 9 (when we moved from an almost exclusively white area to a mixed suburb) of my mother being fearful of and my father prejudiced against black people. Later we had people of all nationalities living in our home as lodgers. On the surface all was polite and friendly and

I believe most of my mother's fears dissipated. In fact relations were mostly warm and affectionate, but in private my father continued to hold generalised negative, stereotyped opinions. I grew up enjoying the company of the richly varied people and cultures within our home. Despite this I had an underlying, unspecified fear, which emerged when I was going up or down the stairs in the dark, that a black man lay in wait, which lasted through most of my adolescence.

If you've experienced oppression, you may stereotype people you're helping. Victims of oppression aren't exempt from this. If you've been part of an oppressed minority, you need to consider how this has affected your attitudes. It may be that you feel anger towards the oppressing majority, or perhaps you've internalised the oppression, leading you to hold prejudiced views against yourself and others from your oppressed group; or maybe you feel a need to 'pass on' the oppression by finding someone lower down the pecking order to feel superior to or to pick on.

Power in the helping relationship

The other person in the helping relationship also holds assumptions. She'll be making judgements and possibly holding prejudiced opinions about you. She'll be influenced by previous contact with authority figures. You're in a position of power and authority in the helping relationship. Some people deny this because they're uncomfortable with the idea that they hold power; some may be unconsciously or consciously pleased to hold power. Examine yourself honestly and think about the following situations and questions.

Imagine, as vividly as you can, that you've approached someone to discuss something that worries you, perhaps something you feel somewhat embarrassed or shameful about:

- ✔ What do you notice about the balance of power in the relationship?

- ✔ How comfortable do you feel with that balance?

- ✔ What impact will the power dynamic have on your ability to discuss the issue?

Now, switch roles and think about being in the helper's place:

- ✔ What impact might there be on the relationship now from being perceived as a person with power?

- ✔ What positive and negative effects are there on you when you're perceived as a person who holds power and authority?

- ✔ How does being perceived as a person with power affect your ability to listen carefully?

Think back to relationships where people have had power over you and reflect on how that has influenced your attitudes towards authority. You're likely to carry traces of these past relationships into present interactions.

Continuing Your Personal Development

You can advance your own personal development in many ways. Whatever personal development methods you choose, the process of reflection, before, during, and after such activities, is most important. You can do the reflective process alone, by thinking and writing. Regularly maintaining a journal or diary is a very useful way of reflecting.

Challenging yourself

Choose activities to challenge you, such as the following:

- ✔ **Fact or fiction, reading is good:** Hundreds of fiction and non-fiction books can contribute to your personal development. Novels can provide insights into the lives, thought processes, behaviours, and emotions of characters who are different from or similar to yourself. Many accounts of people's true life experiences are on the bookshelves. Examples include male and female victims of sexual, physical, and emotional abuse, people who have experience of death, suicide, drug and alcohol use, and so on. On the Internet, you can find Web sites, chat rooms, and blogs that discuss problems and life issues. If you don't know how to find these, your local library may be able to help, or simply type your area of interest into a search engine such as www.google.com. Many magazines have problem pages and newspapers frequently publish articles about relevant issues. Think about how you react to your reading.

You can also read self-help books and textbook accounts of different types of human distress. Textbooks describe theories of human development, which show how problems can arise at different stages of our lives.

Finally, if you want a more academic approach, read journals, such as the *British Journal of Guidance and Counselling*, *Therapy Today*, *Counselling and Psychotherapy Research*, and many psychology and family therapy journals. (Some of these may only be available in college and university libraries or by ordering from your local library.)

✔ **Writing as therapy:** Research shows that writing is therapeutic for a wide range of problematic situations and emotions. Providing you have a place of safe-keeping for your journal or other writing, this can be a medium through which to explore in a very candid way your thoughts, feelings, and reactions. Committing them to paper can clarify what you're experiencing and be *cathartic* (a release). How you choose to write is very personal. It may be 'stream of consciousness' – in other words spontaneous and with as little conscious thinking as possible. Or it could be more formal, using a structure with headings as prompts, or in the form of poetry. A journal may include other people's writing or art which has had an impact on you. You may find Gillie Bolton's *The Therapeutic Potential of Creative Writing: Writing Myself* (Jessica Kingsley Publishers) helpful to read.

✔ **Nonverbal exploration:** Meditation and prayer are helpful aids to reflection for some people. To many people, music and art are important activities that express feeling, or experiences that capture emotion, and can also be aids to reflection. Activities involving movement, such as dance, yoga, or t'ai chi are other possibilities to consider for releasing emotion.

✔ **Stage and screen:** The theatre, film, radio, and television have a long history of exploring people's lives and motivation through documentary and drama. Now that you're focusing on helping others through the act of listening, you can approach these everyday experiences with a more conscious learning intent. Look out for relationships, motivations, actions, and reactions which underlie individual and relationship issues and your own responses. Television has had a number of series focusing on people's emotional and relationship difficulties: for example, agoraphobia, obsessive compulsive disorders, problems with child behaviour, and sex and sexuality. These programmes can challenge your preconceptions, attitudes, and values in a powerful way, as well as sometimes modelling counselling skills.

✔ **Other activities:** Another way to promote your personal development and self-awareness is by trying new and challenging activities. The side-effects from attempting these activities are more valuable for your personal development than the activities themselves. As you struggle to do something new, your self-esteem is likely to increase (providing you do not judge yourself too harshly). At the same time, you come into contact with different people. Reflecting on your own emotions and behaviour, and observing the way others tackle situations, tells you more about how you and others tick.

Working with other people is also a good way of increasing self-awareness and understanding of others. In a situation where all parties have consented to be part of a process of self-discovery, you have opportunities to challenge yourself and receive feedback and therefore increase your open area (refer to the earlier section, 'The Johari Window').

Peer group discussions

Find like-minded people and set up a regular discussion group to focus on relevant issues. You can advertise in the British Association of Counsellors and Psychotherapists (BACP) journal *Therapy Today* or join an online forum (type 'discussion forum self-awareness' into a search engine for example). If you're in a work setting you may have an existing meeting where you can make space in the agenda for discussion and exchange of views. To help the smooth running of such a group, agree on some ground rules. You need to have confidence to reveal more of what you really think is important and get to know each other. You also need to agree on what is, or is not, confidential. Other items you might discuss are:

✔ Keeping to a schedule.

✔ Who, if anyone, will chair the meeting.

✔ How to fix an agenda.

✔ Procedural matters such as not interrupting or speaking over another person (in other words, mutual respect).

✔ How to deal with the presence of a more senior person. Will others feel free to be open and honest?

✔ Practical issues such as whether eating and drinking during the meeting is acceptable; agreeing that mobile phones are turned off; avoiding interruptions during the meeting.

✔ Commitment to regular attendance to increase the sense of safety in the group.

✔ Regular reviews of how the group is working.

Personal Development Through Personal Therapy

You may be surprised to find personal therapy and counselling included as ways of developing yourself. Personal therapy and counselling aren't only for when you have a specific problem. Being on the receiving end of a helping relationship is not only a valuable experience to give you insight into how it can be for a help-seeker, it also deepens your insight into yourself. To be a listening helper you don't have to be completely problem-free and I make the assumption that, like most people, you're likely to have issues at some time that would benefit from a counselling approach. Many people who have experienced life and emotional difficulties go on to become listening helpers themselves because they found such help beneficial.

Peer counselling

Peer counselling is a form of therapy that consists of an agreement between two people (equals who are both interested in self-development) to work in a structured way to counsel each other on a regular agreed basis. Usually meetings consist of a one, or one-and-a-half, hour long session. One person counsels the other and then they change roles.

You can take courses and workshops in an approach to peer counselling called *co-counselling*. The courses prepare and support you to look at patterns of behaviour which can sabotage you. The courses concentrate on the discharge of bottled-up emotions and the reconsideration of who you are, focusing on body and mind, to achieve greater emotional well-being and better relationships. At the same time, participants are having fun and celebrating, not just being problem-orientated and serious. You can find information about co-counselling on the Internet using a search engine.

Group therapy

In some areas, you can find therapy groups. These groups are generally focused on specific issues, such as self-esteem, sexual abuse, and addiction. They're very good in helping you to recognise that what you think and feel are quite normal and they can provide you with feedback on how you come over to others. They also provide a support network. These groups can be challenging, so it is important that the group is facilitated well. Enquire about the facilitator's experience.

A good sign that the facilitator knows her job is when she asks to discuss your situation with you, with a view to making an assessment of whether the group is right for you before offering a place. Groups may be closed (that is, once started, no new members are permitted), open, time-limited, or open-ended. The facilitator needs to establish ground rules for how the groups operate (as in peer-group discussions), so participants can feel safe to share.

Personal therapy

Personal counselling can be used to enhance your personal awareness, facilitate your emotional growth and provide another method of personal reflection. However, most of us *do* have issues in our past or present life that would benefit from personal exploration. If you want to help others and avoid impeding your ability to listen, then you need to be aware of your own emotional baggage. Personal counselling also enables you to understand more fully what being on the receiving end of listening help is like and so to have greater empathy with help-seekers you come into contact with.

If you seek counselling for yourself, be sure to work with someone you feel comfortable with. Research and experience show that one of the most important aspects of successful counselling is the relationship between client and counsellor. Make sure that you feel reasonably at ease and understood by your counsellor so that you can start to trust the counselling process.

A good counsellor never tries to make you do anything that you don't want to do or that conflicts with your values. If you feel under pressure to do something you don't want to do, you need to be able to say so. If not, or if you feel your counsellor persists in pressuring you, immediately stop your counselling and find someone else.

Providing a safe space is the reason why counsellors set clear *boundaries*. Having boundaries means being clear about the contract you're entering into: appointment times, duration, payment, confidentiality, and so on. Abuse by therapists is not unknown (as in other walks of life) and is usually accompanied by serious blurring of boundaries, including inappropriate suggestions, for example to meet socially, or inappropriate touch. You're more vulnerable when you're in counselling because you could be exploring difficult issues, and it is important that you're not taken advantage of.

You may have times when you experience uncomfortable or unusual feelings towards your counsellor which are *not* due to abusive intentions. For example, you may experience unexpected feelings of abandonment, jealousy or anger when your counsellor is away. Mention these feelings to your counsellor as they are a normal part of the process and could help you and your counsellor to understand the influence of past relationships on your life now.

You probably frequently censor your feelings in order to be polite or seem normal. Counselling isn't about being polite – it's a place where you discover your true feelings because they influence your behaviour even when you think they don't show!

Couple/relationship counselling and family therapy

Exploring relationships is a good way of understanding more about yourself for your role as a listening helper (which is about being in a relationship). Generally people enter into these kinds of therapies when they have specific difficulties. However, I've known couples who just wanted to enhance their relationship and who benefited enormously from discovering more about the influences on their relationship and how to communicate more effectively. Couple and family therapy can help you recognise patterns in your own family and show you the ways in which family members relate to each other.

Finding a Counsellor

Here are some places where people look for a counsellor:

- ✔ **GP surgery:** Usually counselling in this setting is time-limited to around six sessions. You may need to be referred by your GP and you may have to wait to be seen. Information passing from counsellor to GP is usually none or very limited but you may want to check this and find out what goes into your medical record.

- ✔ **Voluntary (specialist) organisations:** For example, Mind, Cruse, Relate, and sexual abuse and domestic abuse organisations. Mind, Cruse, and Relate have coverage throughout the UK and you can find them in your telephone directory. You can find other specialist organisations in the Yellow Pages under 'Counselling and Advice'. Many provide longer-term counselling than GP services and some provide services at low or no cost. Find out about the reputation of the organisation by asking friends, colleagues, your GP, or judge from their publicity and literature or by recommendation. Many have Web sites (Chapter 18 has some examples).

- ✔ **EAP and Workplace Counselling:** Some employers offer counselling through in-house facilities or through an employee assistance programme (EAP). Sessions are usually limited to 4 to 6 sessions. Limitations on confidentiality depend on the employer – some employers may require feedback (this could be simply how many sessions were attended). Many schemes have the same confidentiality expectations that private counselling offers.

✔ **Private counsellors:** Counselling is not statutorily regulated in the UK, so anyone can advertise themselves as a counsellor, with little or no training. As in other professions, you can encounter unscrupulous individuals. The safest way is to go by recommendation and/or look for a practitioner who is accredited by, or at least is a member of, a professional body (see next bullet). Such bodies have lists of counsellors and psychotherapists. You can also find counsellors and psychotherapists in the telephone directory and Yellow Pages and in Web-based directories.

✔ **Professional bodies:** The British Association for Counselling and Psychotherapy (BACP) is a major professional association. It has a vetting process for becoming a member and an accreditation scheme which checks that proper training has been undertaken and that supervised practice and training continues. The United Kingdom Council for Psychotherapy (UKCP) has a similar scheme. The Independent Practitioner Network (IPN) operates in a different way. Accountability is through a network of practitioners of equal status rather than a hierarchical organisation: Linked groups offer each other mutual support and challenge. I discuss details of professional bodies in Chapter 18.

✔ **Telephone directory and Yellow Pages:** These resources have sections for psychotherapy and for counselling and advice.

✔ **Web-based directories:** The Counselling Directory www.counselling-directory.org.uk and Counselling Ltd www.counselling.ltd.uk hold lists of counsellors and local Internet trade directories for your area may have listings.

Knowing what to expect

If you decide to go to counselling as a personal development activity or because you have an issue you want to address, bear the following points in mind:

✔ **Appointments:** Although appointments are usually weekly, you can often negotiate different intervals. You need to strike a balance between making a commitment which is sensible for your life circumstances, and making and maintaining progress in counselling – in general you'll make more progress if you attend regularly. Appointments are usually 50 minutes, but some counsellors offer slightly different timings.

✔ **Venue:** Organisations usually have premises where the counselling takes place. Private counsellors often work from home which some clients like; others prefer the neutral ground of an office premises. You need to feel confident that you'll have privacy for your conversation.

✔ **The counsellor:** A good counsellor has:

   Qualifications and training. Expect your counsellor to have a minimum of a Diploma in Counselling. Don't be afraid to ask about the counsellor's qualifications and what they mean. If the issue you want to address is particular, you may prefer a counsellor who has had training in that field (for example, sexual abuse, sexual problems, eating disorders, and so on).

   Accreditation. If your counsellor is not accredited by a professional body, you may want to know whether she is working towards accreditation or why she isn't accredited. Accreditation does not guarantee a good counsellor.

   Experience. Most people would prefer to be dealt with by an experienced practitioner, but all practitioners have to start somewhere. Qualified counsellors have usually undergone rigorous training and been selected for training because they had appropriate qualities and life experience. Unless the issues you have are very particular, then the more important matter is that you feel confident and comfortable with the counsellor.

   Theory. Most counsellors initially train in a particular approach or theory, although most counsellors tend to learn other approaches as they gain experience and further training. For most clients the theory is not particularly important, but you need to understand and be in sympathy with how the counsellor works and what she's likely to focus on and consider important. She should be able to explain her approach to you in straightforward terms.

✔ **Confidentiality:** Counselling is normally confidential between client and counsellor, with some exceptions. The counsellor will tell you about any limits on absolute confidentiality. If the counsellor works within an organisation, the confidentiality may be between the client and the organisation, and the counsellor will make this clear to you. Some normal exceptions to absolute confidentiality exist. For example, all reputable counsellors in the UK have regular supervision where they discuss their work with an experienced colleague, without using identifying details. If anyone is thought to be at risk of harm, especially a child, then information may have to be disclosed to appropriate authorities. In the unlikely event of it being an emergency this may be done without your permission, but normally will be discussed with you (see Chapter 4 for more on crisis and risk).

Most counsellors keep notes to help them think about the work they're doing. You have a right, under the Data Protection Act 1998, to know how notes are kept, how long for, and to view any records held about you.

✔ **Information and advice:** Counsellors are not primarily concerned with offering information and advice. The counsellor's role is not to tell you what to do. However, she may be able to give you relevant information or suggest where you can find it, including books you could read.

✔ **Feeling comfortable:** Initially you're likely to feel unsure and perhaps embarrassed or awkward. However, trust your gut feeling if you feel that the person isn't right for you.

✔ **Payment:** If you're paying for your therapy, you're likely to be asked to pay weekly, possibly one week in advance. Some organisations and private counsellors operate a sliding scale according to income, others have a fixed fee. Some voluntary organisations which charge may have a bursary scheme for people on low incomes.

✔ **Cancellation:** Most counsellors or organisations have a cancellation policy, meaning that you pay for all or part of the session cost if you cancel your session without a reasonable period of notice (usually outlined by the organisation).

✔ **Mode of delivery:** Counselling is generally conducted face-to-face and one-to-one or in a couple or family grouping. However, you can obtain counselling by telephone or email. As with face-to-face counselling, be clear about the contract you're entering into – what exactly is being offered and any limitations.

Understanding when counselling can harm you as a client

In general, counselling is a benign activity that I encourage you to experience as part of your development as a listening helper. However, if you feel unhappy with your counsellor or pressurised in any way, don't ignore these signs. If you manage to discuss your concerns with your counsellor and don't receive a satisfactory explanation or answer, consider stopping your sessions. If your trust is being abused in any way, stop. Sometimes getting a perspective on this by yourself is difficult. If in doubt, talk about it to someone whose judgement you trust. The same is true of group therapy.

Anyone who is seriously depressed may benefit from reading about counselling but needs to avoid being a listening helper until she's much improved and more emotionally stable. If you're severely depressed, discuss with your GP whether counselling is likely to be helpful. You need to be aware that counselling can sometimes lead you to feel worse initially, because you begin to confront the issues rather than blocking them. If you're very low to start with, this may be unbearable unless you have good alternative supports outside the counselling itself. If you're feeling very fragile, group therapy can be intimidating.

Chapter 3

Taking Care of Yourself

· ·

In This Chapter
▶ Knowing the importance of self-care
▶ Recognising what affects you
▶ Thinking about your support network
▶ Becoming appropriately assertive

· ·

*B*eing a listening helper (using listening skills to help another person with difficult issues) can be very demanding and challenging. Although being a listening helper is very worthwhile and rewarding, you need to recognise that potentially thorny issues may arise for both you and the person you're helping, and that you'll need ways of coping.

Not only that, but you need to avoid using the people you help as a way of fulfilling your own emotional needs (to feel loved, needed, and important, for example). Modelling a healthy approach to yourself is a significant aspect of helping others.

In this chapter, I start you off with a quiz to evaluate just how well you're tending to yourself. Then, I tell you things to watch for, how they can affect your own well-being, and how you can call on your support network to help you.

Evaluating Your Self-Care

To find out how you're currently doing in the self-care stakes, complete the following self-care questionnaire. Rate each item with the scores: frequently (2), sometimes (1), or never (0).

Your work

In your work setting (voluntary or paid, or work in the home), how often do you take time for

- ✔ Stepping back and assessing priorities?
- ✔ Social interaction?
- ✔ Giving attention to your bodily needs: proper meal breaks, toilet, fresh air, temperature?
- ✔ Finding opportunities for consultation and peer support?
- ✔ Reviewing your terms and conditions of employment?
- ✔ Ensuring professional development time?
- ✔ Having a quiet time for uninterrupted work?
- ✔ Being clear with yourself and colleagues/family about the limits of your work role and what you can and cannot take on?
- ✔ Making your work space right for you and your work?
- ✔ Taking as much autonomy and control of your own work and decisions as you can?

Your body

In relation to your bodily well-being do you

- ✔ Eat healthily and regularly?
- ✔ Take exercise and other physical activities (but not excessively)?
- ✔ Do things that help you sleep well?
- ✔ Avoid ingesting harmful substances, as well as control levels of potentially harmful ones, such as nicotine, alcohol, recreational drugs?
- ✔ Take time for satisfying sex, alone or with a partner?
- ✔ Take time off from everyday routines for relaxing activities?
- ✔ Do any relaxation, yoga, tai chi, or similar exercises or massage?
- ✔ Act in a timely way about health concerns and routine health checks?
- ✔ Get away from the computer early enough at night and often enough; get off the couch and away from the TV often enough?

Your mind

For your psychological well-being, how often do you have

- Quiet times for rest and contemplation?
- Times when you can share your emotions with people you trust, being yourself and talking about things that concern you or make you happy?
- Close, loving times with a particular person or animal?
- Recreational activities that stimulate you and take your mind off work and stretch you in new directions?
- Time with a supportive social group/network such as friends, church, clubs, and so on?
- Times when other people can be in 'the driving seat' or caring for you rather than you caring for them?
- People around you who you can let your guard down with and show the real you?
- Enough control over your working and personal life?
- Time for holidays and short breaks, away from telephones and responsibilities?
- Time to reflect on your thoughts, feelings and beliefs, perhaps through a personal diary or counselling/psychotherapy/life coaching?

Your emotions

To look after your emotional well-being how often do you:

- Keep in touch with people who are important to you?
- Take time to be with people whose company you enjoy?
- Allow yourself to acknowledge when you have done well?
- Like yourself and treat yourself with respect?
- Allow yourself to experience all your emotions – happiness, anger, sadness, laughter, the whole range?
- Have time with young people or animals, especially in play?
- Make time for listening to music, reading, films?
- Appreciate nature or creative activities?
- Laugh, giggle?

Your spirit and creativity

Thinking about your spirit, do you

- ✔ Notice things that inspire you?
- ✔ Notice beauty in everyday surroundings?
- ✔ Have awareness of what is meaningful to you and take time to acknowledge and celebrate it?
- ✔ Meditate, pray, or contemplate, formally or informally?
- ✔ Find time to be tranquil, maybe in quiet, peaceful surroundings, but also sometimes making that 'space' in crowded, busy times or places?
- ✔ Engage in, or observe, creative or artistic activities such as music, art, and poetry?
- ✔ Develop ways to encourage your hope, optimism, and energy for life?
- ✔ Engage in something where you allow yourself to experience overwhelming joy and passion, to be transported?
- ✔ Engage in a spiritual community or partnership/friendship or something you believe in deeply?
- ✔ Take part in celebrations with your family, friends, community, and so on?

Weighing up the results

There's no 'correct' score – some things give you more pleasure or are more important to you than others and so carry more weight. However, if you have a score that is well below 50 then you need to do more to top up your batteries. Some of the items in the questionnaire may give you ideas of what is lacking for you.

Being Aware of Potential Pitfalls

Being a listening helper isn't easy. Be aware that some aspects of attentive, active listening can lead to stress and worry. For example, you may

- ✔ Find yourself hearing things that you prefer not to hear, that test your ability to accept, or that conflict with your own values.
- ✔ Feel bombarded or overburdened at times, especially if someone is looking to you to provide answers for him.

✔ Face challenges to your role boundaries such as when another person's needs or demands are outside your remit although you feel responsible for him.

✔ Have to say 'No' to someone or give him feedback that he really doesn't want to hear.

✔ Listen to someone when you're having a bad day or period in your own life and when your own emotions and worries are close to the surface. His story may trigger emotions about your own life or previous experiences.

✔ Find that someone is opening up more than is helpful or appropriate in the particular time and place. The speaker may regret revealing so much and you may be left with difficult feelings.

✔ Experience a feeling of helplessness when someone opens up to you or an inability to let go after the conversation is over. When someone opens up to you, you may feel very privileged, but you may also feel overwhelmed.

All of these situations can cause you to worry whether you're being effective or have done enough. You may take the concerns home with you, fret over them, take on too much responsibility for the other person, or you may be left with stirred-up feelings. As a listening helper you need to develop ways of coping. Ensure a good support system for yourself that includes someone you trust to discuss situations with (see 'Increasing Your Personal and Professional Supports' later in this chapter).

Mapping Your Support Network

An effective support system can help prevent you from becoming overburdened, drained, and possibly burning out. To keep your physical and emotional energy levels charged up you need a balance of activities and people to provide support, relaxation, distraction, and release. Some support is *indirect*, such as activities that make you feel better; whilst other support is *direct*, such as discussing a taxing situation with someone you respect and trust in order to reach a better understanding or a more effective way of working.

In a journal, diary, or on a large piece of paper with big coloured pens (probably the best way to really see), map out all the sources of support in your life – personal and professional, people, objects, and activities. One way to approach this task is to depict yourself in the centre of the page with a number of balloons above you representing your supports and some weights holding you down to represent more troublesome areas of your life (see Figure 3-1). Artistic skills not required!

Figure 3-1:
Mapping my
support
system.

Think SMARTER

A useful acronym to use in thinking about what you want to achieve is SMARTER. This stands for:

- Specific
- Measurable
- Achievable
- Realistic
- Timed
- Evaluated
- Reviewed.

An example: I decide I want to feel less lethargic and more fit. Using SMARTER, I ask myself:

- **What *specifically* can I do?** I decide to go running.

- **How *much* running?** Well, ideally 2–3 miles 2–3 times per week.

- **Is this *achievable*?** Theoretically I have time for this but I wonder if I am fit enough.

- **Is it *realistic* then?** Perhaps I need to start with a smaller objective which is more realistic *and* achievable – say, 1 mile run and 1 mile walk. Because I have high blood pressure I ought to check with my GP first.

- **So, when (again being *specific*) am I going to start?** I'll make an appointment with the GP in the next couple of days and if I get the go-ahead I'll do my first run next Tuesday morning (the day that I start work later than normal) between 8.30 a.m. and 9.00 a.m. I'll book days when I'll run into my diary and keep a record of my times so I can measure progress.

- **When will I evaluate and review my progress?** After four weeks, I'll look at my times to see if I achieved my goal and if it was realistic. Oh, and I mustn't forget to celebrate success!

Here are ideas about what you might include:

- Positive contact with individuals, such as family, friends, work colleagues, and with social groups.

- Activities such as walking, swimming, sports, sex, going to the gym, dancing, gardening, decorating.

- More sedentary activities, such as reading, sitting in a hot tub, watching your favourite soaps on TV, relaxation exercises, journal/diary-writing, drawing, and painting.

- Spiritual or contemplative things such as praying, yoga, being in beautiful and natural surroundings, looking at art, listening to music, writing poetry.

- Activities that support your self-esteem, such as trying new challenges and new learning, taking care of your appearance, doing something positive to help others.

✔ Time spent with young people and/or animals (who tend to offer unconditional affection).

✔ Time to reflect in your professional life.

✔ Also include all the things that burden, worry, and weigh you down.

When you've mapped out your sources of support and things that hold you back, consider how to increase areas that support you and decrease areas that are burdensome. Taking time to focus on these areas and making a personal resolution to tackle each issue pays off in reducing stress levels and increasing your energy for the helping role (quite apart from the benefits to your private life and health). Chapter 5 has more on the role of the listening helper.

If you try to tackle everything at once, you're likely to end up disappointed in yourself. A step-by-step approach is usually more successful.

Think about how you're going to keep up the motivation – what is likely to get in the way, for example – and who can support you to keep going. You may find that giving yourself rewards for achieving certain milestones helps. If you haven't achieved what you hoped for, instead of being hard on yourself, think whether the plan was 'smart' enough (see the 'Think SMARTER' sidebar) and try again with less ambitious objectives.

Increasing Your Personal and Professional Supports

You're probably trying to juggle competing demands and current stresses, and deal with your emotional baggage. The quality of support you have in your private life has a direct influence on your ability to manage all this and the demands of listening to the problems of others. Think of the situation as filling a jug and then emptying it – if nothing goes in then nothing comes out. You need to be replenished.

The self-care questionnaire in the section 'Evaluating Your Self-Care,' earlier in this chapter identifies some areas to consider and your support network balloons (head back to Figure 3-1) highlight what support you do have. Consider how you're going to nurture and increase your personal supports.

The following sections offer ideas on how to increase your professional supports.

Consultation, mentoring, and supervision

One way to take care of yourself, and be supported in your listening role, is to identify and make use of people who have experience in this role and whom you trust to give you helpful, impartial advice and feedback. You can use the tools of consultation, mentoring, and supervision to accomplish this goal.

- ✔ **Consultation:** Consultation is often an ad hoc arrangement but it can be useful to come to an agreement with a particular individual, usually a colleague but perhaps a friend who understands your listening-helper role, whom you consult from time to time about specific issues. Bear in mind, however, the need to maintain the confidentiality of anyone you're helping.

- ✔ **Mentoring:** Mentoring is often, but not always, a more formalised arrangement whereby a mentor and mentee meet by prior agreement. The mentoring relationship is usually aimed at offering ongoing support and encouragement to the listening helper and giving information (for example, about the organisation and what it can offer, or where to find resources). Discussion of the details of work with the help-seeker is limited. Some workplaces have mentoring schemes in place; in other situations people often seek out mentors from their more experienced colleagues. You need to be attentive to the boundary of confidentiality, to protect the privacy of anyone you're helping, whether you discuss his situation within or outside the organisation.

- ✔ **Supervision (management and clinical):** In the counselling world a distinction is drawn between management supervision and clinical supervision. *Management supervision* is primarily aimed at meeting the needs of the organisation and is carried out by a line manager. *Clinical supervision* focuses on the needs of the help-seeker and helper. For people who are helping others by using listening skills in the course of their job role, these two types of supervision are frequently merged in the line manager's role. This arrangement can work well but because a line manager has power over his subordinate, developing a truly honest relationship may be difficult. If you are in this position, you may be wary of telling your supervisor anything that you believe could be detrimental to your career or daily working life.

Supervision is an activity that may include some mentoring but focuses much more specifically on the work being done with the help-seeker, and on the helper's needs. The role of the supervisor has been summed up by counselling pioneer Brigid Proctor as normative, restorative, and educative. The supervisor is interested in the helping relationship and what is being experienced by both parties. Whilst the supervisor has an authority function, in that he could and should act if a helper is behaving inappropriately or improperly (the *normative* function), he is concerned to support and encourage the helper in the challenges of the helping role (the *restorative* function). He can also model and teach the role and skills of the listening helper (the *educative* function). Another aspect of the normative function is the transmission of values, attitudes, and professionalism – all of which contribute towards supporting a helper in his role.

Supervision is usually quite formal in the sense that an explicit agreement is made to meet regularly and for a specified length of time. Most often this meeting is face –to face but it is also possible to arrange telephone and online supervision.

Most listening helpers who aren't counsellors do not receive clinical supervision unless their employers recognise that the listening role is demanding and requires time for reflexivity (the capacity to reflect constructively on practice).

You can internalise the attitudes and ways of approaching problems and supportive responses that you have experienced with your supervisors or other significant mentors. For example, you can hold conversations in your head with your 'internal' supervisor and figure out for yourself what to do in a particular situation, or remind yourself not to be so self-critical. (If you're a professional counsellor, you'll continue to have clinical supervision as part of ongoing continuous professional development and ethical practice.)

Replenishing your batteries

Replenishing your batteries in the work situation means making sure that you take proper breaks, improve your working conditions, seek out support, and obtain further training. These are just a few examples, and the self-care questionnaire in the first section of this chapter can give you more ideas. If several people offer listening help within your circle, consider starting a peer support group. I know of a number of peer support groups that started at the end of counselling skills courses and are still continuing to meet years later.

Replenishing your batteries away from the work setting is likely to mean making more time for yourself.

Assertive responses

Here are some suggested scripts for being assertive in tricky situations. In these situations, take a deep breath and count to three before responding. Taking enough time is important to acknowledge the help-seeker's feelings.

Situation A

Problem: A colleague presses you to talk to one of his team. You know you'll end up with an intractable problem and you'll have to refer the person on elsewhere.

Response: 'I know you're worried about your work colleague but I don't think I'd be able to help him, from what you've told me. I think you should suggest that he speaks to his GP or gets professional help.'

Problem: Your colleague continues to press you – a sign that he's finding managing the situation hard.

Response: 'It sounds as if the situation is challenging. How can I help you to deal with it?'

Situation B

Problem: You're just about to leave work for a very important appointment. Someone asks if he can talk to you about a personal matter.

Response: 'I'm really sorry, I can see you're worried about something, but now is not a good time. I won't be able to give you proper attention because I'll be worrying about getting to my appointment on time. Can we arrange a time tomorrow when I'll have time to listen properly? How about 9 o'clock?'

Situation C

Problem: Your friend keeps ringing you to spill out his woes and ask your advice. You're worried about your friend but know that his problems are beyond your competence to deal with.

Response: 'I'm sorry you're having such a hard time, but I don't have the answers. I think you need to seek professional help. Will you do that?'

Problem: Your friend continues in the same vein, in which case you can use the 'stuck record' technique of repeating your response, with increased emphasis and fewer frills each time.

Response: 'You need to get *expert* help. When are you going to do that?'

Situation D

Problem: A young person you know discloses that he's involved in a dangerous situation (abuse or risk-taking for example). He doesn't want you to tell anyone else, but you're aware that it's your duty to involve others, such as his parents or head-teacher. Encourage the young person to talk about his concerns about disclosing to others.

Response: 'I can understand that you're worried about other people knowing and about what will happen afterwards, but it's my duty to take action to protect you from harm. I'm not allowed to keep this secret. Let's talk about how we can handle the situation together.'

Cultivating appropriate assertiveness

Part of taking care of yourself is managing your stress levels, your workload, and the demands made on you. You must be able to say no at times and be clear about what you can and cannot do. Confidence and assertiveness are key. Some people confuse assertiveness with being rude or very challenging and confronting. This doesn't have to be the case, although you must accept that sometimes, if you're straightforward in telling someone what you're unable or unprepared to do, he may not like it. At this stage you need to build plenty of self-confidence and self-esteem so that you're not crushed by his response.

Work out a clear idea for yourself of your role and its boundaries to help you to be clear with others about what you can and can't offer. Working within your limits is an important aspect of safe and ethical practice.

You can read self-help books and attend classes about assertiveness and self-esteem. Look for role models and reflect on how they approach things, and consider individual or group therapy as a way of developing your self-esteem and confidence. For more help with confidence and assertiveness, read *Building Confidence For Dummies* by Kate Burton and Brinley Platts.

Chapter 4

Maintaining Good Practice

*W*orking as a listening helper is a responsible role. Active listening skills are more powerful than is often realised, leading the speaker to open up and reveal issues that can be highly sensitive. As a result you may be faced with potential or actual ethical dilemmas. To be prepared for such eventualities you need to have thought about, and be clear about, the impact of your primary role (say, as teacher, colleague, or mentor) on the boundaries around your listening role. To whom are you accountable? Also consider your own values and how these concur with or differ from the values of the organisation you're employed by or involved with, and of the person who seeks your help. This chapter offers ways to take your thinking further about these potential conflicts.

Monitoring and Reflecting on Your Work

An important part of working ethically is to take time to reflect on what you do, including how the work impacts on you. Such reflective activity can be formal or informal. For example, you may have supervision that provides fixed points when you can consider your work. Peer-supervision arrangements are useful also. Whether or not you have these opportunities, you can make time informally, preferably on a regular basis, or after any helping conversation you have, to think over how the session went. Think about what went well and what was less effective, how you felt, what effects the session had on you, and so on.

Monitoring is an aspect of reflection which is more concerned with measuring, evaluating, and keeping records. Organisations are likely to require monitoring information to be kept. This information may include demographic and statistical types of data, such as age, disability, number of sessions, length of sessions, and so on. Some of this information may be useful to aid reflective activity even when you're not required to keep such details. For example, if you start to notice patterns, such as over-long sessions, then you may want to consider why that is. One reason could be that you're getting sucked into feeling over-responsible for someone. See the later section 'Keeping Records' for more on record-keeping.

Examining Ethical Dilemmas

Ethics refers to a set of moral principles or obligations; guides to your conduct. The *Oxford English Dictionary* describes moral as 'being concerned with goodness and badness of human character or behaviour or with the distinction between right and wrong, concerned with accepted rules and standards of human behaviour, conforming to accepted standards of general conduct.' Morals and ethics are usually arrived at by a consensus of opinion, although everyone weighs principles differently, which is why some ethical dilemmas are particularly challenging. Ethics applied to helping relationships aim to promote well-being and autonomy in the help-seeker, avoid harm to her or others, and ensure that the helper works within her competence.

Boundaries are connected to ethics. Boundaries refer to the limits set on a helping relationship relating to the nature of the contract being entered into by both parties. Although most situations involving the use of counselling skills in a helping conversation don't have a formal contract, an informal agreement exists. This 'agreement' may be *implicit* (not spoken of directly or acknowledged), or *explicit* (spelled out in the form of a clear verbal statement of your limits, especially relating to confidentiality, and/or written information that explains the service you offer and its limits). Having an implicit or explicit agreement is important for your own, and the other person's, protection.

Having an ethical dilemma crop up when dealing with people and their problems is always possible and happens more frequently than you may think. By developing your ethical-mindedness, you're less likely to be caught out when an issue emerges. Being ethically minded means being aware of and alert to possible ethical issues and having some familiarity with how you can deal with them. One way to develop this is to think in every helping situation you deal with what *could* the potential ethical dilemmas be in this situation – they may never present themselves, but this exercise gives you practice in thinking ethically.

The British Association of Counselling and Psychotherapy (BACP), like other organisations which offer personal services to the public, publishes a code of ethics and practice. If you belong to an organisation that has its own codes, you need to become familiar with them. If you don't belong to such an organisation, then the BACP Ethical Framework (www.bacp.org.uk) provides a good foundation for any listening role, not just for counsellors. The document is a *framework* because it sets out principles rather than rules.

A challenge of working as a listening helper is that many situations are individual and complex, and you won't have a 'right' answer. For this reason, avoid making ethical judgements alone and have a model for working through an ethical dilemma when it arises. See the later section 'A model for ethical decision-making' later in this chapter.

Some examples of ethical dilemmas

As you read the following challenges that can arise for a listening helper, take time to think about the implications of the situation.

- ✔ A woman begins to talk about her relationship with her teenage son. She suspects he may be taking drugs and you realise her son may be one of your own teenage son's circle of close friends at school.

- ✔ A person arrives to see you accompanied by a child – the child-care arrangements at home have broken down. The adult starts to disclose details that seem inappropriate in front of a child. Consider whether you'd react differently if the child was a baby, a toddler, of primary school age, or older.

- ✔ Someone talks to you about her relationship and how it's affecting her at work. Her partner also works for the same organisation. Does this raise any potential dilemmas in your mind? Quite independently her partner contacts you and asks to have a chat with you. What are the issues and how will you respond?

- ✔ A colleague has confided in you about the struggles she's facing with her deteriorating home life. She also mentions, in passing, that she has been stealing from work.

- ✔ A young person of 15, during a conversation about her future studies, hints that she won't be able to continue her studies because of problems at home. She says that she plans to leave school and home as soon as she can. You suspect that she is being abused in some way.

Think through these situations so that you're better prepared to make a decision if you're faced with similar dilemmas. The following section provides an ethical decision-making model to help you. The way you think through and deal with some of these examples and the ethical dilemmas arising in two case studies are discussed in Appendix A.

One of the challenges you'll face is that being a listening helper is not your primary role. For example, if your primary role is welfare work in an employment setting, your loyalties may be divided between this and your secondary role as listening helper. Your employer expects you to help the individual back to work as soon as possible whilst you may feel that she needs longer because of her difficult personal circumstances, or maybe even needs to change jobs. Another example is when you have a helping relationship and your social relationships overlap – for example you discover that your children attend the same school. (If you're interested in this topic, take a look at Gabrielle Syme's *Dual Relationships in Counselling and Psychotherapy: Exploring the Limits (Ethics in Practice)* (Sage Publications Ltd).)

A model for ethical decision-making

This model for making decisions about ethical dilemmas describes the steps to work through in arriving at the best possible action in response to an ethical dilemma and can be used by the helper alone and/or with colleagues, or by the helper with the person seeking help.

Step One: Take your time wherever possible

Give yourself as much time as you can to make your decision. That doesn't mean shelving the problem, rather that you don't get panicked into a speedy response. In situations where you recognise an ethical issue exists you may feel under pressure to reach a swift decision, but that may not be necessary. So, your first decision is to think, 'Do I need to make a decision about what to do *here and now*?' In most situations you won't need to decide what to do when you're in the presence of the help-seeker. However, you may need to decide if to let the help-seeker know that you have an ethical dilemma. The situations described in the previous section 'Some examples of ethical dilemmas' can result in different outcomes – in the first two you may initially be able to avoid saying you have a dilemma until you've had a chance to think the situation through. In the other examples you almost certainly have a duty to inform the help-seeker that you have an obligation to take the matter further. You may fear that this will be confrontational and upsetting to the help-seeker. Consider, though, why she's chosen to disclose the information to you when she most likely knows you'll have to do something as a result of her disclosure.

Knowing when not to listen

Sometimes allowing someone to open up is inappropriate, such as when you know you don't have the time to listen because you have a commitment elsewhere. In these instances you need to be assertive enough to interrupt if necessary and be firm about suggesting an alternative. This action is in the help-seeker's best interests as well as your own because to open up and then be left without resolution is unhelpful.

You need to be clear about what you can offer and to recognise the limits of your competence. You may be able to offer sympathetic and supportive listening in addition to other help a person is receiving, but to continue listening to issues that fall outside of what you can deal with is unhelpful, unless it's in order to enable the person to seek appropriate help. Once again, the ability to deal with someone going outside your area of competence requires assertiveness alongside sensitive responses. Sometimes people are resistant to finding more specialised help, which may be what you need to focus your attention on – what it is that gets in the way of the person obtaining the right kind of help. The person may need support and confidence building to tackle this problem.

You may also need to stop someone telling you more about an issue in which you have a bias or interest which would prevent you from being attentive and impartial.

You can be sensitive and collaborative in how you approach the situation by using your counselling skills and by remaining calm.

In instances where you face an ethical dilemma, you may want to take notes – for example, if you're discussing a complex situation it's important to get your facts straight.

Step Two: Gathering information

Make sure you have as much information as you can about the ethical dilemma. If you're in a position to do so, make a list of what you need to know and record the answers. If something crops up unexpectedly (as ethical dilemmas often do) you have to think on your feet, but remember Step One about giving yourself time.

Amongst the things you may need to find out are:

- ✔ All the relevant facts in the situation. Where possible fill in gaps in the help-seeker's story to make sure you have a proper understanding, including all the parties involved (such as other children at risk, or other agencies involved).

- ✔ What is fact and what is hearsay or assumption on the help-seeker's part or your own.

- ✔ The policies, procedures, and codes of ethics available to support you in the situation.

✔ The rights and responsibilities of the help-seeker, yourself, and any other parties involved.

✔ The emotional supports available for the help-seeker and for you during this process.

Step Three: Consultation

Wherever possible take the opportunity to check out your thoughts and any decisions you're considering with a trusted person, or with whoever you're responsible to in your organisation (when a situation arises in an organisational context). This is a time where two heads are definitely better than one. If you haven't informed the help-seeker that you'll consult someone else, then take care to protect her confidentiality as far as possible. Think through the important things in the situation and make notes either by yourself (using the guidance from Step Two) or in consultation with another. Answer these questions in your notes:

✔ What emotions are being evoked in you and how might these influence the process positively and negatively?

✔ What values (for each person involved, including yourself) are important and/or challenged by this situation?

✔ Who, specifically, is at risk?

✔ Exactly what are the risks and how imminent are they (as far as you can reasonably tell)?

✔ Who is (or who are) the person(s) with responsibility in this situation and what is the nature of the responsibility?

✔ What emotional supports will continue to be available during this process for the help-seeker and yourself?

Step Four: Decision-making

List the possible courses of action (even if they seem ridiculous) and their pros and cons, including how they support or conflict with any values and responsibilities you've identified as important to the help-seeker. When choosing the course of action aim for an outcome that everyone involved can be satisfied with. However, this may not be possible and you may need to take an action that puts some values ahead of others (for example the duty of care may take precedence over the help-seeker's autonomy). Take note of your gut reactions and emotions because they're indicators, in conjunction with your thinking, of whether the action seems right. Consider how you'll feel about the decision when you look back on it in a year's time and whether you'd be happy to open up your decision-making process to scrutiny by the help-seeker and the public.

Step Five: Evaluating the process

Always take time to reflect on the process you've been through when you've dealt with an ethical dilemma – this will help you for the next time. Consider what you'd have done differently if you could, what other guidance would have been helpful, and whether procedures need to be changed.

If possible, *always* discuss an ethical dilemma with someone you trust and anyone you are accountable to *before* taking a decision. Keep a written record of such discussions and their outcomes.

Working with Crisis and Risk

Sometimes when faced with a challenging situation that poses issues of safety and ethical responsibility, you can feel pressured to make rapid decisions. For example, you'd feel very worried about the physical safety of a 15-year-old who may be being abused, and have a sense of responsibility to protect her. At the same time you may worry about confidentiality and what the grounds are for breaking confidence in order to protect. In my experience, being in a position of having to make a snap decision by yourself is rare. Generally you have time to consult, and if there's any question of breaking confidentiality, be sure to consult, especially if breaking confidentiality is without the help-seeker's consent.

In a crisis you're stepping outside the normal listening-helper relationship, possibly acting for, or instead of, the help-seeker. In such circumstances you need to sense significant imminent danger to justify making decisions and taking action for the help-seeker, with or without her consent. Normally you expect to encourage her autonomy. Sometimes you can feel pressured or emotionally blackmailed to act as if something is a crisis when it's not. Being infected by the anxiety of another person isn't unusual. Often someone wants to pass the problem to you, so that she can feel better. Be as calm and unhurried as you can and avoid on-the-spot decisions, even if all you do is say you need five minutes to consider the situation before responding.

To discriminate between crisis, urgency, and importance, ask yourself:

- ✔ Do I need to take action right now?
- ✔ Who am I protecting by acting immediately – is it just myself?
- ✔ Do I need to take action today?
- ✔ What harm is likely if I don't take immediate action? Is the risk greater if action is delayed long enough for me to consult?
- ✔ Is there any risk of harm, and to whom, from taking immediate action? Which risk of harm (acting or not acting) carries the greatest weight?

Always give yourself time to think, maybe by taking a short 'time out' from the immediate situation.

Child protection

If you work in an organisation, you may be subject to policies and procedures in relation to protecting children from harm. You must make yourself familiar with these practices if you have any formal responsibility, and you would be wise to do so if you are an informal listener. If the organisation has no policies and procedures and/or training in their implementation, then you would do well to press for them.

If you're not using your listening skills in an organisational context, you won't have rules to guide your actions. In either case, if you're told something that leads you to believe that a child is at risk, you'll be faced with having to make decisions and deal with difficult feelings. Whilst you'll probably never feel fully prepared (every situation is different and throws up new challenges), thinking through some of the potential issues you may face can help you deal more effectively with such situations. This develops your *ethical-mindedness* – your ability to anticipate and think through ethical issues.

Finding yourself in possession of information that leaves you wondering, should I do anything about this?, can be anxiety provoking. Make sure you keep notes of key information, discussion, and decisions, and obtain support.

If you're in a medical context you can discuss the situation with the GP who has responsibility for the patient's care. If possible, obtain the patient's permission to do this. Initially you can also discuss the situation, without disclosing identifying information, with the NSPCC or Social Services, who can provide advice. People are often under the misapprehension that such discussion inevitably means that these services swoop in and remove children from their families. Of course they take child protection seriously but they also have a duty to preserve and support family relationships.

Suicide and self-harm

Believing that a person may be at risk of making a suicide attempt or harming herself is worrisome. Self-harm is often thought of as deliberate acts of abuse such as cutting yourself, but if you think about it more carefully, you'll realise that drug and alcohol misuse, eating disorders, and excessive risk-taking are all versions of self-harm. Of course, the limits are open to interpretation – what does 'excessive' mean for example? Checking your thoughts with others is a good way to think through how seriously you need to take someone's self-harmful behaviour.

The myth exists that people who talk about taking their own lives are not likely to do so. A contrary myth exists as well that talking to a person about her self-destructive urges will make her more likely to take her life if that's what she's struggling with. If someone talks to you about wanting to 'end it' or she says she's tired of life, take it seriously and make time to explore what her real thoughts are. Don't be scared to ask if the person has thought about how she would kill herself – the answer can often give you an indication of just how likely, and prepared, she is to do it.

You need to be clear about your own attitudes to suicide and the sanctity of life. What is more important to you: that you have autonomy to make your own decisions about whether to live or die, or that you're protected from yourself when in despair? Under what circumstances, if any, would you consider it a rational and acceptable decision to end your own life? I pose these as questions without suggesting answers because this is an individual moral choice.

When you're clear about your attitudes and values – as well as any organisational responsibilities required of you – then you can begin to think about and discuss whether you need to take any action to disclose your concerns to a third party, such as the person's GP. It's certainly worth exploring what other support is available to the help-seeker. Always mention and encourage contact with the Samaritans, who are available 24/7 – and not just for people about to commit suicide (see www.samaritans.org.uk, or call 08457 90 90 90).

You may face a dilemma of whether you need to offer more support. Talk this over with someone you trust if you can, but you may feel the need to treat this as urgent. Be cautious about offering more than you can realistically or reasonably manage, but you need to decide in your own conscience what is appropriate in the circumstances.

Keeping Records

Record-keeping is useful and sometimes an organisational requirement. Here are some reasons why.

- Organisations need to monitor whether they are reaching communities they need to reach, and hence need demographic data, which they may require for funding applications if they're publicly funded.

- When an individual is absent for any reason, someone else may need to pick up her work and find the necessary background information to fulfil her task.

- Note-keeping is a way of reflecting on your work.

- Individuals and organisations can find themselves subject to complaints and be required to justify and explain their actions.

Table 4-1 sums up why keeping records is so important.

Table 4-1	Purposes of Record-keeping for Various Stakeholders			
Help-seeker	*Helper*	*Agency*	*Profession*	*Society*
Protection	Aide-memoire	Accountability	Professional standards	Professional standards
Accountability of worker/ agency	Planning	Funding	Complaints processes	Legal proceedings
Best practice	Reflection	Admin.	Research	
Legal proceedings	Development	Audit/research		
	Protection (from complaints for example)	Complaints processes		
	Training			

A number of issues often surround records, including ethical considerations. The BACP lists the following principles to guide good practice: justice, beneficence (kindness), non-maleficence (avoiding harm), fidelity (trustworthiness), autonomy (ensuring the help-seeker remains self-governing), and self-respect. As you think about the following issues, keep these principles in mind:

- ✔ **Purpose:** Always be clear about what you're keeping records for (see Table 4-1). Apart from any organisational requirements, you may want to keep records for your learning, to protect yourself in the event of complaints or queries, and as an aide-memoire.

- ✔ **Access:** Consider who will have access to any records you keep. If you keep notes for your own learning will anyone else be able to see them, and is that appropriate? If you keep such records at home who else might be able to access them? How will you protect privacy and confidentiality?

- ✔ **Data Protection Act:** The previous point will be influenced by this legislation (see the section 'Data Protection' later in this chapter)

- ✔ **Retention and storage:** You may be expected to keep records for a certain length of time, which has implications for how they are stored. If records contain confidential material, this fact needs to be taken into account. If records belong to you, how can you keep them securely?

✔ **Ownership:** If you work for an organisation, any records may be considered to belong to the organisation. Some people favour giving clients/patients ownership of their own records. If you keep records yourself, how will you ensure the privacy and confidentiality of the people whose records you hold?

✔ **Medium:** Records can be paper-based, handwritten or electronically stored. Whatever system is used, records are subject to the Data Protection Act if they are held in any type of filing system.

✔ **Legal proceedings:** Records and notes can be the subject of legal proceedings. Always seek advice (from management, professional body, union, or lawyer) if you find yourself in this situation and before handing anything over to the police or courts.

✔ **Structure:** If you work for an organisation you may be given a prepared structure for keeping records. If you're keeping notes for your own use, and to aid your work, then you could find devising a structure for yourself helpful, although free-flowing writing can be useful sometimes. The structure helps you to control the amount you write. Headings may include the Presenting Problem (PP), other issues arising, what the speaker wants from speaking to you, what emotions were expressed, how you felt, hindering factors, hunches, concerns, any decisions made, and tasks agreed.

If you work in an organisation, always be sure you're aware of what's expected of you in relation to record-keeping. When organisations are new, or setting up new services, they may not have policies and procedures in place initially. They may also not be aware of legislation and ethical implications. I encourage you to bring to the attention of the organisation any issues you become aware of – which is part of your professional responsibility. This chapter may raise your awareness of policies and procedures that need to be developed.

Stick to the facts

As a general rule, if you have to keep a written account of your dealings with someone you're helping, keep the information factual and brief. Always bear in mind how you'd feel if the subject of your records actually read them (as she has a right to do) and how you'd feel if the notes were about you. As a minimum, record the date and key issues discussed and always record any agreed decisions or actions, noting the outcome of any consultation you've sought throughout the process.

If you keep a journal for your own development, write about your experiences in the journal, not in official records. Keep the journal only about you and your learning. Don't include client-related information except in the broadest way. For example, 'I spoke with someone today who had been through a similar experience of miscarriage which brought up all sorts of feelings for me. Her attitude was very different from mine though . . .'

Data protection

In recent years legislation has been introduced to protect people from inappropriate and potentially damaging storage of personal information. The Data Protection Act puts limits on what information can be held and gives rights of access to such information. If you work for an organisation they have a responsibility to inform you of your rights and duties and the rights of any service-users. In a listening-helper role if you are to practise ethically you want to ensure clients' privacy and that any information held is accurate and accessible.

Always bear in mind the right to privacy and confidentiality in all aspects of record-keeping. Avoid using real names in your own notes. Keep identifying details separately.

Part II
The Listening Helper

"Let's see if we can identify some of the problems in your life. You mentioned something about a large wolf that periodically shows up and attempts to blow your house down..."

In this part . . .

I look at all the aspects of how being a listening helper fits with you as a person, and how it affects your life and work. I explore why listening is so valuable, whether it can be harmful, and some common concerns about being a listening helper. I also introduce you to the three-stage model; a helpful structure to guide you as you develop counselling skills.

Chapter 5

Being a Listening Helper

*M*ost people find talking to an interested listener a positive experience. Humans are social beings and find pleasure and release in sharing thoughts and emotions with others.

When you're worried or afraid, confused or churned up, feeling abnormal or angry, unburdening yourself to another person is especially helpful. By doing so you feel less isolated and abnormal. Plenty of research confirms the positive benefits to physical and mental well-being of being listened to by an interested person.

Of course, who that person is and how he listens matters. People who take up counselling skills are often the kind of people others turn to naturally. In this chapter I explain what makes a good listener, how listening can form part of and enhance a helping role, and how developing as a listening helper can affect you.

The Value of Listening

When I'm troubled and muddled I value having the space to air my thoughts and feelings without too many questions and interruptions disturbing my flow. These are some of the things that are important to me when talking to someone:

✔ I want to feel that the person I'm talking to has some idea (empathy) about my feelings in the situation.

✔ I want him to listen carefully and attentively without judging me and show that he cares (offering respect and acceptance), although I'd prefer that he isn't too badly affected or I'd feel responsible for distressing him.

✔ I need him to be absolutely trustworthy and genuine. I'd like to trust him enough that I can reveal some of my deeper anxieties about myself and any shameful thoughts I may have.

✔ Sometimes I want him to offer ideas, but only after I've got the complete story clear in my own mind.

✔ I don't usually want him to take charge and tell me what to do, unless I'm in a complete panic, and even then I'd rather he calmed me by challenging the beliefs that have led to the panic and helping me to get things straight about my choices and resources.

✔ I'm ambivalent about being challenged, but I know that's what I need to get some different perspectives on the situation and realise that my assumptions are just that. Usually, after I've talked it through I have developed a fuller idea of what the issue really is and am clearer about what I want to do.

For me, the ideal listener is someone who can be calm, unbiased, demonstrates understanding and warmth, listens, and shows that he's listening. I need to have a relationship of trust to enable me to be honest about my fears, mistakes, hopes, and beliefs. When I can explore my feelings fully in this way and have space to reflect, I can begin to get a clearer perspective and be better able to make my own decisions. How does this vision compare with what you want from a helper?

Imagine being worried about something. Run an imaginary audiovisual recording in your mind of the conversation you might have with the *ideal* listener (or remember an actual conversation that went well for you). What are the attitudes shown towards you and how do you know that from the person's behaviour? To develop your reflective skills, keep a journal and make some notes. Compare your thoughts with mine and with the following section about the If . . . Then Hypothesis.

The Importance of Your Personal Qualities

Research suggests that the *relationship* between a client and his counsellor is one of the important ingredients of successful counselling and this also applies to other helping relationships. If you reflect back on the reasons why you prefer to talk to *this* person rather than *that* one you realise that the personal attributes and characteristics which draw you to that individual lead to particular relationship characteristics when that person is in helping mode with you. Flip to Chapter 6 for more about the personal qualities of a listening helper.

The If . . . Then Hypothesis

An influential counselling theorist and educator, Carl Rogers, believed from his own observations and his research that effective relationships (of all kinds) required certain characteristics. He set out what he called the *If . . . Then Hypothesis*. Put simply it goes like this:

If I can create a relationship that on my part:

- ✔ Is genuine
- ✔ Is warmly accepting of the other person as an individual
- ✔ Shows a sensitive ability (empathy) to see the other person's world and that individual as he sees himself

Then the other individual in the relationship can:

- ✔ Become more unique, self-expressive, and closer to how he'd like to be
- ✔ Have better self-understanding
- ✔ Find that he becomes more able to function and cope with the problems of life effectively, more self-directing, and self-confident
- ✔ Be more understanding and accepting of others

From my own experience I agree that these qualities (known as *Rogers' Core Conditions* and usually referred to as *respect*, *empathy*, and *genuineness*) provide a sound foundation for helping relationships, which is increasingly recognised by different types of helping. Simply having the ability to use the skills of active listening, such as paraphrasing, summarising, and open questions, isn't enough – an individual may be technically excellent at these but not be the kind of person that you would take your worries to. Using these skills with sensitivity helps to demonstrate helpful qualities and characteristics to the person seeking help.

The Core Conditions sound simple don't they? In practice, to be truly accepting, genuine, and empathic is much more challenging than you first imagine.

What happens when you don't listen

By using the power of your imagination and your ability to reflect, you can discover more about your own reactions. Listening to yourself in this way can help you to understand others. Here's a mental exercise to try.

Can you remember an occasion when you were trying to talk to someone but he wasn't paying proper attention? Close your eyes, recall this event, and notice your sensations and emotional reactions.

When I'm training listening helpers we sometimes do an exercise where the speaker talks to someone who shows he's *not* listening – through inattentive body language and by not showing interest through questions or verbal and non-verbal encouragement. Gradually the noise level in the room dies down – most people find sustaining a conversation in the face of indifference very hard. The emotions people describe range from frustration and anger to a sense of worthlessness. How does this compare to your own reactions in a similar situation? Try this same exercise with a willing partner.

Knowing What It Takes to Be a Listening Helper

Effective listening is the result of the listener being able to set aside his own judgements, preoccupations, and possibly his values, so these don't interfere with the process of listening. Effective listening involves being able to skilfully use a combination of active listening skills discussed in this book, and to selectively draw on life experiences and a range of information and knowledge. All these need to be underpinned by the Core Conditions, or qualities, described in the previous section, 'The If...Then Hypothesis'. Whether you're preparing to enter into a listening-helper role or you already find yourself in that position, you may worry that you don't know enough to be effective. I wouldn't be writing this book if I thought becoming a listening helper didn't require some thought, knowledge, and skills development, but I can offer you some reassurance and encouragement in the following points.

✔ Offering an effective listening ear doesn't necessarily require a lot of knowledge, in the sense of information. Knowledge, experience, and accumulated wisdom are of undoubted additional help. However, more important is the art of being an attentive listener. Experiencing unbiased and truly attentive listening, where the speaker doesn't have to worry about the other person getting his conversational turn, is rare.

✔ Research shows that trainee counsellors are sometimes more effective than trained and experienced counsellors – and that's probably true of people using counselling skills too. The reason is down to the intense interest, enthusiasm, and commitment that people have when they're learning something new. Body language, facial expression, and reactions reflect and communicate these things to the speaker, conveying that the speaker is valued and is being taken seriously.

✔ To some extent you find out about active listening through reflecting on what you read, your life experiences, and practising in your imagination and on friends, family, colleagues, and so on.

The Core Conditions (mentioned in 'The If . . . Then Hypothesis' section) are expressed through using certain skills. You will almost certainly have experienced and even used some of these skills in ordinary everyday conversations, without necessarily realising how they contributed to a helpful conversation. When these skills are purposefully put together in a helping conversation they're called *active listening skills* or *counselling skills.* To help you recognise and identify some of what you undoubtedly already know, try the following exercise.

Imagine or remember a conversation in which you confided in someone or asked for advice and where you felt the listener was listening and concerned. Write about such an experience before you consider the following questions and comments:

✔ **What posture has the other person taken?**

An attentive posture is usually facing you, either square on or at a slight angle so you can look away or keep eye contact. The listener may lean towards you a little to show interest. He may mirror your posture, which contributes to you feeling comfortable to talk and understood.

✔ **What is his facial expression like?**

An attentive expression tends to be serious but not overly solemn, maybe with an encouraging smile, but overall conveying concern.

✔ **What are his eyes doing?**

The gaze will be soft and eye contact will usually be maintained fairly steadily.

✔ **How do you know he's paying attention?**

The listener, apart from his posture, will most likely be using non-verbal encouragement in the form of 'mmm's' and nodding. As well as this he'll demonstrate he's been taking things in by saying some things back to you, sometimes summarising what you said and generally checking out his understanding. By using these skills he'll seem to be in tune with you.

✔ **What proportion of the time are you talking and how much is the other person speaking?**

You'll be doing most of the talking. When the listener speaks, the words are focused on what you've said rather than introducing other topics of interest to the listener. He'll also be interested *in detail* about your thoughts and feelings.

✔ **Does the conversation have spaces for you to think and to experience what you're feeling?**

A good listener leaves space and silences. Sometimes a timely summary gives you the chance to think about what you've been saying. When the listener notices your feelings it can help you to notice them properly yourself.

✔ **Does the listener ask you any questions? What kind of questions are they and do they help the flow?**

A good listener may ask you some questions, but they'll be to clarify and help you expand the issues rather than for him to decide what the problem is and what you need to do about it.

✔ **Do you think the listener understands your situation fully (or reasonably well)? How do you know that?**

When the listener takes care to check out his understanding by summarising, and being reasonably accurate in doing so, and when he identifies what you're feeling, you're likely to believe he understands your situation.

✔ **Does the listener solve the problem for you?**

Sometimes you may think you'd like someone else to solve your problems for you, but you're only likely to be committed to a solution that is of your own choosing. A good listener knows this and doesn't attempt to find the solution for you, although he may try to broaden your horizons and challenge your thinking with suggestions for you to consider. He may also help you find problem-solving strategies that work for you.

✔ **What feelings do you have after you've finished speaking?**

If you feel properly listened to in a helpful way you're likely to have a sense of relief. You may also have a renewed sense of purpose or possibility.

Think again about who you'd like to talk to if you have an issue you need to discuss. This time think about what kinds of things you want from the conversation with this person. Maybe you want different things for different problems. Are any themes common? Make some notes about your thoughts.

Different roles mean differing skills

When you engage in a helping conversation using active listening skills the aim is for the *speaker* to have as much control as possible. However, the balance of counselling skills and other skills reflects the role that you're in with the speaker. In an emergency, when time and action are of the essence, people don't waste time asking how someone feels about it. However, many roles and situations aren't so clear cut. A teacher or nurse, for example, may have to decide when it's appropriate to take control and when it's more fitting to listen and follow the speaker's lead.

Sharing Power in the Relationship

When a person seeks help from another, he almost inevitably puts the helper in control and gives him the power. When someone needs help he tends to feel vulnerable, and to some extent is in a 'one-down' position in relation to any person helping him. Feelings and reactions are coloured by all previous experiences of help-seeking and earlier relationships with authority figures. The help-seeker may even relate to the helper *as if* he's just like a figure from his earlier experience. As a listening helper you need to remember this possibility. Perhaps you can reflect on your own experiences and how you tend to react to anyone who tries to help you.

For the most part, when you use counselling skills as a helper, your aim is to make the relationship even, and give as much power and control to the speaker as possible. The exception is when doing so would be inconsistent with any responsibility you might have for the speaker's safety (or the safety of others who might be affected). The reasons for giving control to the help-seeker are that people are more likely to:

- ✔ Develop their self-esteem and empowerment as an individual through making and following through on their *own* decisions

- ✔ Be motivated and take action when they have decided for themselves

- ✔ Blame you if they can say, 'I did what you told me to' when things go wrong (in their opinion).

In the following types of helping behaviour, you can see that they start from the helper taking most responsibility, and therefore having most control of the situation, to the speaker completely setting his own agenda and taking charge of himself and the situation:

- ✔ **Acting *for* someone:** Taking a decision and acting on behalf of another person puts the helper in a position of authority, responsibility, and control.

- ✔ **Prescribing:** Setting a course of action for the other person (giving solutions, instructions, orders) similarly gives the helper most responsibility, although the speaker may choose not to follow the advice or instructions.

- ✔ **Advising:** Making suggestions is moving towards the speaker taking more control, although, because the helper is often invested with authority by the speaker, he may feel he has to take the advice given.

- ✔ **Questioning:** It may not seem so obvious that the helper is more in control of the conversation and actions here. However, when you ask a question you're setting the agenda, deciding the course the conversation should take. For example, the speaker may say, 'I'm thinking of giving up the course I am taking.' The helper might respond by asking, 'What's wrong with the course?' The speaker is directed by this response into telling the helper about the course when the problem is possibly elsewhere – perhaps the speaker is under pressure at home or work, feeling depressed, or suffering from anxieties about being in groups. Some speakers may say, 'Oh, it's not the course that's the problem it's . . .' However, some people worry about revealing what the real problem is.

- ✔ **Summarising:** By summing up what a speaker has said you're staying largely with his chosen direction. However, you've decided the point at which to intervene, decided what's important, and condensed what you've heard, possibly using your own instead of the speaker's words. Summarising in this way is not necessarily wrong; indeed it can be very helpful to the helping process, but you need to recognise that it subtly alters and shapes the conversation.

- ✔ **Clarifying:** Clarifying can be extremely helpful, but also gives the helper a degree of control of the conversation. You're identifying things that interest you or puzzle you – they may or may not be of particular interest to the speaker.

- ✔ **Reflecting:** Reflecting back specific words (especially feeling words) to the speaker, which is often a helpful intervention, again gives the helper some power in the conversation – you are deciding which words or feelings are worth noticing.

- ✔ **Listening:** Empathically listening by showing positive attention through body language and facial expression is least likely to put the helper in control, yet even here are subtle encouragements or discouragements to the speaker. A change in expression, an 'mmm' here or there, can suggest you're interested in hearing more, or not.

The last five helping skills form part of the package of skills called 'counselling skills'. The first three are things that may be included in your primary role, but aren't normally helpful in the kind of listening-helper role described in this book because they tend to take power away from the help-seeker.

The appropriateness of your response as a helper – the degree of control and power you exercise in the situation – depends on the nature of your primary role in relation to the person who's seeking your help. If you're using counselling skills as part of another role you face dilemmas about where you need to be on the spectrum of responsibility and control. For most counsellors the difficulty is to decide whether taking *more* control is appropriate, because in general their aim is to create an environment where their client has as much control as possible and is encouraged to take responsibility for his own life.

For the person using counselling skills as part of another role, *relinquishing* control may be harder. If you're a teacher, for example, you may face questions in your own mind about your responsibilities for a young person's safety and your potential loss of authority when you appear to step out of your normal role. You may also feel that, as an adult, you believe you know better than the young person. As a friend, you may have strong feelings about the speaker's situation and what you think he should do, which affect your ability to simply listen. You may also have information that the speaker doesn't have (for example you may know your friend's partner is cheating on him). Other professions or types of relationship with a person seeking help pose similar challenges and choices.

You can avoid some of the dilemmas facing you by being clear about your role, its purpose and limitations, and by making these clear to the speaker at the outset. The process of arriving at an understanding of what's being entered into by both parties and creating some boundaries around the relationship can be done in informal discussion and this forms part of the skills that a listening helper needs to develop. I look at this kind of informal contract making and boundary setting in more detail in Chapter 8.

Figuring Out How Being a Listening Helper May Affect You

Developing and using the skills of active listening can have an impact on you in a number of ways. Your personal and work life and relationships are likely to be affected in positive and rewarding ways, but relationships and your emotions may also be disturbed. This situation is true of any personal, study, and career development. You need to recognise this possibility and to realise that your friends, family, and colleagues may not understand the changes you're undergoing as you discover more about yourself and challenge your previous ideas and beliefs (and possibly theirs).

If you decide to pursue this role of listening helper be aware of both the benefits and the potential personal challenges of listening. Being a listening helper brings rewards, satisfaction, disturbance, and benefit to you because:

- ✔ Through listening to the problems of others you may find your own difficulties are put into perspective.

- ✔ You can be in danger of ignoring your own issues when you focus on those of others – noticing the struggles (or failings!) of others is always easier than noticing your own. In the short term you may feel better, but overall ignoring your own issues isn't helpful to you or the people you're trying to help. However, through reflection and experience you may come to realise when this is happening and understand yourself better. (Refer to Chapter 2 for more on the role of self-awareness and self-development.)

- ✔ Studying about and working with people leads you to understand that your own emotions and actions are usually normal, which helps your self-acceptance.

- ✔ Finding out about listening involves self-examination and increased self-understanding, which can be of great benefit to self-acceptance and emotional well-being. However, you may also become disturbed as you realise new things about yourself and the way you feel, think, and behave – you'll almost certainly develop a new kind of relationship with yourself. Because of this potential disturbance you need to take care of yourself and use whatever supports are available to you (see Chapter 3 for suggestions).

- ✔ You'll be challenged to recognise and to consider changing aspects of yourself that get in the way of relating to others, such as your prejudices and assumptions. You may currently be unaware of your beliefs about people that are based purely on prejudice and fear. (Flip to Chapter 7 on defences and Chapter 13, which includes more on prejudice and oppression.)

- ✔ Your self-esteem will rise if you're able to take responsibility to help and actually be helpful to another.

- ✔ Receiving positive feedback from someone you've helped is a good feeling.

In your job role

Using counselling skills as part of your job role can have some highly positive benefits, but can also bring some challenges:

- ✔ Your relationships with others improve because you listen more carefully, you become more aware of what people are really saying and meaning, and your own communications become clearer.

✔ You find that people gravitate to you to discuss more personal issues because they recognise that you're a good listener (this may happen already of course!). The extra demands on your time and energy mean that you need to have ways of limiting such demands and of taking care of yourself.

✔ You develop a better understanding of why people, including yourself, react and behave in the way that they do. As a result you become less defensive and more tolerant of others.

✔ You, your colleagues, and any person you're in a helping relationship with need to be clear about the boundaries around your job role. If you and they are unclear then you may find yourself in problematic situations where there are unreasonable expectations of you.

✔ As you develop your self-awareness and skills you find that you become more assertive. Whilst this change in you may prove personally beneficial, those around you may not be happy that they can no longer take advantage of you.

In your personal life

As in your job role, becoming a better listener in your personal relationships can have both an up and a down side:

✔ Your family and friends become aware that you're easier to talk to and you find that relationships improve.

✔ On the down side, family and friends may accuse you of 'counselling' them or becoming too assertive. Perhaps you become too close for comfort or are perceived as behaving unnaturally – playing the role of counsellor in a self-conscious way. Maybe your new-found awareness means that you spot patterns of behaviour and point them out (not always welcome!).

✔ As with work, you may find you become burdened with other people's problems and need to find a way to say no, to switch off, and not to take undue responsibility.

✔ When you embark on new study, especially when it involves personal development, it's likely to have an impact on your relationships. Finding out about active listening skills involves understanding more about yourself and this means examining your life and experiences. For some people this leads to self-questioning and reflecting on the life and decisions they have made, which can disturb close relationships in positive and negative ways.

In your career

Increasing your capability with the communication skills involved in active listening has a positive effect on your career and is likely to increase your career satisfaction:

- ✔ Sophisticated communication skills, in the form of active listening or counselling skills, are extremely relevant and helpful in many job roles and are likely to increase your effectiveness.

- ✔ Some employers positively value knowledge and experience of using counselling skills.

- ✔ However, if you work in an environment where these skills aren't valued you may become more dissatisfied. This could motivate you to change direction.

- ✔ Although you can find out a great deal from reading and informally practising listening skills, the best way to develop your skills and knowledge is in a group in a work, college, or university environment. Through such environments you can also obtain certificated learning.

- ✔ Having a place where you can use your developing counselling skills is important. For many people this is best done in a voluntary sector setting. Undertaking voluntary work benefits your CV while giving you valuable and varied experience. Making a contribution to the community can also enhance your self-esteem.

On your personal resources

Acquiring and developing counselling skills make demands on your personal resources because of the commitment and time involved. Using counselling skills can also be emotionally draining. For these reasons you need to:

- ✔ Have a good support network.

- ✔ Not be afraid to say 'no' if you feel that you can't cope with additional responsibility.

- ✔ Take care of yourself physically and emotionally.

You can find out more about looking after yourself in Chapter 3.

On your emotions

Some aspects of attentive, active listening may lead to challenges for you:

✔ Active listening can lead to people opening up more than is helpful or appropriate in the particular time and place. You need to be in a fit state to resume your primary role when you return to your other activities.

✔ Someone opening up to you can be a very privileged feeling, but it can also be overwhelming. What the speaker has revealed may trigger emotions related to your own experience.

✔ The speaker may become angry or upset with you, possibly because you cannot give him what he wants, perhaps because he regrets telling you so much, or because he has difficulty with an authority figure in his life and you represent authority.

✔ You may find yourself feeling helpless or anxious during the discussion and/or unable to let go after the conversation is over, perhaps taking your worries home with you.

For all of these reasons you need to have somewhere appropriate to offload your concerns and share any anxieties raised by the work. In Chapter 3 I say more about self-care and the role of support, consultation, and supervision.

Thinking about Other Concerns

A number of situations can crop up where the support of someone who understands the listening-helper role would be very helpful for you. Knowing a little about some of these situations helps you to feel more prepared. Here are some particular concerns that tend to worry listening helpers, especially at the beginning.

The speaker gets upset

As an empathic listener you may find that the speaker's feelings suddenly burst out. For the listener this can be scary. Although you have responsibility to manage the situation so that the speaker can eventually leave the conversation able to face the world outside, expressing emotion can be very helpful – pent-up emotions block people from thinking and recognising what's truly important to them. If you're uncomfortable with this kind of situation you may try to prevent the speaker expressing his emotions by being sympathetic and saying (actually or in effect), 'There, there, don't cry,' or by moving into solution-finding mode too quickly. If you find being present when others express emotions difficult you need to think about why this is so, whether being a listening helper is right for you, or if you can eventually accept emotion (or particular emotions). To achieve acceptance of others' emotions means you become more aware of where your own feelings come from.

Sometimes people worry that to open up sadness may make the speaker worse or depressed. In general this doesn't happen. However, if the depth of someone's sadness or despair worries you, recommend that he sees his doctor and check what other supports he has or knows about (friends, family, place of worship, Samaritans, and so on). Whenever you're anxious about something like this, consider *asking* the speaker if he'd prefer to express or hold back his feelings.

From training many people in counselling skills, I know that the skill of talking about what's going on in the mind of the help-seeker at that particular moment is very challenging, and may take you some time and practice to develop.

The speaker gets angry

Many people are uncomfortable with anger – their own and other people's. This discomfort may be more apparent if you're a woman because, in general, women in our society have been socialised to keep their anger under wraps. The concept that anger is bad, rather than natural, is acquired early on. You have formative experiences of the anger of authority figures when you were little, such as your primary care-givers or teachers, which may leave you scared of anger.

Alternatively you may have experienced oppression and have accumulated a well of anger and a sense of injustice that is triggered when you're with others who are oppressed. You identify with them and want them to stand up for themselves. This identifying with the help-seeker creates a tricky situation for a listening helper. You have to tread a fine line between helping a person identify that he's being oppressed and offering him support, and fulfilling your own agenda by inciting him to vent his anger. Remember: being a listening helper is about the speaker's agenda, not yours. This kind of situation could have unforeseen consequences and the speaker may later regret his actions (and possibly blame you).

As you may realise, understanding your own attitudes and habits in relation to anger is useful if you're to be open to the other person without your own baggage intruding on the helping relationship.

Bad behaviour is still bad behaviour: What you do with your anger is important. Anger has energy and can be the force for change. So, on the positive side, when a speaker gets in touch with his anger he may get the energy and impetus to initiate change. Anger may have a negative side if the speaker can't control its manifestation. If the anger is turned inwards he may become self-destructive and/or depressed. If the anger is turned out he may vent his spleen on you or others. If someone is self-destructive, suggest that he sees his doctor and check what other support he has. If the anger is directed outwards you may need to check what his intentions are towards people and property. If you have any concerns that the anger is going to be directed at you in an aggressive way then you need to ensure your safety first and foremost – never take risks. In both these scenarios consult a trusted colleague about appropriate action.

In more than 20 years' practice as a counsellor I have never experienced a client being worryingly aggressive with me, but clients are sometimes angry with their counsellors. This situation can arise because the counsellor has done something that merits an angry response, or because the client has projected an aspect of his past experience onto their counsellor, and this becomes part of the counselling work to explore. However, in a counselling skills relationship you may have more than one relationship with a speaker (for example as a line manager) and these roles have a potential for conflict, which can cause angry feelings to be aroused. You need to be aware of these issues when entering into so-called 'dual relationships'. Be clear about the boundaries of your role.

When the speaker harms himself

Self-harm takes many forms. People tend to think of self-harm as people attempting suicide or cutting themselves. To these examples you can add dangerous levels of alcohol, tobacco, and other drugs (prescription, over-the-counter, and 'recreational'); other addictions, such as cyber-sex, serious over- and under-eating (eating disorders such as anorexia and bulimia); other forms of serious risk-taking; workaholism; spendaholism; and probably many more. You need to treat these activities seriously without being unduly focused upon them – a difficult balance. As a listening helper these issues are beyond your scope and you need to encourage the speaker to seek appropriate help. You may be able to locate such help but generally the speaker needs to seek the help himself, possibly with a great deal of support and encouragement from you. Approaching a professional person or organisation and admitting that help is needed takes a great deal of courage. Speaking to you is a helpful rehearsal. You may be able to find out about the services on offer so that you can allay misconceptions and anxieties.

Avoiding harm as a helper

Conscientious helpers frequently worry that they might inadvertently cause harm. On the whole, active listening is a benign activity. However, it is possible to do harm. Most of the ways of causing harm are related to taking on more than you capable of and/or not recognising that referral is called for. This kind of situation often happens out of the best of motives. Good support and consultation can help you avoid harm. (See Chapter 11 for more on referral and Chapter 16 for discussion about things that can go wrong.)

You can cause harm by being a listening helper inappropriately, for example:

- ✔ In some dual relationships where the roles and expectations are blurred.
- ✔ By getting more involved (in your concern and enthusiasm to help) than you can realistically manage.
- ✔ By not referring on appropriately when you find the situation is more complex than anticipated.
- ✔ By fulfilling your own needs; for example, enjoying being needed and therefore unconsciously encouraging dependence.
- ✔ By gaining satisfaction from the other person's emotions or actions.
- ✔ By using your skills to open someone up and not taking adequate time to help him come back to his everyday life and responsibilities.
- ✔ If you don't recognise when a person needs additional or more in-depth support through his doctor or other agencies.
- ✔ If you don't have adequate support for yourself.

You can safeguard yourself to some extent by making sure you have good supports and opportunities to discuss your work. Refer to Chapter 4 for more discussion about safe practice.

The speaker becomes too dependent

The idea for the speaker becoming dependent can be seductively dangerous for either the speaker, or the listening helper, or both. The listening helper can be enticed into the guilty pleasure of feeling needed and the speaker similarly can be attracted to feeling cared for. Whatever your helping role, your aim needs to be to assist the speaker to develop his own resources. Some experts decry dependence but my own opinion is that some dependence is likely – preferably only for short periods of time – and you need to be alert to the issue and deal with it sensitively. As in all the areas of concern, having a trusted person to discuss such things with is helpful, always being mindful of the speaker's rights to privacy and confidentiality.

Thinking on the Fly

Has anyone ever said to you (ominously), 'Have you got a minute?' You'll sometimes find that a person approaches you to talk at an inconvenient time and it immediately becomes apparent that he wants to discuss a pressing problem. Alternatively, towards the end of a conversation you may realise that he's worried about something (perhaps bringing the subject up has

taken courage) and you don't have the time, the energy, or the patience –
or it may not be appropriate – to take the matter further. You need to be
assertive and confident enough to make a quick assessment of how urgent
and desperate the problem is and to make a decision about if and when you
can offer an alternative time to talk.

Rehearse some phrases that can help in this type of situation, for example:

- ✔ 'I'm really sorry, I can see that you're worried. I don't have time right
  now to be able to discuss this properly with you. Can we meet/speak on
  the phone at . . .?'

- ✔ 'I'm due at a meeting and it sounds like you need a little time to talk this
  over. Perhaps it would be better to arrange another time. How about . . .'

- ✔ 'This sounds like something I can't help you with. The person you need
  to talk to is . . . or would you like me to find out who you'd be best to
  talk to?'

The important things are to acknowledge the person's feelings and to be specific about what you can offer. Whether you explain why you cannot talk just
then is up to you. The danger of doing so is that if your commitment elsewhere sounds negotiable, and the speaker may try to persuade you to stop
and talk.

Reflecting on Practice

Whenever you come across something new when working with counselling
skills, take time to reflect. Reflecting on practice means thinking about:

- ✔ The skills you've used and how effective you've been in using them.

- ✔ Any feedback you receive from the speaker, a 'witness', or someone you
  discuss things with afterwards.

- ✔ What knowledge you might need to develop.

- ✔ The feelings that were aroused in you during any interaction.

- ✔ The subsequent impact on you of the work you've done.

- ✔ Any concerns you have that you may need to consult about.

If you have the possibility to discuss your observations and questions with
someone, then make use of that opportunity – doing so is not a sign of weakness but shows you're reflective and willing to learn from experience.

One way of reflecting on practice is to keep a journal. If you like writing, journal-writing is straightforward. If, like me, you find that writing a diary or journal is a challenge, give yourself a short time limit (no more than 10 minutes) and simply keep writing anything that comes into your head, even if it's nonsense. Try not to censor yourself or judge what you're writing as you go, or what you've written when you've finished. The writing is for you alone. You'll be surprised at how often something useful comes out of this exercise. If you really can't contemplate writing, use a dictating machine to make verbal notes.

Chapter 6

Qualities, Skills, and Knowledge for Listening

In This Chapter
▶ Discovering the personal qualities needed to be a listening helper
▶ Using a three-stage model to guide you
▶ Sourcing other knowledge that can help you

*B*eing a listening helper is demanding. You need to develop self-awareness (covered in Chapter 2), be aware when your personal resources are being depleted (Chapter 3 gives you an insight into this area), and ensure that your working situation is safe (see Chapter 4 for advice on this subject). If you're going to spend time listening to the problems of other people, you need to develop resilience, courage, awareness, and good practice (all of which are supported by the topics discussed in the aforementioned chapters).

In this chapter I talk about the *personal* qualities that the UK's professional body for counsellors, the British Association for Counselling and Psychotherapy (BACP), has identified as necessary for listening helpers These personal qualities form part of your resourcefulness.

Developing Your Personal Qualities

The BACP has identified the essential characteristics of a counsellor which are set out in their *Ethical Framework*. People who use counselling skills as part of another role will find these apply just as much to their work as well.

According to the BACP, the qualities of a good listener (explained in detail in the following sections) are: empathy, sincerity, respect, integrity, humility, fairness, wisdom, courage, resilience, and competence (knowledge and skills).

A tall order! I would add assertiveness to the list, as well.

A sense of commitment

To be an effective listening helper, you need to be committed to the role and to the individuals you're listening to. Being a listening helper requires the development of certain personal qualities, and these demand commitment. If you find yourself losing your sense of commitment, you may simply be experiencing a temporary situation – maybe you're tired and need to take time out for a while, for example. If the lack of interest and commitment endures, consider whether counselling is really what you want to do or if some other impediment, such as dissatisfaction with your work or personal life, requires attention (refer to Chapter 3 for more about these situations). A help-seeker is highly likely to spot a lack of commitment and feel less able to trust you and your ability to hear what she has to say.

If you decide to talk to someone about a situation that matters to you, what are your reasons for choosing that particular person? Why do you trust her? What qualities does that person have? What makes her a good listener? Take some time now to make notes so that you can compare your ideas with some of the suggestions in this chapter.

As you read about each of the following qualities, you may find that thoughts and memories about being in a speaker, listener, or observer role during a helping conversation occur to you and these would be good to reflect upon, again making notes. Notice that these characteristics are interrelated and depend on each other.

Empathy

Recent research has shown that empathy is a very important aspect in successful helping relationships. *Empathy* has been described as the ability to step into another's shoes, to see her world from her perspective while not losing sight of other points of view. To feel empathic means being able to concentrate on gaining understanding of the other person and the way she experiences her life. It also means reaching inside yourself, drawing on your own experiences, particularly of emotion. Gaining an internal understanding of the other person's experience is important but you also need to communicate your understanding through body language and verbal responses.

Here's an example of how empathy is distinguished from other possible attitudes. Imagine a person who has fallen in a ditch. The unsympathetic passers-by either pass without comment or else berate the unfortunate victim for being stupid in the first place and pathetic for not getting herself out. A sympathetic passer-by sits on the bank and cries with her, bewailing her fate. The empathic passer-by shows that she understands how helpless the victim feels, holds out a hand to the person in the ditch, and helps her scramble out, without commenting on how she got herself there in the first place.

Being empathic involves accepting the other person, and making a connection with her, demonstrating rapport and thereby enabling the person to open up and explore the issues she's struggling with through the development of trust.

Sincerity

Sincerity is often referred to as genuineness, and sometimes authenticity, and means that you are what you seem. You're probably not always genuine in daily life because you appraise a situation realistically and decide that being honest is not in your, or someone else's, best interest. Alternatively you may have learned, possibly, but not always, from your family of origin, to fear the reactions of others. You defend yourself emotionally by using *defence mechanisms* – for example humour, avoidance, sarcasm, put downs, and so on – to guard yourself. In this way you attempt to deflect another person's potential reaction or cover your true feelings.

As a listening helper the masks you wear tend to get in the way of the helping process. A help-seeker can usually spot the person who is not being sincere with her. I find I'm reluctant to disclose anything important to someone who lacks sincerity or genuineness, because I cannot gauge whether I'm being accepted or judged. See Chapter 7 for more about what stops you from being genuine and how you use defences.

Being a critical thinker

An important quality of a listening helper is the willingness to think critically about your own ideas and the ideas of others. I encourage you not to believe everything you read. All theory and research are approximations, flawed attempts to reach helpful explanations which can guide our thinking, understanding, and actions. Human beings are socially and psychologically complex and any theory or research, however helpful it appears and however eminent the author, is not The Truth and the last word. Also, what works for one person or a certain situation may not work for another. Compare what you read with your own experience and be prepared to criticise what you read as well as your own ideas and ways of working.

Respect

Respect is also referred to as acceptance, although the two are not exactly the same. To enable someone to talk to you freely, you need to cultivate an attitude of acceptance, valuing her and giving respect to her and her struggles. You can see the link with empathy here. Accepting, valuing, and respecting yourself are all related attitudes.

Individuals who are very critical of others lack self-esteem, even though this may not be immediately obvious to those around them. Often the thing you most deplore in others is what you most fear or dislike in yourself. If you become more accepting of yourself, then you are less likely to judgemental of others.

You'll come across the term *non-judgemental* in other books about counselling skills. Personally I find this a clumsy and misleading word because it's not possible to be without judgement. You can become less judgemental by tackling your prejudices and assumptions (see Chapters 2, 7, and 13) but you're unlikely to rid yourself of judgement. Develop an awareness of the judging part of yourself and so minimise its effects.

Integrity

You're expected, as a listening helper, to act in good faith, with honesty and moral uprightness in your dealings with those you try to help. *Integrity* is connected to respect and genuineness in that all three are based on honesty. The word also suggests that the person with integrity is integrated, that she's consistent and reliable.

You may spot a potential problem with some of these qualities – what if you don't respect or feel able to accept the other person? Should you be honest? Some people distinguish between a person's behaviour and the essential humanity of the person and find that helps them. Some find that they can suspend judgement until they know the person better, when the behaviour becomes more explicable and therefore easier to accept.

You may think that only the obvious and 'big' things are difficult to accept. For example, many of my students say that they would find working with child abusers or rapists difficult. Certainly you need to decide whether you're able to help people that you have made fundamental judgements about and where you have a serious conflict with your values and beliefs. However, often the smaller things cause most difficulty for the listening helper, such as feeling critical of people who are overweight or who have treated their family or partner inconsiderately.

ANECDOTE

Embracing difference

As a supervisor I once facilitated a group where someone brought a situation that she found difficult to deal with. I suggested that she try playing the client whilst someone else took the helper role to see whether that gave her some ideas about how to work with her client in the future. The change of role brought out some interesting aspects of how to handle the situation. After this role play someone else said, 'Can I have a go?' She approached the 'client' in a very different, but equally effective way. Everyone in the group realised that no single correct way of helping the client existed, and I hope the experience led to increased acceptance and respect of each others' differences, and greater humility.

You may also believe that concealing negative reactions is best, and just get through the conversation – and in some short-lived helping relationships that may be possible, the most appropriate, and the least damaging way. Remember though, that the person you're trying to help may already perceive your negative feelings, so avoiding what some people call *the elephant in the room* (the thing that everyone knows about but that remains unacknowledged) may endanger your relationship.

Most people are quite astute at picking up when someone feels negatively or indifferently towards them. You need to be truly accepting of a wide range of people, which takes self-examination and self-development (I discuss self-development in Chapter 2).

Resilience

Helping people through dialogue is more demanding than many realise. You need to develop the ability to be open-hearted and yet protect yourself. Being resilient means having the strength of character to cope with demands made on you. Make sure that you have ways of recharging your batteries, through rest, relaxation, other absorbing activities, good supportive relationships, and generally taking care of yourself (refer to Chapter 3 for more about self-care).

Humility

You may only see other people as the ones who have problems but remember that, as human beings, everyone is susceptible to losing confidence, making mistakes, being defensive, acting foolishly, and so on. If you're experiencing problems, would you rather talk to someone who seems to have everything in her life completely sorted or someone who can understand what it's like to feel vulnerable? Considering your own failings and recognising that you aren't superior to the help-seeker is a form of humility that helps to put the other person's problems in perspective.

Seeing yourself as the competent one with all the answers, knowing best, can be very seductive. However experienced and competent you are, you cannot automatically assume that you know what is right for another person. Remember, you always have more than one way of approaching a problem.

Fairness

Fairness is about treating people as equal, but society and individuals can behave in oppressive ways. As a helper, strive to recognise any tendencies to behave unfairly and overcome them.

Keeping a diary is a good way of developing self-insight. One of the things you can reflect on in your diary with honesty is fairness. If you're a listening helper within an organisation consider whether staff and any service users are treated in an egalitarian and respectful way. You may need the other qualities discussed in this chapter to challenge organisational practices or other people's actions that are unfair.

Wisdom

The dictionary tells me that *wisdom* involves judgement and prudence. The definition also refers to knowledge, common sense, and learning as well as speculation and spiritual perception. These definitions suggest that wisdom involves being well informed but also having an open mind and the ability to be discerning.

When I think of the people I believe to be wise, they also have an attitude of thoughtful reflection, not rushing to conclusions and judgements. Think and make notes about someone you judge to be wise and what makes her so.

The inclusion of a spiritual dimension is interesting because spirituality has become a topical issue in the counselling and psychotherapy field, with increasing recognition that spirituality or religion is an important part of people's lives, to be taken into account when working with problems. Many of the issues that people struggle with are connected to some degree with the problems and mysteries of existence.

Courage

Listening to people's difficult experiences often requires courage. Sometimes you may feel out of your depth. Having courage means taking risks, exposing your own doubts, fears, uncertainties, and mistakes. Often you have to contain your own anxiety and make decisions by yourself. You may be faced with situations where you must compromise on one value in favour of another, for example, breaking confidentiality to ensure a child's safety (refer to Chapter 4 for more on good practice and ethical decision-making). You may also find yourself in a situation where you need to challenge the behaviour of an organisation or colleagues.

Competence

Competence is a combination of knowledge and skills, and knowing when to use them. The pool of knowledge that could be useful in helping others is vast and knowing all that might be relevant is impossible. What you *can* do is continue to update and develop your knowledge and the art of listening through reflection, relevant reading, and further training. What the speaker mainly needs from you is for you to listen carefully so that she can work out for herself what the problem really is and what to do about it. Developing the confidence to admit *not* knowing is valuable – the speaker then has to explain and explore in more depth, which helps her understand herself better and find her own resources. Later, however, you might go away and attempt to find out relevant information for her. However, what she needs may be beyond your capacity. Understanding your own limits is an important part of working ethically (refer to Chapter 4 for more discussion of good practice and ethics).

Assertiveness

Assertiveness means the ability to stay true to yourself and what you think is right (so it's related to integrity); to believe in yourself; and to speak plainly and directly when necessary, without being aggressive or imposing your ideas on another. It involves taking responsibility for your own position and reactions (for example, by using 'I think/believe . . .'). Assertiveness also includes the ability to hear what another person has to say without feeling overly defensive or destroyed by it.

You need to be assertive at times, both directly in the encounter with someone who is telling you her troubles and in your role as a listening helper outside of those conversations, such as when you maintain the speaker's confidentiality or act as an advocate.

Working with Active Listening Skills

Developing courage, fairness, integrity, and so on means working on your self-awareness. However, communicating these qualities relies on certain skills, sometimes called *active listening skills*.

What follows is a model of listening divided into stages. Different skills are attached to each stage. This framework helps you to identify the components of a helping conversation. First I take a look at the stages and what each stage is attempting to accomplish. Later in this chapter the individual skills are identified. Subsequent chapters discuss them in more detail.

Initially, as you begin to deconstruct your normal conversational skills, you will probably feel *de*-skilled. This is quite normal. Like a tennis player who goes to a coach to improve her game, everything at first goes to pieces as the player's game is broken down into its component parts. Later, greater mastery is acquired through practice and the skills can be put together again.

Realising that a helping conversation differs from ordinary conversation

Active listening, *communication*, and *counselling skills* are all terms used interchangeably and denote much the same set of skills. These communication and relationship-building skills are used intentionally in a helping conversation. Using techniques of everyday, casual conversation, but with a different emphasis, these exchanges differ from normal conversation in the following ways.

Active listening:

- ✔ Is a deliberate helping conversation with an understanding about confidentiality, unlike everyday conversations.

- ✔ Has the intention of *one person mainly responding to the other*, in a purposeful, accepting, unbiased manner. Normal conversations tend to consist of a more interactive style with mutual sharing of stories, thoughts and opinions and the subject matter is usually less focused.

- ✔ Usually intends to help the other person work towards an outcome or goal.

- ✔ Uses a conscious discipline of putting aside your own preoccupations to concentrate as fully as possible on what the other person is expressing, using a high level of self-understanding. By contrast, everyday conversation is often rather casual, inattentive and lacking in self-awareness.

- ✔ Involves one person taking care to understand very accurately by double-checking, summarising, and repeating some of the content of the speaker's communication, all of which may feel unnatural.

The skills of normal conversation are, so to speak, *reconfigured* for helping conversations. Certain skills are more prominent and others are used rather less – for example, drawing attention to emotions through the skill of reflection and staying with silences are both more common than in everyday conversation. Also, particular skills are more useful at different times in the helping encounter; for example, relationship-building skills are vital in the early stages and towards the end problem-solving skills may come into play. These skills are identified in a framework of a three-stage model of exploration, understanding, and action, as shown in Figure 6-1.

Figure 6-1: The three-stage model framework.

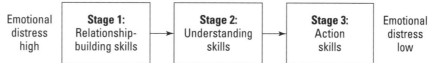

These stages are a way of structuring a helping conversation and the acquisition of the relevant skills to undertake it. When conducting a helping conversation, keep this structure in mind to help you manage the time and process of the encounter.

The model implies a sense of purpose and a linear progression. While I encourage you to have a sense of purpose, in real life helping conversations and the helping process don't follow such a neat linear progression. You may well experience helping conversations that do take such a path, but you will probably feel confused, that the stages are not always clear, and that you seem to be going backwards sometimes! However, when you reflect at a later stage, seeing that you and the help-seeker have progressed through these stages may be easier.

The three-stage model: The aims of the stages

Each stage of the three-stage model has a purpose. At the beginning of a helping encounter you aim to set the scene, enable the help-seeker to engage in the process, and begin to explore her issues by using the relationship-building skills of Stage One. As the relationship develops you deepen the exploration for you and the help-seeker to gain further understanding, using the more challenging skills of Stage Two. Towards the end of Stage Two you assist the help-seeker to identify what she wants to achieve so that in Stage Three you can use problem-solving and action skills to move towards a conclusion. Table 6-1 gives a summary of the stages.

Table 6-1	The Three-stage Model: The Aims of the Stages	
Stage	*Skills*	*The Help-seeker*
One	Relationship-building	Feels valued, understood, prepared to trust the listener, and able to tell her story.
Two	Exploring and clarifying	Is able to talk and explore, understand more about how she feels, consider and choose options.
Three	Action and closing	Can develop clear, achievable objectives and action plans, do what she needs to do, and manage the ending.

Stage One: Relationship building skills – exploration of help-seeker's story

Stage One is concerned with meeting the help-seeker, beginning to form a productive relationship with her, and reaching an understanding of whether and how you can work together on the problem she wants to discuss. This involves using particular qualities and skills to create an environment of trust and openness where the help-seeker can tell her story.

Relationship-building skills help develop rapport through:

- ✔ Contracting, which means discussing the purpose and limits of the helping relationship in relation to the issue the help-seeker wants help with.

- ✔ Meeting, greeting, and seating.

- ✔ Respect, empathy, and genuineness (the *core conditions*).

- ✔ Understanding and working with the client's frame of reference.

- ✔ Paraphrasing and summarising, which show you are paying attention. They also slow the process down so you and the speaker can consider what has been said.

- ✔ Reflecting thoughts, content, and (importantly) feelings.

- ✔ Mirroring body language (with subtlety).

- ✔ Non-verbal communication to show warmth, encourage speaking and convey that you are tracking the speaker's talk and emotions.

- ✔ Careful observation.

- ✔ Open questions that encourage the speaker to elaborate and that develop the story and fill in gaps.

- ✔ Probing and prompting.

- ✔ Timing and pacing.

Stage One skills continue throughout the encounter, providing the foundation for the other stage skills. These skills are often underestimated, especially summarising, reflecting, and paraphrasing. You also build the relationship by showing that you're listening and endeavouring to understand. Contracting skills not only provide safety by offering clarity about issues, such as your role, the time you have available, and confidentiality, but also help in conveying respect and contribute to managing the session.

Stage Two: Exploring and clarifying skills – understanding the help-seeker's story

These skills help to open exploration (in conjunction with Stage One skills) and lead to focusing on what really matters in the situation by:

- Clarifying through asking open questions.
- Encouraging concreteness (concrete examples of what the speaker is describing).
- Encouraging specificity.
- Using immediacy – sometimes called *you-me talk*.
- Challenging – offering alternative perspectives, challenging negative-self talk.
- Confronting, such as pointing out discrepancies.
- Appropriate self-disclosure.
- Identifying key issues.
- Giving feedback.
- Identifying objectives.
- Helping to identify and maintain motivation.

These Stage Two skills enable a deeper understanding of the issues so that there isn't a premature rush to the third stage, a common fault in listening helpers at the beginning of their training.

Stage Three: Action and closing skills – ending the relationship

These skills move the speaker towards action and ending (including Stage 1 and 2 skills) and include:

- Action planning
- Problem-solving skills and strategies
- Supporting and encouraging
- Addressing blocks
- Renegotiation

✔ Evaluating

✔ Future proofing (helping the speaker plan for future challenges)

✔ Ending management.

These Stage 3 skills not only move the whole process towards a productive conclusion (if you have more than one meeting) but also help manage the closing down of a single session. Management of the ending of a session or sessions relates to the contracting skills of the first stage, where the boundaries (such as session duration) would be discussed. If contracting has been neglected, managing the ending will be more difficult.

I discuss all of these skills in detail in Chapters 8–11.

Managing the helping process

Managing a listening session involves several aspects, such as:

✔ **Managing the beginning:** The opening of a helping conversation is often crucial. In these moments a person seeking help makes judgements about whether to disclose personal details and feelings (and how much), and whether she can trust you. The meeting, greeting, and seating are important elements, especially if the person isn't already familiar with you.

✔ **Managing the timing:** Managing the timing of a listening session is important. Helping conversations can happen when you least expect them and take longer than you anticipate. Think about how to deal with unplanned, as well as planned, sessions so that the speaker feels adequately heard and not left unable to cope with what has been opened up in the conversation.

✔ **Managing the duration:** Speaker and listener can wind up exhausted and frustrated if a session lasts too long, or left dealing with difficult emotions and thoughts if the session is too short.

✔ **Managing the boundaries:** Boundaries is a jargon word used in the counselling and psychotherapy world to describe the limits on the counselling contract (refer to Chapter 4 for more on this).

✔ **Managing the story or content:** Some people are able to tell a coherent story which leads straightforwardly to resolution. Others need help to relate the issues in a way which can progress to being resolved.

I explore these techniques in more depth in Chapters 8–10.

Encouraging self-direction and motivation

When starting out, listening helpers often assume that anyone who chooses to discuss her situation is seeking change. Be aware that the situation is often more complex than that. Some people are quite definitely looking for change, although needing some support, but sometimes they may be seeking to change someone else. You must recognise that changing someone else, especially if that person isn't present, isn't possible so don't attempt to do so.

The person in front of you is the person you are working with.

Some people know that they need to bring about a change in themselves. This change may be purely an internal change, a difference to how they feel inside, perhaps to be more self-accepting, or perhaps admitting to themselves that their situation may not be open to change. Alternatively they may be ready to embark on changing aspects of their external life.

Other people are not open to change. Perhaps they don't recognise that change is necessary – they may be scared of the unknown, or of success (better the devil you know, however painful, as it apparently makes fewer frightening demands).

Psychologists Prochaska and Di Clementi devised a model known as *the cycle of change model*, shown in Figure 6-2, which can help you to assess a person's readiness for change.

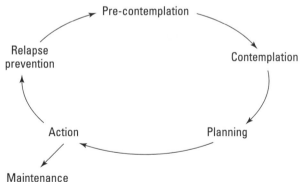

Figure 6-2:
The cycle of change model.

The cycle of change model identifies that people move through stages when dealing with change, at each stage having a different attitude towards the change and readiness to engage with it. When change is unexpected, imposed, or the person doesn't recognise the necessity for it, she's at the pre-contemplation (not yet ready to think about it) stage. After she acknowledges that change is needed she moves into contemplating the issues, then on to planning what to do and taking action. Having made a change she needs to consider how to maintain it and what can help prevent relapse to the earlier behaviour or situation. Change can highlight that further changes need to be made and so the cycle comes back to the beginning.

Recognising where someone is in this cycle when she seeks help is useful. If a person is at the pre-contemplation stage in relation to her problem, for example, she won't engage in thinking about it seriously. In terms of the three-stage model, the skills of Stage One can assist a person to move from pre-contemplation to the next stage; contemplation encompasses Stages One and Two, while planning and action, maintenance, and relapse prevention are part of Stage Three.

The cycle of change model reminds you that if someone is seeking change then she needs to plan carefully and consider how she's going to maintain the actions that promote or support that change. The model also acknowledges that relapse is normal and needs to be planned for. In reality, people don't move neatly through each stage of this cycle. They may move backwards and forwards. For example, in attempting to make a change it may become evident that this is not the change that really needs to be made. This model has been adopted by workers in the drug and alcohol field in particular because it fits their experience with their clients very well.

Recognising internal change and resistance to change are both important progressions that you may underestimate as a listening helper. If you're a beginning helper you may feel you've failed if a noticeable change in circumstances doesn't come about because of your help. As a consequence, you may consciously, or unconsciously, push the speaker towards solutions which may at best be irrelevant and at worst bullying.

You must be able to recognise where someone stands in her attitude to change (skip to Chapter 10 to find out more about encouraging motivation and change). You also need to understand how emotions are related to transition and change in people's lives (not least your own). Look at Chapter 11 for more on this subject.

Developing Other Helpful Knowledge

The areas of knowledge that may be useful for a listening helper are almost limitless. One of the things that makes being a listening helper so interesting is that you're always learning. Having some basic understanding of the following areas, which I expand upon in other chapters, will prove helpful:

✔ **Ethics and good practice (Chapter 4 and Appendix A):** You need to work within an ethical framework which contributes to a safe environment for you and the person seeking help. You may think of yourself as an ethical person. However, ethical-mindedness is an attitude and skill that needs practice and development. The kinds of ethical dilemmas you may face are many and varied – no two situations are ever the same – and are generally quite demanding. Chapter 4 provides a model for assisting ethical thinking and Appendix A has some case examples.

✔ **Transition, change, and loss (Chapter 11):** Most problems in counselling practice involve change and some kind of loss. Transitions and changes in life are stressful and involve recognised patterns of reaction and emotion. All changes and transition in life bring stress. When trying to understand a speaker's difficulties, you need to recognise the impact of such events and give them due weight.

✔ **Common personal problems (Chapter 12):** Understanding the effects of a range of life experiences and circumstances, for example, illnesses and addictions, is very helpful in counselling work. You can update your knowledge by reading appropriate books, journals, newspapers, and magazines, attending seminars, and listening to and watching relevant radio and TV programmes (but remember your critical thinking for all of these).

✔ **Social influences (Chapter 13):** Sometimes the effects of the wider world on your life, such as the part that oppression can play, are under-estimated or overlooked. Conversely, external support you can find may be crucial to the person you're trying to assist – even though she may need help to see that support and to access it.

✔ **Human development: (Chapter 14):** Theories about psychological development help you to understand how people's responses are shaped by patterns in their earlier experience. Sometimes people haven't broken free of restraints that are a consequence of earlier experiences, and may be unaware that they're so restrained.

✔ **Resources that are available (Chapters 11 and 18):** As a listening helper you're frequently in a position where you have a limit to the help you can or should offer, so knowing about other resources and services is invaluable. Remember that you're not responsible for solving everything and that you can encourage the person you help to avail herself of other resources.

Don't be overwhelmed by this list. Developing the art of listening and your knowledge of safe practice are most important. Some appreciation of the implications of transition, the origins of personal problems, and the influence of social pressures will undoubtedly help you to be a more understanding listening helper – but this is a long-term project. You can develop knowledge of services and resources as issues come to you. Enjoy researching some, or all, of these topics!

Chapter 7

Recognising Your Own Barriers to Listening

*Y*ou bring your own history of relating – including your defences, atti-tudes, and values – into the listening-helper role, which can be a help or a hindrance. This chapter looks at obstacles to listening – if you can understand these obstacles, you'll not only listen more effectively but you'll also better understand other people's behaviour and psychological blocks. (Check out Chapter 14 for more on understanding people from a psychologi-cal perspective.)

Getting Acquainted with Defences

When talking about your own listening barriers, the word *defences* is very apt. Defences are the way that you protect yourself – emotionally and in regard to your value system – from perceived and actual attack. When devel-oping defences, you don emotional armour to shield yourself from being wounded or undermined.

Although defences are necessary for your emotional survival, you can pay a high price for them. People tend to:

✔ Be unaware of their defences.

✔ Overlook when their defences outlive their usefulness, at least in certain situations.

⨯ Fail to notice, or find it difficult to change, when their defences interfere with their capacity to engage with the world, or particular people in the world.

You mostly learn defences by example or through experience when you're young, impressionable, and especially vulnerable. The ways in which you respond become patterned and habitual. Many great minds have tried to determine how far people are influenced by nature, genetics, and personality and how far by upbringing and experience, without reaching a definitive answer. A balance of both nature and nurture seems to be likely, so some people may be more predisposed to anxiety, and therefore defensiveness, than others.

What is known about defences is that they:

⨯ Are usually automatic, unless a person chooses to become aware of and determined to change them.

⨯ Exert powerful control within each of us.

⨯ Have a profound impact on relationships. Many people who seek help have interpersonal difficulties, which are a cause or a consequence of other problems that they face, but defences almost certainly play a part.

⨯ Often influence the helping encounter, which is based on a relationship.

Take some time to notice and reflect on those occasions when you recognise that you react in a blocking, defensive way. If you feel strong enough, ask family and friends for feedback about when *they* perceive you as being defensive. For any one example, try to identify whether you're reminded of a situation from your past. Go back to the earliest memory you have of a similar feeling. You may be able to recognise that your current feelings are a transference of feelings from the past. Something in the present may trigger old feelings in an unconscious, knee-jerk, habitual way. Pay attention to any body sensations you get at the same time. Underneath your defensive response is usually some deep anxiety or fear (of being abandoned, humiliated, rejected, overwhelmed, and so on). Childhood memories may be the basis for your fears and may not be realistic for you nowadays.

Knowing How Defences Operate

People use their defences to avoid feelings that they find painful and difficult, as well as to avoid situations that may trigger such feelings. Defences tend to work in a cyclical fashion which simply reinforces the defence mechanisms.

Take a look at Figure 7-1. Imagine that the speaker is telling the listening-helper his story – it's all about the feeling that 'nobody cares for me'. Because the speaker wants to hide his neediness and fears that the response will be rejecting, he uses the defence of keeping the listening helper at bay. The principle is that if the listening helper doesn't get too close then he can avoid the pain of possible rejection. Imagine how you'd experience this person if he came to you for help. Most likely, try as you might, you find staying interested in what he's saying difficult. You may even feel bored. You hope that he doesn't notice because, as a listening helper, you don't want to be perceived as not caring. Because of your own needs (to be liked, needed, helpful), you may end up feeling useless and hopeless.

Sometimes the speaker acts completely in the opposite way. Rather than responding in a manner that pushes others away, he tries to attract people to himself. For example, when a person cannot bear the pain of loneliness or being alone with himself, he may draw others to him in a desperate bid to avoid these feelings. He hides aspects of himself and clings in an attempt to keep the person with him. Sadly, this behaviour often drives the other person away, confirming the underlying fear 'I am worthless/unlovable/useless.'

Another aspect of defensive behaviour is the use of things like alcohol, drugs, and obsessive and compulsive behaviours, all of which people employ to keep deep fears at bay.

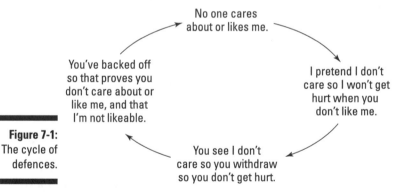

Figure 7-1:
The cycle of defences.

Responding When You're Defensive

Some sayings in everyday speech recognise defensive behaviour. You've probably heard variations on, 'I'll just go home and kick the cat', or 'I think I'll go and eat worms' and the recent one, 'Speak to the hand 'cos the face ain't listening.' Kicking the cat is a classic defence; the individual feels powerless or too afraid to deal with the source of irritation and anger, so instead finds a less powerful person or object on which to take out his frustration. This behaviour is called *displacement*, because the original feeling is displaced elsewhere than where it belongs.

Finding out more about your own defences

This exercise helps you reflect on your defensive behaviour. The more in touch you are with the feelings lying below your own behaviour, the better you can understand the feelings others may be experiencing. By understanding your own defences and the source of your anxiety you can work towards being less defensive. Also, by understanding that other people aren't necessarily attacking you when they behave defensively, you'll be freer to truly listen to the other person in a helping conversation, even if it is challenging to you.

1. Think of a feeling that you don't like to display or reveal to others.

2. Imagine a situation where you could be in danger of showing that feeling. Try to immerse yourself in that scenario and your feelings and really experience the anxiety of letting your true feelings show. What behaviour do you use to manage the anxiety and other feelings aroused in this situation? How will other people experience your outward behaviour?

3. Now think of a belief or value that you hold dear. Imagine a scenario in which you have your belief or value challenged by another person, indirectly through his behaviour and speech or directly through him attacking or disagreeing with your view. What behaviour do you use to manage the feelings aroused in this situation? How will that person perceive your reaction?

When people are in situations that create anxiety and a sense of powerlessness they have characteristic ways of *managing* their feelings, especially when they don't want the anxiety to show. Everyone uses patterns of behaviour to cover anxiety or relieve feelings without revealing their true source. Some people are so used to covering up the anxiety that they almost don't know it's there any more. The anxiety may be the result of real events in the present, or may be an out-of-proportion reaction to real or imagined events. In some situations the defensive behaviour is the sensible response, for example when your boss gives you a dressing down and you shut off instead of biffing him on the nose. In many situations though, especially in closer relationships, defensive behaviour can get in the way of a productive relationship and may be more a reaction to past hurts than present ones.

Many people are unaware that the behaviour that they don't like in another person (such as being aggressive, aloof, arrogant, obsessive, belittling, ingratiating, or patronising, among many others) is frequently a cover for anxiety. They react to the defence rather than the underlying anxiety. Furthermore, many people criticise in others the very behaviour they are themselves are prone to (which is a defensive behaviour to avoid recognising unpalatable truths).

You, as a listening helper, aren't an exception – everyone has these patterns – and the behaviour of the people you listen to in a helping conversation is likely to trigger your defences. To understand defensive behaviour, and to be a better listener, you need to deal with your own defensive behaviour. This section gives you an idea of the range of people's defences. You'll probably recognise a few from your own experience of other people and from yourself, so take time to reflect on situations that arouse these responses in you.

People tend to react to their anxieties in several common ways. Some of these defences will apply to you; you even may find that some are old favourites that you use over and over again; others are held in reserve for certain types of people or situations.

Everyone uses listening blocks, so don't worry if a lot of these are familiar or if you recognise several of them in yourself. Take the opportunity to become more aware of your blocks at the time you actually use them. Think about who in particular evokes that defence in you.

Here are some examples of defensive, blocking behaviour (with thanks to my colleague Ali Harrison):

- ✔ **Advising:** You're the great problem-solver, ready with help and sugges-tions. You don't have to hear more than a few sentences before you begin searching for the right advice. However, while you're cooking up suggestions and convincing someone to 'just try it', you may miss what is most important. You didn't hear about the person's feelings and you didn't acknowledge his pain. He still feels alone because you couldn't listen and just be present.

- ✔ **Being right:** Being right means you'll go to any lengths (twist the facts, start shouting, make excuses or accusations, call up past sins) to avoid being wrong. You can't listen to criticism, you can't be corrected, and you can't take suggestions to change. Your convictions are unshakeable. And because you won't acknowledge that your mistakes are mistakes, you just keep making them.

- ✔ **Comparing:** Listening is hard because you're always trying to assess who is cleverer, more competent, more emotionally healthy – you or the other person. Some people focus on who has suffered more, who's a bigger victim. While someone's talking, you think to yourself, 'Could I do it that well?' or 'My children are so much brighter.' You can't let much in because you're too busy seeing how you compare.

- ✔ **Derailing:** This listening block is accomplished by suddenly changing the subject. You derail the train of conversation when you get bored or uncomfortable with a topic. Another way of derailing is by joking. This means that you continually respond to whatever is said with a joke or quip in order to avoid the discomfort or anxiety in seriously listening to the other person.

✔ **Dreaming:** You're half-listening and something a person says suddenly triggers a chain or private association. For example, your neighbour says he's been laid off, and in a flash you're right back to when you got sacked for playing cards during work-time. Your mind starts drifting and you're gone, only to return a few minutes later as your neighbour says: 'I knew you'd understand, but don't tell my wife.'

✔ **Filtering:** When you filter, you listen to some things and not to others. You pay only enough attention to see if somebody is angry or unhappy, or if you're in emotional danger. Once assured that the communication contains none of those things, you let your mind wander. One woman listens just enough to her son to learn whether he is fighting again at school. Relieved to hear that he isn't, she begins thinking about her shopping list. A young man quickly ascertains what kind of mood his girlfriend is in. If she seems happy as she describes her day, his thoughts begin wandering.

✔ **Identifying:** In this blocking mechanism, you take everything a person tells you and refer it back to your own experience. He wants to tell you about a toothache, but that reminds you of the time you had oral surgery for receding gums. You launch into your story before he can finish his. Everything you hear reminds you of something that you've felt, done, or suffered. You're so busy with these absorbing tales of your own life that you have no time to really hear or get to know the other person.

✔ **Judging:** Negative labels have enormous power. If you prejudge someone as stupid, or mad, or unqualified, you don't pay much attention to what he says. You've already written him off. Hastily judging a statement as immoral, hypocritical, fascist, or crazy means you have ceased to listen and have begun a knee-jerk reaction. A basic rule of listening is to only make judgements after you've heard and evaluated the content of the message.

✔ **Mind-reading:** You don't pay much attention to what people say. In fact, you often distrust it. You're trying to work out what the other person is really thinking and feeling: 'He says he wants to go to the show, but I bet he's tired and just wants to relax. He might be resentful if I push him when he doesn't want to go.' You pay less attention to words than to intonations and subtle cues in an effort to see the truth. If you're a mind-reader, you probably make assumptions about how people react to you: 'I bet he's looking at my bad skin,' 'She thinks I'm stupid,' 'He's turned off by my shyness.' These notions are born of intuition, hunches, and vague misgivings, but have little to do with what the person actually says to you.

✔ **Placating:** 'Right . . . Right . . . Absolutely . . . I know . . . Of course you are . . . Incredible . . . Yes . . . Really?' You want to be nice, pleasant, supportive. You want people to like you. So you agree with everything. You may half-listen, just enough to get the drift, but you're not really involved. You're placating rather than tuning in and examining what's been said.

✔ **Rehearsing:** You don't have time to listen when you're rehearsing what to say. Your whole attention is on preparing and crafting your next comment. You have to look interested, but your mind is going a mile a minute because you have a story to tell, or a point to make. Some people rehearse whole chains of responses: 'I'll say, then he'll say, then I'll say . . .'

Another way people filter is to avoid hearing certain things – particularly if threatening, negative, critical, or unpleasant, although some people filter out positive feedback. It's as if the words were never said: you simply have no memory of them.

✔ **Sparring:** This blocking mechanism has you arguing and debating with people. The other person never feels that you heard him because you're so quick to disagree. In fact, a lot of your focus is on finding things to disagree with. You take strong stands and are very clear about your beliefs and preferences.

One sub-type of sparring is the *put-down*. You use acerbic or sarcastic remarks to dismiss the other person's point of view. For example, Helen starts telling Arthur about her problems in a biology class. Arthur says: 'When are you going to have the sense to drop biology?' Or Ali is feeling overwhelmed with the noise from the television. When he tells Meera, she says: 'Oh no, not the TV routine again.' The put-down is the standard block to listening in many marriages. It quickly pushes the communication into stereotyped patterns where each person repeats a familiar hostile litany.

Another type of sparring is *discounting*. Discounting is for people who can't stand compliments: 'Oh I didn't do anything, really,' 'What do you mean I was good, I was rubbish,' 'It's nice of you to say, but it was really a very poor try.' The basic technique of discounting is to run yourself down when you get a compliment. The other person never feels satisfied that you really heard his appreciation. And he's right – you didn't.

Be honest about recognising yourself in any of these examples and make notes about your reactions to reading about these blocks. How would you react to someone who used one of the above responses when you were trying to help him?

In a helping situation your own defences may show themselves in slightly different ways, such as:

- ✔ Finding a quick solution
- ✔ Not noticing or acknowledging the speaker's emotions
- ✔ Asking too many questions
- ✔ Not challenging or confronting discrepancies and gaps
- ✔ Not being able to cope with silence
- ✔ Wanting to do too much
- ✔ Transferring your own anxiety to the speaker
- ✔ Making too many allowances for the speaker's approach to life.

See the later section 'Realising What You Can Do about Your Defences' for some pointers for overcoming these blocks to listening.

Recognising the Interactive Effects of Defensive Behaviour

The cyclical nature of defences and interaction (refer to Figure 7-1), in which both parties are unaware of their own defences, may operate to reinforce the defences of one or both parties. When a help-seeker talks to you, he will continue to use these blocks with you. You may even be affected by your own defensiveness.

A help-seeker might behave towards you as if you're a figure from his past. This phenomenon is known as *transference* and is one of a number of unconscious processes.

Because you represent authority (whether you like it or not) this person from the help-seeker's past probably also represents authority. The help-seeker may see or experience you as a judging parental or teacherly figure or expect you to have some similar characteristics. He may anticipate that you'll be parental in a nurturing and supportive way or in an intrusive sense, or see you as angry or rejecting, for example.

Positive transference can enable a helping encounter go well at the start. For example, initially a help-seeker may feel very in need of nurturing. Mostly the transference doesn't interfere with the helping process. At other times it can be unhelpful or even disastrous. This is especially the case if your reaction plays into the transference. For example, if the help-seeker behaves in a childlike, dependent manner and you respond in an overly maternal or paternal way, then the help-seeker is less likely to take charge of his life and may eventually resent you.

If you think about being on the receiving end of the 12 blocking responses listed in the preceding section, you may find it difficult to maintain a neutral stance and not get drawn into an unhelpful set of interactions. As a listening-helper you need to work on your ability to understand and connect with what lies below the defensive behaviour.

Notice when you feel unusual reactions within yourself because these could be indications that an unhelpful transference is taking place. Also reflect on what it is in you that responds to the particular transference – usually some internal hook from your own past and your insecurities. The aim is to move the encounter into an adult-to-adult relationship. If this seems to be impossible then the help-seeker can probably benefit from more in-depth work in counselling or psychotherapy.

By contrast with the negative potential of unconscious processes, if a help-seeker is able to make use of a genuine, respectful, and empathic relationship, he may be able to suspend or undo his learned responses.

Realising What You Can Do about Your Defences

A person's relationships with significant others, especially (although not exclusively) in his early life, is potentially transferred onto everyone he meets, notably in this case, the listening helper. His relationship with the listening helper may follow the same path as it does with others, but he has an opportunity for change if you, the listening helper, don't react defensively yourself. If you look for your own defences and their causes, you can start to dismantle them through changing your thinking habits, building self-esteem, seeking feedback and other self-development activities (refer to Chapter 2).

How can you accept a person for who he is and for what he's saying even if it conflicts with your own ideals and prejudices? If you can, this may break the cycle for him. If you can find a way to value a person for being different and unique and accept him as he is, that person could then begin to feel worthwhile, valued, and able to work towards what he can become. To achieve this change you need to be aware of your own values and prejudices, have a willingness to suspend them, and be able to give complete attention to the other person. If you find doing so difficult, you're creating an obstacle in the listening process.

Facilitating a helping relationship requires a different style to that of everyday communication. It requires you to respond in a way that focuses on the other person so that he feels heard. You may find the speaker behaves towards you with hurt, resentment, resistance, and reactive or retaliatory behaviours when your intention had been to communicate understanding and sensitivity. Remember that these behaviours indicate underlying fears and hurts which are not always to do with you. If you, as a listening helper can understand your own defences then you may understand those of others, take them less personally, and react less defensively. Then the individuals you help will be better able to undo their own defences.

Many of the defences described in this chapter are related to:

- Low self-esteem and lack of self-acceptance (for example, the Comparing, Sparring, and Judging defences)
- Lack of confidence (Rehearsing)
- Fear of attack (Placating)
- Difficulties with trust (Mind-Reading)
- Fear of being vulnerable (Advising and Being Right)
- Other unresolved emotional issues and repression of feelings (for example, the Dreaming, Derailing, and Identifying defences)

To overcome defences you need to accept yourself more fully and undertake activities that can increase your self-worth or express your emotions (refer to Chapter 2 for ideas). In the meantime, work on your basic skills, focusing especially on reflecting, summarising, and communicating empathy (see Chapters 8 and 9). These apparently simple skills are powerful antidotes to defensiveness.

Seeing Defences in Action

Here's a statement by a help-seeker, followed by a number of defensive responses where the listener has responded by imposing his or her own values or emotional needs. These values or needs have got in the way of what the speaker is saying. The listener needed to respond in a way that enabled the speaker to feel his needs had been met.

Speaker: 'I just can't cope, everything is getting on top of me – there's no point to anything. . .'

Mr Bossy: 'Now, come on, stop feeling sorry for yourself; just get out and do something to take your mind off it.'

Miss Browbeater: 'You had better be thankful you're as well off as you are. In the old days, things were really bad.'

Mr Moraliser: 'You keep talking like that and you'll get yourself in trouble. You should be grateful for what you've got.'

Miss Teacher: 'Start thinking of yourself in other ways. Why don't you do a mind map, I'll show you how.'

Mr Adviser: 'If I were you, I'd talk to your priest.'

Miss Critic (judging): 'You're just making things worse for yourself by thinking that way.'

Mr Nice (praising, agreeing): 'Many people feel that way; I can see your point. You must feel terrible.'

Miss Reassurance: 'In time you will feel a lot better, don't worry.'

Mr Name-caller: 'Listen mate, don't be a wimp, you've got to face up to it like a man.'

Miss Interpreter: 'You're just unhappy because of what happened in your childhood.'

Mr Questioner: 'Why do you feel that way?'

Miss Sarcasm: 'The point is don't whinge, binge, that's what I say!'

Mr Mindreader: 'You just think you can't cope. Of course you can cope. I expect you have just got a bit down and blown things out of proportion.'

Miss Dreamer: 'Mmm? Oh, I know . . . yes, awful . . . mmm.'

Mr That-Happened-to-Me: 'I know just how you feel, I felt just like that last year. I did feel terrible. Did I tell you . . . ?'

Although exaggerated, all the preceding responses are close to the truth of how anyone might respond. They are *closed*, cutting off opportunities for further exploration of the problem. They all:

✔ Communicate a lack of respect for the other person

✔ Show poor listening

✔ May cause reactive or retaliatory behaviour

✔ Can produce resistance rather than openness to change

✔ May be damaging to the recipient's self-esteem

✔ May make a person feel hurt and later resentful.

Revisit the statement 'I just can't cope, everything is getting on top of me – there's no point to anything . . .' Remember that people tend to show only a fraction of what they're feeling. You need to notice body language, tone of voice, and facial expressions to infer what the person is feeling. In this case the individual may feel desperate. Think about what response would reflect the speaker's message in a way that shows you have heard both the feelings and the content. Aim to communicate your attentiveness and empathy non-verbally as well as in your speech. You can pick up on the sense of despair by saying something like, 'You sound overwhelmed, and as though it's hope-less?', or 'Mmm . . .[communicating empathy non-verbally] no point?', or 'It's all too much for you right now'.

People also use their defences to protect and maintain their own values, preju-dices, and attitudes as well as their emotional vulnerabilities. As a listening helper, you're encouraged to be more accepting of others by becoming more self-accepting and by understanding the influence of your attitudes and values.

In this exercise (with thanks to my colleague Mike Wilson) make a note of the following examples in which you could listen to the person with ease, and those you'd find difficult:

- ✔ A husband who says, 'My wife promised to obey me and that's what she must do; there's nothing to discuss'.
- ✔ A woman who says, 'I want to leave him; he's so boring and I've found someone younger.'
- ✔ A drug pusher who works the local primary school.
- ✔ A woman who batters her baby.
- ✔ A woman who discloses that she is lesbian and promiscuous.
- ✔ A woman who feels that her partner should make all the important deci-sions in the relationship.
- ✔ An angry person.
- ✔ A person who complains about her life all the time, but is unprepared to make changes.
- ✔ A teenager who is tense and withdrawn and who has contemplated suicide.
- ✔ A frail, elderly widow who is lonely, depressed, and weeps a lot.
- ✔ A single young man who says his preferred lifestyle is to live on income support.
- ✔ A heroin addict.
- ✔ A person who talks non-stop, but never about his feelings.
- ✔ A person who is very tearful.

Identifying blocks

Part 1: Use the following incomplete statements to examine what helps and hinders how you listen to people. Don't spend too much time thinking about each sentence; try to be spontaneous and honest as you complete each one. When you've finished, reflect back on what you've written and then go to Part 2.

I feel comfortable listening to someone when . . .

I enjoy listening to someone talk about . . .

I find it irritating when someone . . .

I find it embarrassing when someone talks about . . .

I get defensive when someone talks about . . .

I get bored when someone talks about . . .

Words and phrases that annoy me are . . .

I find it difficult to concentrate on what someone is saying if I am . . .

I get bored when . . .

I feel drawn to someone I am listening to who . . .

If someone who is talking does not give me a chance to contribute, I feel . . .

When I'm listening to someone I get frustrated with myself when . . .

If someone is talking to me for a length of time, I find myself . . .

If someone is talking to me about something I disagree with, I find myself . . .

Interrupting someone while they're talking is . . .

Part 2: Think about the answers above then complete the following statements:

To improve my counselling skills I need to . . .

Things I do when I'm listening to ensure that I'm actively listening are . . .

Things I can do when I'm listening to ensure that the speaker is also actively listening are . . .

(With thanks to my colleague, Ali Harrison.)

Take time to reflect on your responses to each of the previous situations. Imagine now that each of these people has suffered a recent tragic bereavement. Would you be able to work with any of these people if you were presented with such a scenario? What enables you to empathise with one more or less than another?

There are as many different ways of seeing the world as there are people. Your view is not necessarily any more valid than the help-seeker's. Don't judge others by your own set of values. Take time to explore how the other person sees his or her world.

Part III
Structuring a Helping Conversation

The 5th Wave   By Rich Tennant

"If we're going to have a conversation, then
we've got to do it in some way other than
messages left on the refrigerator with
these tiny word magnets."

In this part . . .

I look at the structure of a helping relationship and how you use a sequence of particular counselling skills to deepen the relationship. This part covers the beginning, middle, and ending stages of the helping relationship and describes the various skills and how to use them productively.

Chapter 8

Establishing a Helping Relationship

*R*esearch and experience show that one of the most important aspects of successful helping conversations is the quality of the relationship between speaker and listener. In this chapter, I look at what underpins a good helping relationship and how to get the conditions right for the helping to take place.

Getting the Relationship Started

A helping relationship starts from the very first glimpse a help-seeker has of you, and sometimes well before that, such as in the contact she's had with the organisation you belong to, or in any preliminary telephone or email conversations. Even at these initial contact stages impressions are formed that may or may not be conducive to the trust needed for a helpful relationship to ensue.

You need to consider when and where you undertake your listening-helper activity and how your answers to the following questions are likely to influence the process and outcomes:

✔ How does the speaker initially make contact with you – personally, by phone, through a third party, by email?

✔ How does the setting influence the speaker's expectations and your response?

✔ How can you separate this role and any other role you may have in relation to this person?

✔ How will you ensure privacy? Privacy doesn't just mean that no one can overhear, but may mean taking steps so that others don't even know that the conversation is a helping one.

✔ What can you do to make the environment as appropriate as possible?

On occasions you may be taken off guard, perhaps switching from one role into a listening role, so make sure that you take the necessary time to ensure the meeting, greeting, scene-setting and seating are managed as well as possible.

Meeting

In a situation where you're using active listening skills as part of another role, you may have little or no control over the manner of meeting a help-seeker. You possibly already know the person who chooses to seek your help. If she's approaching you for help this may be because she sees you as someone good to talk to. However, her approach may not be overt or previously planned. The conversation may evolve into a helping conversation when she's plucked up courage or checked you out first by asking questions or dropping hints. Occasionally someone is so full of what she's experiencing that she can't contain herself and the emotion spills out. You become more adept at picking up the signs with practice.

After you become aware of the change in the nature of the discussion you may consciously move into the sequences of greeting and seating. You could be in a situation where someone is directed to talk to you, which brings other factors into play.

If you're making the approach, perhaps following a request to meet, you have time to think about the meeting stage and the impression you give – are you demonstrating that you're approachable through your demeanour, body language, tone of voice?

Greeting

Reflect on how you'd like to be greeted by someone with whom you intend to discuss a problem. Most people respond to an open posture, some eye contact, and warmth, but over-friendliness can be off-putting. A client recently told me that the welfare officer she spoke to at work smiled too much right from the outset – it made her feel that the listener wasn't taking her seriously enough. So try to convey an appropriate level of warmth and concern and, most importantly, take action to ensure adequate privacy. If the meeting is planned, you might make reference to that fact in the greeting.

Imagining how the speaker feels

Thinking about your own experiences of first-time meetings is a useful exercise. If you cast your mind back to the most recent time you met a group of people new to you (new job, course, or social group, for example) and recall your thoughts and emotions you can get some insight into how a help-seeker could be feeling when she approaches you, particularly if you don't already have a relationship with her. Think about what you feared and hoped for from that set of new relationships, how you thought you might be treated and all the assumptions you made.

In many settings nowadays the use of first names is the norm. Whilst many people are quite happy to be greeted in this way, think about the appropriateness of the use of different types of address in particular settings and with different cultures and age groups. Remember, not all people are comfortable with such informality.

If you're meeting someone for the first time consider:

- ✔ Would it be more respectful to use her surname or full name to start with? Follow up by checking out how she'd prefer to be addressed.

- ✔ What is your own preference for how you like to be addressed?

- ✔ Unless you're working with children and young people in a formal setting, aim for equality of address.

A decision may have to be made about touch. Should you shake hands, touch the person's arm, or avoid touch when greeting? Touching relates to how you are as a person, what you naturally tend to do, and being comfortable with it. However, also consider the possible reactions of the help-seeker. In general a cautious attitude to touch is preferable because you cannot know what significance touch has for the person seeking your help. Many touches seem innocuous but can convey subtle messages, such as 'I'm in charge,' or can be perceived as threatening in other ways, perhaps due to an abusive experience.

If someone's been in an abusive relationship, especially if she's been sexually abused in childhood, touch (beyond a formal handshake) is likely to be associated with difficult emotions.

Seating

In some situations organising appropriate seating arrangements can be tricky. The ideal is two similar seats of the same height, square on or at a slight angle, with enough distance between them so that your legs don't meet and with no other barriers, such as desk or table. In some situations you may not sit at all, or the help-seeker may be in bed or a wheelchair.

Cartoon depictions of scenes in a counsellor's or psychiatrist's office frequently show the professional behind a desk, which is highly unusual. The helping conversation needs to remove barriers and create equality, hence the avoidance of physical barriers and unequal height differentials. In situations where active listening skills are used it can be difficult to achieve the ideal conditions, but think creatively to minimise the barriers.

Barriers aren't only to do with furniture. If you're much taller or larger than the other person, consider how you can reduce your presence through your posture or seating arrangements. Whatever the situation, think how you can equalise it by trying to be as near as possible in each other's eye-line. Commenting on the physical situation is sometimes appropriate, especially if you feel uncomfortable with it. Often, speaking about the discomfort can help to dispel an awkward situation and prevent it from interfering with your listening.

In addition, the proximity of chairs is important. Culturally and personally we all have our own comfortable distance (personal space). If possible invite the speaker to choose her seat so that she can make it as comfortable as possible for herself, and don't be afraid to ask if the seating arrangement is right for her. However, always put your safety first. If you're meeting an unknown person for the first time you may want to consider whether you can make a quick exit if the need arises. Such incidents are rare but never be complacent.

In some situations the safety of both parties is an issue, for example when an adult is working with a child. If you're working within an organisation you need to check any policies (for example, some may have an 'open-door' requirement).

Setting the Ground Rules

In situations where you're using active listening skills to help another person, a formal agreement or contract probably doesn't exist, unlike in a formal counselling relationship. Nonetheless, thinking in contract terms, however informally, is part of managing the helping relationship, ensuring safety for both parties. You need to take responsibility for the time and any other constraints, including confidentiality, by informing the help-seeker about them. This is known as setting *boundaries* (a counselling-jargon term that I explain in the following 'Managing other boundaries' section).

As a general rule, helping conversations using counselling skills usually last for up to half-an-hour, although on occasions may be longer. Formal counselling sessions normally last for 50–60 minutes. When you know you don't have time to get involved in a complex conversation, postpone the meeting (to a specified time) rather than enter into a session. Don't be afraid to interrupt a conversation to explain that now is not a time when you can give undivided attention. If possible, give an alternative specified time.

When a help-seeker is unaware of the time you have for the conversation she may embark on telling you things, and revealing feelings, that can't be easily contained in that time. So be clear about how much time you have available as soon as possible in the conversation.

One way of helping to manage the duration is to think of the session in three parts (such as the three-stage model discussed in Chapter 6). If you have more than one session with someone, then the whole period of contact also falls into three parts:

- **Beginning (Relationship-building):** This stage is the meeting, greeting, seating, settling down, and dealing-with-boundaries part of the session. It includes the start of telling the story and the relationship-building skills.

- **Middle (Exploring and Clarifying):** Here you help the speaker to open up further, to explore and clarify the situation so that the real nature of the problem can emerge, and the beginnings of an outcome start to be seen.

- **End (Action and Closing):** You support the speaker in imagining how she'll implement any decisions, offering guidance and support as appropriate. Then you give attention to how the session will end and what future sessions, if any, are needed to evaluate what has been done. Sometimes no action as such needs to be taken. The speaker may realise she doesn't want to take any action, or perhaps any action would be inappropriate: The therapeutic effect of simply being listened to may be enough. The session may be the beginning of two or more sessions, in which case the action and closing may consist of making an arrangement to continue the conversation at another time.

While it isn't a good idea to have a rigid clock-watching approach, having a feel for a session roughly in thirds helps to manage the time. One of the common problems experienced by listening helpers is not being able to close the conversation down and end the session. By having a clear timescale at the outset, bringing a session to a close becomes much easier. A longer session isn't necessarily a more productive one and can be detrimental to both parties. See Chapter 11 for more about ending the conversation.

Is a friend in need a friend indeed?

When I was fairly new as a counsellor I had a client who wanted to be friends when the counselling finished. I discussed the situation with my supervisor but she did not give me clear guidance. I did have misgivings but I found it hard to identify and articulate them. I also didn't know how to say no to the client without seeming rejecting. I met the client for coffee and quickly knew that the meeting was a mistake. Although I liked her, she wasn't the kind of person I would normally make friends with. I knew a lot about her, whereas she knew little about me, so the relationship was skewed. I hadn't fully appreciated the power dynamics inherent in the counsellor-client relationship, which would be difficult to move away from: I felt she would always look to me for emotional help rather than just being a friend. The situation was even harder to handle after we had met socially. I had to get my courage and an explanation together to extricate myself. This experience made me cautious about changing the nature of the relationship.

Managing other boundaries

Boundaries are aspects that need to be considered, in addition to timing, such as confidentiality and its limits and the separation of this relationship from other relationships like friendship (for example, whether meeting for coffee or going out together is appropriate). All these boundaries are intended to foster a climate of safety, honesty, and trust, which underpin the kind of relationship where people can make disclosures.

In many helping relationships, unlike in counselling, befriending someone may be entirely appropriate but always think through such decisions. The boundaries need to reflect the primary relationship and the context that you share with the help-seeker. If in doubt about what limits to set, discuss the situation with a trusted colleague and also with the speaker. Always ensure that you're beginning with the same understanding about the 'rules of engagement' as the help-seeker.

Explaining the limits of confidentiality

Be clear within yourself about confidentiality and its limits and make sure that you give an unambiguous message about it to whoever you help. The limits depend, to some extent, on your setting:

✔ If you work with children or vulnerable adults, your responsibilities for their safety mean a narrower definition of confidentiality.

✔ If you have a management responsibility you may have a duty to reveal disclosures to other members of the organisation.

Always check the protocols, guidelines, and expectations in your agency.

As soon as you recognise that you're in a helping conversation, you need to find space to explain what confidentiality means so that the speaker isn't under any misapprehensions. Ideally do this at the start of the conversation. If the speaker discloses things to you before you've been clear about your responsibilities to disclose certain things to other people, you can end up in a difficult position. Even if someone is upset, gently intervene to make a brief statement.

These are some of the potential limitations of confidentiality:

✔ **Safety of children:** Remember that this aspect applies equally whether you're talking to a child or an adult because the adult may mention a child who is at risk or a situation where a child could be at risk. Examples include: parents who are rowing, perhaps including domestic violence; an alleged child abuser from the person's past who may still have easy access to children; a young adult who has been abused and who has younger siblings still at home. (Refer to Chapter 4 for more about child protection.)

✔ **Organisational responsibilities:** Check the policies of your organisation. For example, although you may believe that a person has the right to take her own life or self-harm, your organisation may require you to disclose such risks. If a person's job responsibilities are jeopardised by her lifestyle (drug-taking, use of alcohol, and so on) you may have a duty to disclose. Other people may be involved in a person's care so some organisations offer confidentiality *within* the organisation.

✔ **Supervision and consultation:** If you're lucky enough to have supervision, disclose this information to the help-seeker and explain what it means. For example, in my supervision I don't disclose identifying information such as names when discussing my work.

✔ **Records:** Your organisation may require you to keep records. Data and service-users have rights under the Data Protection legislation. If you keep records of helping sessions you need to disclose this fact to the help-seeker and be prepared to answer questions about the security and privacy of, and access to, such records.

Developing a confidentiality statement

Write yourself a short statement covering what you need to say about confidentiality and other boundaries such as how much time you can offer. Rehearse the statement until it feels natural and part of you. Try it out on someone if you can or tape-record yourself. After you've internalised it, you'll be able to stop worrying about the words and pay attention to how the other person is receiving them.

For example: 'Before you go any further, I need to tell you that what we talk about is confidential within certain limits. If you tell me something that leads me to believe that you, or anyone else, especially a child, is significantly at risk, I may need to break that confidentiality.' You may need to add other things specific to your situation, for example about record-keeping and supervision or responsibility to management.

Being clear about issues of safety and privacy helps to build trust between you and the help-seeker. Some people are uninterested or too upset to be bothered with such things, whilst others are very concerned about their privacy. Refer to Chapter 4 for more information about working ethically and safely, which includes more on limits of confidentiality.

Managing the Story or Content

Quite often, when someone seeks help, all the person needs is someone to listen carefully and with empathy to what she wants to discuss and explore. When the help-seeker knows roughly how much time they have in a session, she can manage her story-telling to her own advantage. As for the helper, discovering what the speaker is expecting from the session is useful – but not necessarily right at the beginning.

After setting the scene and handling the boundaries, you can move into helping the person. Sometimes you need no more than a questioning pose, gesture, gaze, or smile. You'll have picked up some signals from the help-seeker that help you gauge how active you need to be. If the help-seeker looks as though she needs you to prompt her with an invitation to speak, here are some examples of how you might open, not forgetting non-verbal warmth and encouragement:

- ✔ Would you like to say what brings you to speak to me today?
- ✔ Perhaps you'd like to tell me what's brought you?
- ✔ What would you like to talk about today?

If this is a second or subsequent meeting, you can use the last of the previous list or:

- ✔ What's uppermost for you today?

- ✔ Where would you like to begin today?

- ✔ When we met last time, you talked about [brief summary/headlines]. I wonder if that's what you want to focus on today or something else?

Although summarising what happened in the last meeting can be helpful, sometimes it's not. If the help-seeker has moved on since then, revisiting previous discussions may be at odds with where the help-seeker is now and may divert attention and use up time better spent on more pressing or timely issues. Asking if she'd like a summary of what you talked about last time may be helpful to the help-seeker if she has any hesitation about starting. You could ask what has been happening since you last met. However, you run the risk with this approach that each time you meet you'll hear a blow-by-blow account of the events of the intervening time – which may not be purposeful. On balance I suggest avoiding this kind of invitation.

Working with confusion

Sometimes stories seem to be circular and repetitive, which may reflect the confusion of emotions and thoughts that the speaker is experiencing. The temptation to rush to solutions is counterproductive. Sometimes the emotions haven't been sufficiently explored or maybe the listener isn't listening carefully enough to pick up what is really being said. Sometimes, however, the speaker doesn't reveal what she thinks and feels below the surface because she doesn't yet trust the listener enough.

Occasionally people are just not used to telling a focused story. They ramble, give excessive and inconsequential detail, not because they're hiding true feelings, but perhaps they've never learned how to focus or because they don't yet know what's important for you to know. This can be confusing and frustrating (to me anyway!). Focusing uses skills from Stage One (head to Chapter 9 to find out about the stages and to see how reflecting, paraphrasing, summarising, and probing can help) and some from Stage Two (see Chapter 10 for these more challenging skills).

People often *feel* when they tell their story that it's jumbled, incoherent, and a mess, although for the listener, this may not be the case. The telling of the story itself helps the speaker to see some order and begin to make sense of it. The active listening skills of paraphrasing, summarising, reflecting and clarifying, and asking open questions help to construct a comprehensible and comprehensive story. A 'good' story is one that includes the speaker's thoughts, emotions, sensations, and behaviour and it uncovers attitudes, beliefs, or values, and possibly spiritual aspects. When you listen, you're listening not only to what is said, but also to what is left out and to the *manner* in which the story is told. For example, the pace and style of delivery can indicate how the speaker feels about her story and her developing relationship with you.

The story is likely to include imagery and metaphor, reference to the speaker's relationships, and sometimes information about bodily things like sleep patterns, eating habits, illnesses, addictions, exercise, and activity.

Telling the story so as to include many of these aspects is therapeutic in itself (see Chapter 12 for more on using the *BEST-I BEST-R model* which elaborates on these aspects).

Noticing assumptions and prejudices on both sides

As a listening helper your aim is to set aside judgement in order to enable the speaker to talk as freely, without fear, as possible. Therefore, discovering your stereotypes and assumptions through your personal development is most important so that you're less influenced by these things (you may never get rid of them entirely).

The speaker comes to a discussion with preconceived ideas about you as an individual through the role you have and through her previous experience of others. She's also likely to project onto you, and believe that you hold the judgements that she has about herself. Everyone tends to do the same. To find out more about assumptions and prejudices, look in Chapter 13.

I find that reminding myself that I don't know this person fully or even very much helps me to set aside my judging self. The person may remind me of someone else or another situation that I've experienced and I may not recognise this, or the effects of it, until afterwards. If I realise that I'm reacting uncharacteristically, it's a fairly sure sign that I may be relating to this person as if she were a figure from my past. In that case, I would want to discuss and explore this with someone I trust (my supervisor usually).

Noticing uncharacteristic responses

You may find yourself feeling or acting in the way the speaker unconsciously wants you to. For example, if you find yourself taking on an unusual level of responsibility for the speaker, it could be that she's representing herself as highly vulnerable, in effect saying, 'Take care of me or else I'll go under/die/hate you . . .' As you may imagine, recognising and dealing with such things with sensitivity takes reflection, skill, and courage.

These issues continue in the middle stage of work as a listening helper, and would be most pertinent to explore in a *counselling* relationship. However, even when using counselling skills in a listening-helper relationship, understanding that such mechanisms operate can help you recognise why these relationships sometimes go awry, why you get burdened or feel resentful.

Practising Core Conditions

The three main *core conditions* that are fundamental to the success of most helping encounters are: *Respect*, *empathy*, and *genuineness* (refer to Chapter 6 for more on these core conditions). Although they can be described separately, they're interlinked – one cannot work without the others.

Respecting the speaker

The other terms that are used interchangeably with respect expand on what this value means: acceptance, unconditional positive regard, prizing. At the very least respect involves treating the individual with care. At a deeper level respect means offering a relationship that accepts and values the individual, warts and all.

A way of thinking about how to be accepting is to think about some non-acceptant responses:

- ✔ Ordering, directing
- ✔ Probing, questioning
- ✔ Warning, threatening
- ✔ Moralising, preaching
- ✔ Reassuring
- ✔ Teaching, lecturing
- ✔ Advising, offering solutions
- ✔ Psychoanalysing
- ✔ Criticism, judging
- ✔ Over-praising
- ✔ Sarcasm, humour
- ✔ Name calling

Whilst *some* responses may be appropriate when used in a timely and supportive fashion (such as teaching, advising, humour, probing, and questioning), all these responses can be indicative of the helper's defences, or blocks. They may not be outwardly expressed, perhaps just being part of a person's inner dialogue or self-talk. Nevertheless, they are often picked up by the helpseeker and tend to have negative effects on the helping relationship. They tend to:

- Have an accusing 'you' component (you *should*, you *must*, and so on).
- Have an 'I'm the expert and you are inferior' tone.
- Make people feel guilty.
- Cause reactive or retaliatory behaviour.
- Produce resistance rather than openness to change.
- Create dependency or compliance rather than develop independence and autonomy.
- Be damaging to the recipient's self-esteem, inducing feelings of inadequacy.
- Make a person feel hurt and later resentful.

Recognise non-acceptant reactions in yourself and notice what the blocks are that you tend to have in relation to yourself and others. Being in a helping role can be particularly effective at tapping into some of them. Try to be open to acknowledging your own negative impulses (be *self*-accepting). Everyone has blocks and learning to be less defensive is a lifetime's work.

Communicating empathy

Empathy is the ability to imaginatively enter another person's experience, feel it *almost* as if it were your own (but you need to keep in touch with your own perspective too) and, most importantly, communicate that understanding. In some situations having empathy for someone is easy, even too easy occasionally (this is called *over-identification*). In other situations gaining such understanding can be quite difficult. However, even the endeavour to understand is almost always perceived by the speaker as a therapeutic experience. Empathy is crucial to the formation of the helping relationship and important in the whole helping process because empathy identifies emotions which are vital to problem identification and to problem-solving.

An extremely important aspect of communicating empathy is non-verbal communication. Think about the kind of person you yourself would go to for help. Recall this person now – picture and hear in your mind this person's demeanour, body language, and non-verbal vocalisations (ums, ers, uh-huhs, mmm's, and so on) and how they all fit together. You now get a model of the communication of empathy. Essentially these non-verbal behaviours show:

- ✔ Attention.

- ✔ Interest.

- ✔ Attunement to the person.

- ✔ Understanding through mirroring of facial expressions and body posture.

- ✔ Encouragement to continue.

Mirroring the speaker – that is, adopting similar expressions, posture, and gestures – can help to build rapport, but only if done in a spontaneous and genuine way. Otherwise mirroring could be interpreted as caricature or manipulation, demonstrating that the core conditions must operate in conjunction with each other.

As well as conveying encouragement and the fact that you're paying sincere attention through non-verbal communication, you need to develop the ability to communicate understanding through verbal responses which pick up not only on facts but also, and most importantly, on the emotional content of the speaker's experience. In a listening-helper role, because your involvement is usually relatively brief, practise picking out highlights or key emotions.

Next time you have an opportunity to listen to someone telling you about an experience or worry, focus on conveying non-verbal empathy; listen for and remember up to three key emotional words. At an appropriate moment say,

> 'It sounds like . . .' *or* 'I'm sensing that . . .' *or* 'From what you're saying I get the feeling that . . .' *or* 'You felt . . .' *or* 'You're feeling [the key emotions that you have noticed].'

Resist doing anything else for most of the conversation, apart from repeating this formula. Afterwards reflect on how the conversation went: What happened after your intervention? Did it help the conversation flow? Did it lead to deeper exploration (as it often does)?

You can take the communication of empathy further by highlighting particular feelings but also identifying what could be called a *core message* in the person's story. As well as picking out key emotions, you can also identify important aspects of the speaker's story, and make links between the two. Pick out links from what you've heard but not to *diagnose* that the speaker feels a certain way because of something you've identified. Chapter 9 talks more about the skills of *reflecting*, *paraphrasing*, and *summarising* which contribute to communicating empathy.

Another aspect of empathic responding is noticing and speaking about what you observe during the helping conversation (one form of *here-and-now talk*) which invites the speaker to say more. For example, having noticed tension in the speaker's body language and manner of speech (perhaps some breathlessness or rapid speaking) you may comment:

> 'You seem very anxious as you tell me about this.'

This kind of response is also an example of one form of *reflecting*, in this case reflecting a feeling. Such responses show that you're paying attention to what the speaker is saying and enhance rapport. Chapter 9 covers more about the foundation (Stage One) skills involved in here-and-now talk, and Chapter 10 discusses the more challenging aspects of commenting on what you're experiencing (Stage Two skills).

Being genuine

Showing respect and communicating empathy contribute to building trust. Being genuine is also key. Genuineness is sometimes known by other names, for example *authenticity* and *congruence*. These alternative names suggest what genuineness means:

- Authenticity implies the listener is 'real'.
- Congruence is a matching of your inner and outer self so that your visible responses are in tune with your inner self.

The revealing of your true self is known as *self-disclosure* or *transparency*.

Dealing with challenges of genuineness

Of course the idea of transparency brings its own potential problem because you're expected as a listening helper to accept, respect, and show empathy towards the help-seeker, but you may find this very hard to do for a variety of reasons. You may feel irritated with a person's inability to make a decision, for example. So, do you reveal what is *really* going on inside of you? In this situation you have opposing values (*acceptance* and *genuineness*) and no correct answer exists. Your irritation could be a reflection of what the speaker is feeling about her situation or herself, or it could be your own impatience. Developing your ability to reflect on these kinds of experiences, discovering the source of your feelings, and considering whether revealing them is likely to be helpful to the helping process is all part of your personal development as a helper and takes time (refer to Chapter 2 for more on personal development).

Not everything you think or feel is necessarily relevant to the help-seeker. The help-seeker doesn't need to know about every passing reaction you have. She needs to feel that you're reasonably consistent. In short-term helping relationships you may have to compromise the genuineness while you do your best to be as accepting and empathic as you can. In longer-term or deeper relationships it becomes even more important to be genuine and to find ways of facing the dilemma of experiencing the help-seeker negatively, and being congruent, without destroying the relationship. You can find more about this kind of situation in Chapters 10 and 15.

I hope you feel relieved to hear that you don't need to be perfect. Turning to someone who's an expert can sometimes seem reassuring but you can also be left feeling more incompetent and foolish. In a listening-helper role you need to view the help-seeker as the expert on herself and work to assist her in becoming more autonomous. You build her self-esteem in this way.

You may find that revealing to the speaker that you're feeling confused or uncertain encourages and enables her to explore what she is experiencing in more detail. She then finds herself clarifying things on her own. Gaining understanding herself is far more important than you having complete understanding. Owning up to mistakes (and apologising) also brings together and demonstrates respect, self-acceptance, and genuineness and leads to greater equality in the relationship.

Modelling self-acceptance and normalising experience

When you're real and honest in the relationship, disclosing doubts, mistakes, and admitting that you also struggle to understand sometimes, but not beating yourself up about it, you're modelling self-acceptance. Through the example of you being real and self-accepting the help-seeker finds risking being real with you easier. The anxiety about being judged lessens. The end result is that the speaker has a great sense of relief and becomes more accepting of herself.

You may imagine that other people are well-adjusted, problem-free, sorted, and that only you are foolish, plagued by anxiety, unable to make a decision, and so on. One of the benefits of listening help is in discovering that other people also have problems, maybe not experienced in exactly the same way, and that what you experience is *normal*.

Being cautious about self-disclosure

Having encouraged you to be aware of your own reactions and to be genuine and honest, here's an opposing principle.

Self-disclosure is potentially harmful to the helping relationship.

Self-disclosure comes in two types:

- ✔ Telling the help-seeker about your personal life and/or experiences.
- ✔ Telling the help-seeker about your reactions and observations from the interaction in the helping relationship.

How often have you told someone about an experience only to have her cap it with one of her own which is *more* in some way (more exciting, more dreadful, and so on)? Does this kind of response invite you to say more? Do you feel listened to? When you're preoccupied with a difficulty of your own does it help you to hear every last detail of how the other person solved her problem?

Self-disclosure that takes attention away from the help-seeker and her experience is not helpful. Self-disclosure that can be helpful includes:

- **Normalising:** Many people worry that they're uniquely mad, bad, or sad and so hearing that their feelings are not abnormal is a helpful experience. As long as it doesn't take away the uniqueness of the speaker's own experience such normalising can be useful.

- **Brief stories:** They can give hope that change is possible.

- **Disclosure:** Enables the speaker to recognise and explore her own emotions. For example, you may notice that you feel sad or angry when someone tells her story, while she expresses little emotion. Mentioning your feeling and wondering how she feels can lead to her realising she's been bottling up her emotions.

In all cases you need to monitor how the speaker is responding, using a light touch with your self-disclosures and only disclosing just enough to achieve the desired effect.

Chapter 9

Stage One: Beginning the Discussion

*W*hen you begin as a listening helper, managing the situation and the process can feel daunting. You might feel that you're expected to control or guide the meeting but feel unsure how to do it; or conversely the speaker might seize control and gallop off on his story, leaving you trailing behind.

In this chapter, I suggest a structure to help you. Within this structure, I identify and explain key skills associated with the beginning of the helping relationship.

Having a Structure in Mind

When you're in a helping conversation keeping a structure in mind helps you to guide and contain the process. The structure introduced here identifies three stages that the process goes through (this is the three-stage model introduced in Chapter 6):

✔ **Stage One – Encouraging exploration:** The aim of the first stage is to enable the speaker to explore the issue he has brought to the discussion. Setting the scene for establishing the trust necessary to enable the speaker to speak freely, and helping the speaker begin, are discussed in Chapter 8. In this chapter, I turn to the skills that express or convey the core conditions and begin to give the helping conversation purpose and direction. This is the beginning of the process, when you and the speaker are settling down and starting to open up the story that has brought the speaker for help.

✔ **Stage Two – Increasing understanding:** In this stage the speaker is encouraged to delve and disclose at a deeper level. You, as the listener, require the supportive qualities and skills from Stage One as well as the use of more challenging interventions. The aim is to ensure that the speaker develops a fuller picture of his situation, including less obvious aspects that he may not have considered or been aware of. In this stage the possible goals or outcomes should begin to become clearer.

Development of Stage Two skills is probably the hardest for beginning listeners. You may have a tendency to rush from initial exploration to problem-solving and action, which can be doomed to failure because the true nature of the issue hasn't been revealed. When the problem is better understood, the speaker can move more readily and purposefully to naming, evaluating, and choosing some goals for himself. I discuss these Stage Two skills in Chapter 10.

✔ **Stage Three – Facilitating action:** During the action stage you support the speaker in carrying out and reviewing what he has decided. In a one-off session in which you ascertain that referring on is more appropriate, the session includes all three stages. All the qualities and skills of Stage One and Stage Two contribute to this closing part of the helping relationship, along with problem-solving and evaluation skills and management of the ending. Check out Chapter 11 for more on Stage Three skills.

The idea of three stages isn't new; it has been used in the counselling field for decades. Some authors have elaborated on it but I'll stay with a simplified version. You can also find an outline version of the whole three-stage model in Chapter 6. The stages coincide with beginning, middle, and ending.

A helping conversation is a process, not a collection of stages and skills which fit neatly together in a linear progression. In real life the helping process often appears to be disorganised and non-sequential, so don't feel you've failed if what you experience doesn't progress in a smooth fashion. As you work with someone and he develops trust in you, the conversation deepens and new areas of exploration open up, resulting in revisiting an earlier stage. If something happens to disrupt the relationship, you find yourself going back to the beginning stage to re-establish trust. So the structure is flexible and is experienced as cyclical in many situations.

The three-stage process applies to individual helping conversations as well as to a series of sessions. Within each conversation is a beginning, middle, and end stage; the same is true of the whole of a longer helping relationship.

The simple three-stage structure which approximates to beginning (exploration), middle (understanding), and end (action), can help you keep an eye on the process and manage the time. If you keep the idea in your mind that any session, and any series of sessions, falls roughly into three parts then you should keep on track. The understanding section usually takes longer than the exploring and action stages, so you might think in terms of:

- ✔ **First quarter:** Exploration
- ✔ **Middle half:** Developing understanding
- ✔ **Final quarter:** Action and ending

Eventually most people develop a kind of internal clock or sensor that gives them an approximate sense of where they are in any session. It isn't flawless though! Many counsellors can tell stories of how they went well over time in a session. It's always worth thinking, 'Why did that happen with *this* person?'

At all times, keep theory at the service of the process, not driving it. Always strive to be sensitive to the needs of *this* person at *this* time and place. The structure is a guide but listening sessions don't always fit neatly into the structure – they may go backwards and forwards between the stages as the relationship develops and the understanding of the issues deepens, perhaps as the speaker feels increasingly able to trust you and the process and so disclose more of what he really feels and thinks and how he behaves.

You'll face many occasions when help-seekers conceal the true nature of their difficulty, either consciously or unconsciously. Often other difficulties are discussed safely whilst the real issue lies waiting. An example is a woman I counselled who was having difficulties in her relationship – all the blame seemed to be on her partner and she had a catalogue of complaints about her. After a number of sessions she admitted that she had a problem with her own angry feelings and had been emotionally and physically abusive to her partner. We could have worked on the other issues without ever getting to this admission, which she was ashamed of. In the cases of sexual abuse survivors, they frequently don't reveal their abuse until well into therapy when they have built up sufficient trust.

Forming the Relationship

A crucial part of the beginning stage of the helping process is forming the helping relationship. Three key qualities known as the *core conditions* – respect, empathy, and genuineness – underpin the relationship. The core conditions aid the help-seeker to begin to

✔ Feel valued and accepted

✔ Feel understood

✔ Trust you

✔ Tell his story fully and coherently

✔ Express and identify emotions

✔ Connect different aspects of his experience.

The core conditions are demonstrated through the facilitative active listening skills I describe in this chapter. To hear the help-seeker's story, you need to offer encouragement and manage the process using these active listening skills, which continue throughout the helping encounter as well as providing the foundation of the helping relationship.

The skills you use at this beginning stage help to slow down the process and give space and time for reflection. Sometimes you'll yearn to speed up the process (which might be more about your own discomfort with silence and slowness than that the process *needs* to be faster). More often, though, the difficulty for beginning listening helpers is enabling enough reflective space. The speaker needs to hear his own story and process in order to fully understand what the problem really is. From this position he'll be better able to reach his own solutions.

Conveying the Core Conditions

You can convey the key attitudes of empathy, respect, and genuineness to the speaker through developing your attentiveness; verbal and non-verbal encouragement; picking up on and reflecting emotions and thoughts; and careful questioning, pacing, and timing.

Demonstrating acceptance and empathy

Part of the exploratory process is forming the relationship. Even if you already have a relationship with the speaker, you may need to create a new one if the speaker doesn't know whether you're approachable about this particular issue on this particular occasion. When people experience difficulties, they often feel muddled, churned up, and concerned that they're going mad or will be seen as bad or stupid. The speaker sometimes tests the water to discover whether you're going to judge him. Because the story at this juncture often feels incoherent to the speaker, and because he may be concerned about being judged, receiving encouragement, prompts and feedback is important for him, providing evidence that you're listening with empathy.

Empathy, which can be described as the ability to communicate that you can see the world from someone else's perspective, has a number of different levels, ranging from none at all (sometimes called *subtractive empathy,* because the listener's responses *remove* strength of feeling) to what is called *depth,* or occasionally *advanced empathy.* At this stage of the process the most useful empathic responding is a basic recognition and acknowledgement of the speaker's feelings, which helps to build trust. (I discuss deeper levels of empathy in Chapter 10.) Here is an example of a help-seeker's statement and some different responses you might make:

> 'I just sat there, stunned. I couldn't believe that she could say those things. I still feel stunned. Now I don't know what to do – part of me says, "Leave the job," and the other part says, "Hang in there, other people know you did a good job."'

A subtractive response might be:

> 'So you're thinking, "Shall I stay or shall I go?"'

Only the thinking part is picked up. A basic empathic response might be:

> 'So you're still shocked and wondering what to do?'

The questioning tone conveys that you're checking your understanding.

Another would be:

> 'It sounds as though you were shocked, and still are (pause) . . . and you're in two minds whether to stay or leave the job?'

The preceding statement includes several skills: reflection (of feelings and thoughts) in a paraphrased mini-summary. Although the words matter, whether the recipient feels your response is empathic depends a great deal on the non-verbal accompaniments.

Empathy is important for understanding the speaker's *frame of reference,* meaning that you gain a sense of the speaker's world from his perspective. Only when you have this understanding can you fully appreciate what the speaker's difficulties are really about and later, when moving into problem-solving and solution-finding is appropriate, what strategies are likely to be helpful and acceptable to the speaker.

Communicating non-verbally

A high proportion of your judgements about other people are formed through non-verbal information and perceptions. Whilst it may be less true for some, for example those with Asperger's syndrome or other forms of autism, most people are adept at picking up on minimal gestures, posture, and expressions, and understanding (sometimes misunderstanding) their meaning. Conveying the Core Conditions of acceptance and empathy (refer to Chapter 8) needs to take into account your non-verbal messages – which makes being a listening helper very challenging. Because your non-verbal behaviour is largely automatic and unconscious, you can easily betray a lack of empathy and acceptance. To be a highly effective listening helper, you need to accept others, which means understanding yourself (which is why I put an emphasis on personal awareness in this book, especially in Chapter 2).

Giving full attention

Think for a moment about what someone is doing when he gives you his full attention. Can you picture his posture and stance, his expression and eye contact, non-verbal communication and non-speech vocalisations? Most people find it uncomfortable being face-to-face square on, but find that being at a slight angle to each other so that each can avert his gaze easily if he needs to is better. Maintaining eye contact shows that you're listening and a soft gaze can communicate empathy.

Fixing your gaze intently could be counter-productive, perhaps being perceived as threatening or piercing. In some cultures eye-to-eye contact is considered rude, so you do need to be sensitive to the other person's culture and body language. If you're ever in doubt, ask the speaker.

When I work with couples on their relationship, I often teach them active listening skills with a communication exercise. On one occasion I explained that the exercise involved one partner showing that he was listening whilst the other talked about something that mattered to her. The woman was upset and angry with her partner afterwards because she said he hadn't been paying attention and wasn't listening properly because he was looking up at the ceiling. He responded by explaining that when he concentrated, he tended to look up so he wouldn't get distracted and didn't realise how it made her feel. This story illustrates how we make assumptions about what other people's behaviour means and how even appearing not to listen affects communication. When this happened at home, the couple rapidly descended into bickering, not realising what the root of the problem was. When we talk about something important, we need to know that the other person is listening.

The distraction of internal conversations

Internal conversations (conversations you have in your head, often while supposedly listening) distract you from giving attention. Try to put them aside. When you're new to counselling skills, you'll almost certainly find yourself having dialogues in your own head such as: 'Oh, I shouldn't have done that,' 'I wonder what the time is,' 'Should I be suggesting some homework?' 'I don't know anything about this subject, will I seem stupid?' and so on. When these thoughts come into your mind, accept that this happens sometimes and then put them away and focus on being empathic to redress the balance.

Sometimes feeling distracted, such as when you're bored or irritated, means that something is going on in the relationship between you and the help-seeker. Don't berate yourself, but take time after the conversation to reflect on what these feelings could mean. Perhaps the help-seeker bores and irritates other people in his life so try to find a non-threatening way to help him understand how he affects you. Or perhaps your distraction is a sign that the help-seeker is concealing uncomfortable feelings, for example that he's furious about something but feels unable to say so and covers up by being bland.

Often after a skills practice a trainee will say something like, 'I didn't know whether the speaker's relationship with his son was more important or the problem at work, so I didn't know which way to go.' If during a helping conversation you find yourself having a separate conversation in your head about what to do, consider having it out loud with the help-seeker. These internal conversations are very distracting to your attention and you don't have to take all the responsibility: By sharing it with the speaker you demonstrate respect. In this example the trainee could have said, 'I'm feeling confused about which direction you want to go – you came saying you wanted to talk about work but actually, now, you're talking more about your son.'

Using encouragement

Make sure that your whole context and demeanour create an encouraging environment. Use appropriate nodding to add to this encouragement by showing that you're following the speaker as he speaks.

Avoid turning into a nodding donkey – too much head movement can not only be distracting but also can lead the other person to feel sick or develop a headache. Non-speech and minimal vocalisations such as 'mmm,' 'uh-huh,' 'yeah,' and so on can punctuate the conversation so that the other person knows you're following – but don't overdo it. A pet irritation of mine is too much repetition, particularly the word 'right'. Try to notice if you have similar verbal mannerisms. Audio-recording conversations (with permission) is a good way of reflecting on your skills.

Your facial expressions and tone of voice can also provide encouragement. When they are training as listeners or counsellors, some people think they should be expressionless and appear unshockable and emotionally uninvolved.

They then come across as wooden and unresponsive, somewhat inhuman, which is very discouraging for the speaker. Emotions are like an iceberg – what is displayed on the surface is a fraction of the iceberg. People who have lived in an environment where their emotions and experiences are discounted learn to mask and even dissociate from their own feelings, leading to stories bleached of emotion. Your facial expressions convey empathy and can enable the speaker to recognise his own squashed feelings.

Communicating attention through posture

Relax your posture, but without being too laid-back, in order to show receptiveness and attention. Some people advocate a slight forward lean, but be guided by the speaker's posture. Mirroring the speaker's posture promotes rapport, but needs to be subtle. If the speaker is tense and on the edge of the chair you might begin by initially mirroring his posture in a less intense way and then gradually relaxing your own stance.

Sometimes people imagine that as a listening helper you're supposed to be absolutely still, not waving your arms about and gesturing. While maintaining a relaxed and relatively still posture is generally a good idea, you don't have to be unnatural and stiff. Check out any repetitive habits you might have though, as these can be highly distracting, for example bouncing your foot up and down or jingling money in your pocket (get feedback from colleagues or friends if you can). If you maintain good attention, minor gestures will probably be unimportant to the flow although they may still be noticed; people almost always notice when you consult your watch, for example.

Picking up on emotions

Displayed emotion is almost always a fraction of what is felt. Unless you're one of the minority of people who wears his heart on his sleeve, in most situations you edit your feelings for public consumption. This concealment of emotions is the reason why I use the analogy of the iceberg; most is below the surface and a hazard for the unwary. Not only do we hide our feelings but conveying them in words tends to reduce their intensity.

If the help-seeker senses that you're uncomfortable with particular feelings, for example the expression of anger or tears, he'll be far less likely to reveal these feelings to you, especially if he's already learned to think of them as unacceptable. Concealing parts of the emotional experience can impede the work you're aiming to do as a listening helper, once again highlighting the importance of your personal development.

How do you express your feelings, using words and without using words, in the following situations?

- ✔ When you're bored with what's going on.

- ✔ When you feel very annoyed with someone with whom you want to build a better relationship.

- ✔ When someone hurts you.

- ✔ When you're asked to do something you're afraid you can't do well and want to hide your inadequacy.

What you express is likely to depend on who you're with and how comfortable you feel being open with him. Notice what makes the difference in terms of the kind of relationship you have and the other person's responses. With someone you don't feel comfortable showing your feelings to, how do you manage your feelings, what do you do instead of showing your true feelings? These responses are called *defences* (Chapter 7 has more about defences).

This exercise, used by my colleague Ali Harrison, touches on a few areas where some people find it hard to reveal their feelings. Perhaps you can think of others. Think about what behaviour you use to manage your feelings in order to avoid revealing them. Such reflections can help you understand a help-seeker's reticence and also some of his defensive behaviour.

Developing a repertoire of emotional language

You need to develop your own emotional vocabulary so that you can paraphrase, summarise, and enhance the speaker's ability to describe and express his emotional experience, and so you can convey an understanding of the nuances of that experience. Many people have limited words to describe feelings. (For more on paraphrasing, see the upcoming section 'Paraphrasing and summarising.')

Think of all the feeling words you know (or use a thesaurus) and write them down under the following headings: Mad, Bad, Sad, Glad, Afraid, and Others (sorry I couldn't continue the rhyme). You may find some words are alternatives to each other, or indicate a subtle difference in feeling. Notice how many emotional words hold several feelings inside them. An example is 'jealous', which can include insecure, anxious, worried, angry, and more.

Table 9-1 shows an example of some words grouped under headings. You may not agree with where the words are placed. People feel differently about feeling words. When you've compiled your own list, use the words more often to help you increase colour and richness in your descriptions of feelings.

Table 9-1		Feeling Words			
Mad	*Bad*	*Sad*	*Glad*	*Afraid*	*Others*
annoyed	belligerent	broken	cheerful	anxious	bold
cross	cruel	crushed	elated	hesitant	curious
enraged	devious	flat	enthusiastic	insecure	in-tune
furious	envious	gloomy	excited	panicky	loving
losing it	jealous	heartbroken	festive	scared	proud
out of control	rebellious	suffering	jubilant	shaky	sensual
sullen	sulky	tortured	merry	terrified	tender

Reflecting experience

The picking up of key parts of a person's experience and putting them back to the speaker is called *reflecting*. Reflecting generally means using the exact same words that the speaker has used, whilst avoiding simple parroting. Reflecting takes practice to master but is very effective at keeping the control and direction in the speaker's hands, so that you don't impose your own agenda, through questions, for example.

Three types of reflection are:

- ✔ **Reflecting facts and thoughts:** By picking up facts and thinking and reflecting them back to the speaker you can help clarify the story or issue. As well as showing attention, the process also helps to focus the conversation, for example highlighting the dilemma someone faces.

    A way of practising is to listen carefully to someone as he speaks and store up between three and six keywords or phrases in your memory. As soon as you can find a space in the conversation after you reach three to six keywords, say, 'The key things I'm picking up so far are . . . [listing the words or phrases].' This can be rather artificial but you can develop other ways of saying it. The technique is useful for slowing things down and keeping track.

    Here's an example of a part of a conversation where someone has been talking about feeling unsettled at work, with some keywords highlighted: 'There are things I *love* about my job and things that *drive me mad*. I find the contact with people is *rewarding* but dealing with the paperwork and the financial side is very *stressful*. I've found myself browsing the job adverts, but I don't know what I want really.'

    This person has a dilemma which he's thinking through. You might reply: 'The key things I'm picking up are that *some* of your job is very rewarding, but other parts are stressful, they "drive you mad" and so you're unsure whether to change jobs?' This summary is perhaps a little long (always strive for economy), but it tries to capture what has been said mostly using the speaker's words.

✔ **Reflecting feelings:** Picking up on feelings and reflecting them back to the speaker is a powerful tool, belying its apparent simplicity. As an example, the speaker says: 'It was awful, I felt so churned up and I thought, I've got to get out of here, I was so het up I didn't know what to do with myself, whether to cry or scream at them or run away.'

You could use a very simple reflection here: 'You felt 'het up'? or 'You felt churned up?' This kind of response, although so simple that it might seem simplistic, is very effective at encouraging the speaker to tell you more about what 'het up' feels like and means to him. Notice the question mark – a question in the voice invites more. You may very well guess what feelings go into the 'het up' category but two points are important here:

- Never assume you know what an emotional term means to someone else, especially portmanteau words (words that potentially contain a lot, in this example a lot of emotions) such as *jealousy, guilt, upset, confused*, or *het up*. Your understanding of the word may differ subtly or significantly from the speaker's.

- By questioning the meaning you draw the speaker into exploring his feelings more fully so that he increases *his* understanding of what is going on for him. 'Het up' might include: emotions such as anger, frustration, irritation, dismay, betrayal, anxiety; and physical sensations like stomach knots or churning, tension, feeling hot, nervous energy and so on.

Occasionally someone reacts with annoyance, as if it is *obvious* what he means; you must be a simpleton if you don't understand. This kind of response provides a good opportunity to say that people experience things differently, and you want to understand how it is for *him*. Usually simple reflections are interpreted as indicators that you're truly trying to understand. Reflecting slows the process down, enabling the speaker to listen to himself.

✔ **Reflecting observations:** Noticing, and reflecting back, aspects of the speaker's body language or facial expressions is a useful practice. Look out for contradictions such as the speaker describing feeling angry and yet smiling, or saying that he's fine but with his eyes welling up or his fists clenching. Check out Chapter 10 for more on picking up contradictions and discussion on more challenging interventions, and see Chapter 12 for more on the significance of body language.

An example of reflecting an observation is: 'As you were talking about being fed up, you looked very sad.' Such an observation encourages the speaker to elaborate and recognise the complexity of his feelings. Often people don't realise that they're stuck because they're caught between conflicting emotions.

These different types of reflection have different functions, although all demonstrate careful listening. In practice they may be difficult to separate out.

Paraphrasing and summarising

When developing listening skills, people often don't realise or forget how helpful the skills of paraphrasing and summarising are. *Paraphrasing* is when you take a small part of what someone has said and reflect it back in your own words. *Summarising* generally comes after hearing more and is when you pick up on key things that have been said and you probably use the speaker's own words. Paraphrasing and summarising slow the pace, which is often helpful and gives time for reflection. The speaker can hear his own story when you reflect, paraphrase, or summarise. When someone has been churning something around in his mind with no one to speak to, gaining a perspective is hard. When his story is spoken aloud, and then reiterated, the speaker has time to reflect on what he's saying. Time for reflection is one of the great benefits of speaking to a listening helper.

If in doubt – summarise!

Paraphrasing

Paraphrasing can be an extension of reflection and a kind of mini-summary. For example, if the speaker shows agitation through his pace of delivery, breathlessness, and gestures and says, 'The funeral was dreadful. My brother and sister started arguing over who should have done more for Dad, who was entitled to what from the house. I wanted to tell them to shut up but I couldn't get the words out. I was feeling so upset about Dad dying suddenly like that, even though we knew it would happen. I just had to run out of the house and cry.'

You might reply, 'It sounds like you were really upset.' This paraphrases and could communicate empathy with the right tone and expression. However, because it *reduces* the identified feelings to a bland word (*upset*), it could close down the opportunity to invite the speaker to say more and go into more depth about his feelings. At times such closing down is useful (when you're trying to end a session for example).

By contrast, a paraphrase can open up by helping to *increase* the identification of feelings. For example, by picking up on the non-verbal signals, you could say, 'It sounds like you had really *mixed* feelings, such as hurt and anger at your brother and sister (pause) . . . and also shock and sadness, perhaps some other feelings in there too?'

Like reflecting, paraphrasing slows the interaction and gives time to connect with emotions. Understanding the emotional undertow is important for understanding the problem. From this snippet of conversation you cannot know what has brought this person for help or what might lie underneath. The speaker may seek your help because he simply needs to off-load his feelings by telling you the story, or it may be that with careful listening for underlying emotions, you recognise that he's looking for help with a deeper issue, leading you into Stage Two (Understanding Stage) of the helping process, which I discuss in Chapter 10. Maybe the speaker has a history of being unable to verbalise feelings, or of being, say, the youngest, whose opinion was not sought or valued so that his self-esteem is poor.

The underestimated value of summarising

Beginning listening helpers often fall into the trap of asking too many questions (see the later section 'Mastering the Art of Questions' for more on this). During a silence the listener can feel uncomfortable and responsible for keeping things going. Hunting for a solution, the listener searches for a question to ask. What can happen is that the speaker is then responding to the listener's agenda and/or gets into a series of question-and-answer interactions where the listener becomes ever more desperate to keep the conversation going.

The much preferable alternative is to summarise (although see the later section 'Probing, clarifying, and filling in the gaps' about working with silences as well). Mini-summaries at intervals help to maintain focus and show that you're attending. Longer summaries provide a punctuation point, a place to pause and think, for both speaker and listener. I find a lot of people in training fear that they won't remember everything. Summaries help you to remember. Practise making a mental note of keywords and when you run the risk of not being able to recall them all, stop the speaker and summarise what you've heard so far.

Summarising is a way of clarifying and focusing that assists in bringing direction and purpose to the helping encounter.

Summarising enables you to identify and convey the core messages in a speaker's story. To gain practice, the next time you're listening to someone telling you an incident (it could be an everyday incident experienced by a friend, colleague, or family-member) concentrate on the following:

1. **Listen carefully.**

2. **Identify one or two of each of the key experiences, behaviours, and feelings experienced.**

3. **Use these to communicate a statement back to the speaker that summarises the core message of the story of the incident.**

4. **Check out your understanding with the speaker.**

Exploring the Presenting Problem

As well as the qualities and skills mentioned in earlier sections in this chapter, you can do other things to assist the telling of the story. These skills fill out the detail and begin to expose some of the possible underlying issues. Very often, what is presented (called the *presenting problem*) is not the whole or real story. The presenting problem may mask deeper difficulties or may be a way of testing you to see if you're trustworthy. Most of the skills which lead to deeper levels of understanding are in the next chapter because they're more challenging and need the basis of a good relationship to be effective, but the following sections highlight some slightly more challenging skills which are part of this exploring stage.

Probing, clarifying, and filling in the gaps

Most people omit things from their narrative. They make generalisations and assumptions about what the listener understands. One of the dangers of empathy is that you may understand all too readily, but usually not being too clever and not assuming is helpful for the listening helper because the help-seeker is forced to explain his story (as much to himself as to you). Hidden emotions and patterns of thought can be highlighted through the speaker having to tell his story in detail. Table 9-2 offers an example where you might probe or prompt for more in order to clarify the difficulty and what contributes to it.

Table 9-2	Filling the Gaps
The speaker says:	*What is missing?*
I get frightened . . .	Of what? When?
. . . Of being with people . . .	Which people in particular? When?
. . . People I don't know very well, especially at work.	What is it that frightens you?
	Is there anyone specific?
	Does it always happen?
Making a fool of myself.	How would you make a fool of yourself?
I would probably say something stupid.	And then what would happen?
	How would you feel then?
	How would you know it was stupid?

The questions in the right-hand column of Table 9-2 are probing and potentially challenging. They're possibilities, not a recommendation that you bombard the speaker with all these questions. The questions are examples of *Socratic questioning*, which means asking questions so that the help-seeker finds his own conclusions. Of course, you may prefer to couch your questions differently, less abruptly, such as, 'What is it that scares you?' 'Is there anyone in particular that you're scared of?'

Prompting

In a similar vein as probing, prompting helps to deepen the exploration. Releasing and recognising your emotions is therapeutic and yet most people tend to edit and minimise their feelings. Asking 'How does that make you feel?' has become a cliché, so you need to find ways of eliciting more about the way a person feels whilst avoiding the cliché if possible. Some methods previously discussed (such as non-verbal encouragement and reflection, paraphrasing, and summarising) can all prompt elaboration. To add variety to your interventions and/or if the speaker doesn't pick up and elaborate when you try those methods, you could say:

- ✔ 'You mentioned you felt . . . [for example, guilty]. Could you tell me a bit more about that?'

- ✔ 'When you said you were . . . [for example, upset], I was wondering what other feelings you had.'

- ✔ 'You used the word . . . [for example, jealous]. What does that mean for you exactly?' (Other examples are: 'What feelings go into that?' 'What is it you feel when you feel jealous?' 'How does jealousy feel? And so on.)

- ✔ 'You've told me all about what your friend said and did but what effect did that have on *you*?'

No one *makes* you feel anything. At times others may *try* to make you feel something, manipulating you to induce guilt or needling you to anger for example. However, how you feel is largely up to you and depends on your patterns of thought. If you don't hold internal messages that you're responsible for another person's happiness, for example, then you're not likely to be manipulated into feeling guilty. I'm not advocating that you confront a help-seeker with this idea (certainly not at this stage), but you don't need to collude by asking how someone else *made* the speaker feel.

Interrupting appropriately

Interrupting sometimes seems disrespectful. However, sometimes you need to interrupt. Here are good reasons why interrupting may be helpful:

- ✔ This is supposed to be a helping conversation. If the speaker wanted to be uninterrupted he could have simply spoken out loud to himself. Asking what the speaker wants from the conversation is quite legitimate – you might want to check out if he simply wants to offload, for example.

- ✔ Once people get into full flow they can generate strong feelings which are hard to suppress. You need to allow time for the speaker to gather himself together to face the world outside.

- ✔ When the story emerges very rapidly the speaker can get carried away and reveal more than he meant to. Sometimes people don't return for further sessions for this reason.

- ✔ When the speaker is running away with his story so fast that you can't get a word in edgewise there's no space and time for reflection. As a result neither you nor the speaker can explore things in depth – which may be what the speaker wants, of course, consciously or unconsciously.

Interrupting can take courage, assertiveness, and confidence in your role and its purpose. Here are some examples of phrases you can use. You may need to begin with a gesture, such as a raised hand.

- ✔ 'I'm sorry to stop you but I'm finding it hard to keep up. Can I check that I am understanding you properly?'

- ✔ 'Can we stop there for a moment?' (leading to a summary).

- ✔ 'It seems you have a lot you want to say, but I want to make sure I'm following you. Can I tell you what I've heard so far?'

- ✔ 'It sounds like you've been bottling things up for a while. Can we take stock for a moment?'

- ✔ 'I need to stop you because I'm aware that we only have a short time left.'

Working with silence

Undoubtedly one of the most difficult aspects of being a listening helper for most people is tolerating silence. What seems like a long and painful pause when you are the listener is often experienced as very short by the speaker or observers. What tends to happen in silences is that the listener panics, imagining that the speaker is looking to him to do something, and starts to hunt for questions. Of course, at times the speaker *is* uncomfortable and wants you to rescue him; sometimes it does help to break the silence. For now, though, especially if you become aware that you find staying with silence difficult, practise holding back.

When a silence occurs, try to turn off your inner voices and pay attention to the speaker's body language, especially his eyes:

▶ If he's looking up then he's most likely imagining or picturing something.

▶ If his gaze is unfocused or focused in the distance he's likely to be having an inner dialogue.

▶ If he's looking down he's probably immersed in his feelings.

While any of these is happening, resist the urge to interrupt. After the gaze returns to your face, notice the expression. Again, resist the impulse to immediately ask questions, reflect, paraphrase, or summarise – take your time.

Don't use the previous pointers as a sure indicator of what's going on when someone is silent. Always remember that each person is an individual with his own characteristics and any guidelines are only potentially helpful.

If the speaker's facial expression seems to indicate that he's come to a stop, or that he's looking to you for a response, consider the following examples of responses that stay with his process:

▶ 'I wonder what was going on for you then?'

▶ 'You seemed to be thinking deeply about something then?'

▶ 'I feel like you're looking to me now to say something?'

▶ 'I get the feeling you've come to a stop.' (pause) 'What would you like now?'

The first two are inviting reflection on what was going on during the silence, while the second two are commenting on the here-and-now experience and inviting the speaker to take the lead. Sometimes people look away because they feel uncomfortable and it might help to talk about how uncomfortable they feel and what is causing that. Sometimes (I find particularly with young people) they just don't know where to start and prefer a helping hand in the form of some questions. You need to practise judging these subtleties.

Mastering the Art of Questions

The role of questions in a helping relationship is complex. Asking questions is potentially extremely helpful and, equally, possibly disastrous. In a listening-helper situation a special kind of conversation is happening where one person is encouraging another to open up so he can explore whatever issues are troublesome. The aim is to enable the speaker to be in charge. I encourage you to reflect on how to help this process with alternatives to carefully judged questions.

Asking questions is a normal part of everyday conversations and of interviewing. The aims are to:

- ✔ Show interest
- ✔ Gain information
- ✔ Form a hypothesis or theory
- ✔ Keep the conversation going
- ✔ Gain control

If you reflect for a moment you'll realise that if one person is predominantly the questioner he'll almost invariably and inevitably set the agenda and hold control. People are well trained to answer questions as well as ask them, but they don't always do so willingly.

Notice conversations – especially those where you can sit back and observe. You need to:

- ✔ Think about the purpose of the conversation.
- ✔ Notice who asks questions.
- ✔ Consider who's in control of the conversation.
- ✔ Decide what is the effect of the questions.

Television dramas and soaps are good material for this exercise. Take notes to help your reflections.

Making notes isn't a good idea when you're trying to get someone to open up to you, but doing so afterwards *is* a good idea, to help develop your reflections.

Listeners who lack experience or confidence often resort to questions when other responses would be more helpful to the process. The dialogue can degenerate into an interrogation. The listener feels increasingly desperate, searching for the right question to open things up, expending effort on his own internal processes (anxiety and desperation) instead of being free to pay proper attention to the speaker's experience. Meanwhile, the speaker retreats into defensive, monosyllabic responses, possibly feeling hounded and misunderstood or that he isn't meeting the listener's expectations, or perhaps pleased to be avoiding the issues that brought him for help in the first place! The relationship can become skewed, so that the speaker becomes passive, abdicating responsibility and seeing the listener as the expert, or alternatively, the speaker becomes resentful and frustrated.

Of course, being curious and interested in the people that you're trying to help, and being fascinated by them and their stories and seeing how they tick, is all part of the motivation for working with people. However, an unhelpful motivation for asking questions is so that the questioner can work out what the problem is and provide a possible solution. This temptation to come up with theories about the speaker is potentially dangerous – you may believe your theories are the truth and try to make the speaker fit them. Questioning that leads to the *listener* controlling the content of the session undermines the principle of self-determination. Self-determination is central to listening-helper situations for a very good reason – it works!

Finding alternatives to questions

Next time you have a conversation, make a conscious effort to avoid asking any questions. To manage this you need some alternatives:

- ✔ Reflect feeling words that the speaker uses and don't be afraid to use the speaker's own words.

- ✔ Observe and reflect non-verbal cues (which signal underlying emotion), such as: 'I notice your eyes welled up when you said that,' or 'Although you were smiling you were clenching your fist then.'

- ✔ Draw on empathic understanding that notices how the other person is feeling, such as: 'You seem to be . . .' or 'I'm wondering if . . .'

- ✔ Use 'I' statements, for example: 'When you told me about that I felt quite sad.'

- ✔ Use minimal verbal and gestural encouragers, such as 'mmm', 'uh-huh', nodding, and smiling.

- ✔ Use 'you feel . . . because . . .', a form of mini-summary which picks up on feelings and links them to their apparent cause.

- ✔ Use mini-summaries and paraphrasing. In general, using the client's own language helps to convey your understanding and helps you get inside his skin, but paraphrasing – summarising in your own words – is also useful.

- ✔ If in doubt, summarise.

Not asking questions feels very strange but is good practice. The purpose of your conversation is to help the speaker open up and explore so that he can come to understand himself and his situation better.

Working with a partner, each find a picture (from a magazine for example) that evokes some emotions for you. Don't let the other person see your picture. Take it in turns to find out about your partner's picture – without asking any questions! Doing this exercise is quite hard but it makes you realise how reliant you are on questioning and helps you recognise the internal pressure that you feel to ask questions.

Using questions constructively

Questioning is a skill to be used with care and purpose. Sometimes questions can be appropriate or helpful. Open questions can legitimately control the process of a listening session. Also, you may need, or be required, to ask particular questions at the assessment stage to establish the level of risk, or to check that help in this place at this time is likely to benefit the help-seeker. At times a speaker may find speaking too difficult and may prefer you to ask questions. I've found this particularly with young people, who sometimes ask me to help them out by asking them questions.

If you must use questions, use caution and purpose.

Helpful questions are invitations to:

- ✔ Elaborate. Enabling the speaker to give more detail is usually helpful.

- ✔ Fully explore and join up the experience of the help-seeker – thinking, feelings, and behaviour. People often leave out areas of their experience.

- ✔ Specify. Questions can help the speaker to move from generalisations to specific examples. For example, you can gently challenge the person who says, 'Everyone thinks I'm stupid,' by asking 'Who, exactly, thinks you're stupid?' Hopefully the reply will give something that can be worked on.

- ✔ Be more concrete. For example, when someone says 'I'm always so stupid,' you might ask him to tell you exactly when and where he gets this feeling. Again, the answer opens up areas (patterns and themes) that you can work with.

- ✔ Uncover hidden assumptions and maladaptive thinking. These assumptions can be discovered through helping the speaker to specify and be more concrete or by asking 'dumb' questions. Don't jump to 'understanding' what the speaker is saying too readily – by inviting him to give more detail he will uncover his assumptions and faulty logic (for example, the speaker may say 'He said . . . so he must hate me.')

- ✔ Give personal reactions. Many people omit their own feelings, behaviour, and thoughts from their stories.

Why not why?

Imagine a time when you were questioned about something you were perhaps ashamed of. You may have been asked, or asked yourself, why you did it. What reactions do you get as you imagine being asked this? Most of us feel anxious and defensive and possibly obliged to explain ourselves when we may not even understand our actions. This questioning is likely to put us into a one-down position (and the listener,

therefore, in a one-up position) which gets in the way of resolving the issue in question.

Statements and inferences you make can be checked out with the speaker by using an upward, questioning inflection in the voice, for example, 'You were feeling frustrated?', which invites further elaboration.

Helpful questions are helpful by being:

- ✔ Open
- ✔ Tentative
- ✔ Checking out.

Open questions tend to help the speaker elaborate and disclose more. A poem by Rudyard Kipling starts with:

> *I keep six honest serving men*
>
> *(They taught me all I knew);*
>
> *Their names are What and Why and When*
>
> *And How and Where and Who.*

Kipling makes a good point: Open questions in a listening-helper situation often begin with how, what, when, who, which, where – but *not* 'why?' (See the sidebar 'Why not why?')

Closed questions are questions that lead only to a Yes/No choice or effectively close down the conversation.

Always approach questioning in a tentative way – usually indicated in the upward lilt in the voice – when checking things out. Taking this stance gives the speaker the signal that he can disagree with and correct you and your assumptions. In this way the help-seeker is seen as the expert on himself and therefore in charge of his life.

Here's a list of the beginnings of tentative statements. You can alter them to fit your own language style better. Add more of your own and try them out in a conversation.

- ✔ 'It sounds as if . . .'
- ✔ 'I get the feeling that . . .'
- ✔ 'Could it be that . . .?'
- ✔ 'I wonder if . . .?'
- ✔ 'Correct me if I'm wrong, but is it . . .?'
- ✔ 'Perhaps you're feeling . . .?'
- ✔ 'This maybe a long shot, but I'm wondering if . . .?'
- ✔ 'I'm not sure that I follow you. Do you mean . . .?'
- ✔ 'I'm not certain I understand; you're feeling . . .?'
- ✔ 'As I hear it, you [. . .]. Is that the way it is?'
- ✔ 'I get the impression that . . .'

As you see, many of these questioning statements include *reflection* and some are evidently going to *paraphrase*, whilst some seem to lead to *mini-summaries*.

Closed and open questions in a dialogue

In this example, the person is talking about his relationship with his son. Imagine what the conversation (and the helping relationship) would be like using the different styles of questioning: closed, open, and more open.

Closed questions:

'Did you speak to your son, as you planned? Did you say any of the things we talked about? Did it go well? Has he agreed to tidy his room?'

Open questions:

'You said last week you intended to speak to your son about tidying his room. How did it go? What did you say to him? How did he react? What effect did that have on you?' (You wouldn't ask all of these in a row like this of course.)

More open questions:

Listener: 'You said last week you intended to speak to your son about tidying his room. What were your feelings about it afterwards?'

Speaker: 'I was pretty nervous, because he's been so bolshie and abusive before, but I was determined to do it'

Listener: 'Nervous but determined?'

Speaker: 'Yes, after we talked I felt better about having a go and I thought that something's got to change'

Listener: 'Mmm?'

Avoiding unhelpful questioning

The following common habits take self-monitoring to change:

- ✔ **Too many questions:** This can lead to feelings of being interrogated and thus defensiveness.

- ✔ **Two questions at once:** The speaker has to choose which to answer and it will probably be the least interesting or useful.

- ✔ **Closed questions:** Not just questions that lead to Yes or No, but those which effectively close options for responding and can also lead to a sense of interrogation.

Train yourself to ask one open question at a time: Take time to decide what question is appropriate. Here are some more examples of questions that can block progress:

- ✔ **Leading questions:** These impose the listener's frame of reference and put the speaker under pressure to answer in certain ways. A famous example is 'When did you stop beating your wife?'

- ✔ **Why questions:** These tend to put the speaker on the defensive so he tends to respond by justifying or giving intellectual explanations.

Both *leading* and *why* questions suggest the listener has an agenda of his own. Here are more examples of questioning that can disturb the helping process:

- ✔ **Over-probing questions:** These cause anxiety by putting the speaker under pressure to disclose information when he may not yet have developed a sense of trust.

- ✔ **Inappropriate information-seeking questions:** Here attention is taken away from the central concerns of the speaker; the speaker's feelings about the information are ignored. This type of questioning tends to lead to resistance. An example is when someone talks about his relationship with his partner and the listening-helper asks if the speaker is married. Necessary information usually emerges naturally, given time.

- ✔ **Poorly timed questions:** Questions that may be useful in themselves, but which come at the wrong moment, may disrupt the flow and the speaker's concerns. These include questions that interrupt a thoughtful silence, that change direction, or that open up big emotional areas at the end of a session when you don't have time to follow through.

The following questions are part of a dialogue where the speaker has been talking about experiencing panic attacks and mentions an accident. The listener asks these questions, which I hope you can now see are phrased in such a way that they lead nowhere. Can you think of ways of enabling the speaker to open up the same areas using a more relaxed and encouraging style?

- ✔ 'Did the panic attacks start before or after the accident?'
- ✔ 'Didn't you feel hurt when she said that?'
- ✔ 'Is it your work that's causing all this stress?'

Responding to questions

Help-seekers ask questions too and it's worth considering what approach you'll take to such questioning. Turning questions back on the questioner has become a therapy cliché. For example the help-seeker asks:

'Do you have any children?', or

'You look very young, how old are you?'

to which the listener replies:

'I wonder why it's important for you to know that.'

Being on the receiving end of this reticent approach can be puzzling and frustrating and it puts the listener firmly in control. But good reasons for being reticent about yourself are:

- ✔ To keep the focus on the speaker and his concerns and feelings.
- ✔ To maintain your own privacy.

You may have valid reasons for disclosing information about yourself. For example, by disclosing an experience or reaction of your own, you might normalise the help-seeker's experience and give hope when he feels 'abnormal' for his experience or reactions. Always consider personal disclosures carefully though, because they're potentially harmful to the helping relationship and process. If you disclose something about your own life in the hope of normalising the speaker's experience, he may hear this as, 'I got over it; so should you.' One way of dealing with a personal question is to tell the speaker whether you're willing to answer it (you may or may not be), and why, but that you're also interested in what lies behind the question. Questions about age and children probably cover an anxiety, such as 'Do you understand what it's like to be a parent? Are you going to judge me?' or 'Do you understand enough about life to help me?', and these underlying concerns are the ones that need addressing.

Here are some alternatives to answering a question focused on you (remember your *tone* is important):

- ✔ 'I'm quite happy to answer your question, but before I do can I ask you what lies behind the question?'

- ✔ 'I notice you keep asking my opinion, as if you don't trust your own judgement?'

- ✔ 'You seem to be interested in me and my life and I'm wondering what that's about?'

- ✔ 'I prefer not to answer questions about me because this time is for you and your concerns.'

Give yourself time to consider what a help-seeker is really asking you when he asks a question.

Chapter 10

Stage Two: Deepening Understanding

. . . .

In This Chapter

▶ Getting a deeper understanding

▶ Achieving deeper empathy

▶ Using more challenging skills

. . . .

*A*fter you've established a relationship with the help-seeker and enabled her to begin telling her story, you move into the second stage of the helping conversation – also referred to as the middle or understanding stage. (Chapter 8 covers the first stage, about how to foster a good start; and Chapter 9 shows you how to build on that with Stage One skills). In Stage Two, which I talk about in this chapter, you help the speaker to deepen exploration in order to help her reach a fuller understanding of herself and the issue that she's bringing to you. After the help-seeker arrives at this understanding, you move on to the Stage Three skills of decision-making, including choosing priorities and identifying goals, which I discuss in Chapter 11.

Often beneath the issue that the help-seeker first presents with are core concerns or deeper anxieties yet to be revealed. When the relationship is established, with a measure of trust, the help-seeker can, with your assistance, take more risks to uncover the complexity of the problem, using the middle stage's more challenging skills. Because the skills of the understanding stage pose more of a threat to the help-seeker's view of the problem and her world, you need to tread with care to convey acceptance and empathy effectively, so you need to minimise the risk of her feeling judged. This continuing foundation of respect and rapport, established through Stage One skills and attitudes, encourages the help-seeker to reveal feelings, self-perceptions, and behaviours that are usually private. The speaker runs the risk of feeling shame, embarrassment, and inadequacy and is likely to defend herself with her habitual defence mechanisms (refer to Chapter 7 for more on defence mechanisms).

If you achieve satisfaction from feeling superior, being competitive, or acting like an expert or a bully you have plenty of scope here. These traits aren't just confined to other people who you can dismiss as nasty but are often a disliked and/or disowned part of oneself (refer to Chapter 2 for more about personal growth). Challenging skills bring a responsibility to be self-monitoring, self-aware, and alert to reactions in the help-seeker.

Getting Below the Surface

Stage Two (Understanding) of the helping relationship utilises all the qualities and skills of Stage One. Added are other, more challenging, skills to help you and the help-seeker get below the presenting issues. These skills are listed in Table 10-1 and then described in more detail later.

Because the middle stage is the most substantive part, you may be tempted to think of it as more important than the beginning or the end. The middle can only be a productive stage of understanding if it's wrapped in a solid relationship involving all three stages – establishing the relationship and beginning exploration in Stage One; deepening exploration and understanding in Stage Two; and moving towards action and closure in Stage Three. If the speaker feels accepted, through effective use of Stage One qualities and skills, she's open to increased understanding through deepened exploration by being challenged in Stage Two.

Often trainee helpers baulk at the words 'challenge' and 'confrontation' because they sound aggressive. Many listening helpers want to be helpful to and liked by the speaker, so prefer to avoid challenging or being challenged. If, though, you're to help more effectively you must be prepared to be honest where it is in the help-seeker's best interest. You can use particular skills to challenge the speaker in a supportive way, provided the challenge is embedded in Stage One skills and a positive helping relationship, A challenge is more likely to be heard as having a supportive intention if you're conveying empathy, respect, and acceptance through your careful use of listening skills (reflecting feelings, summarising, and non-verbal encouragement for example).

As a listening helper you must be able to challenge and confront in as timely and unthreatening a way as possible. The speaker needs to be ready to receive the challenge, sometimes called the 'edge of awareness'. In other words, the speaker is almost there and less defensive. However careful and skilful you are you can come unstuck: You may hit a raw nerve or mistime or misjudge your intervention, leading to defensiveness. If you have a positive relationship you can probably retrieve the situation. Admit the mistake, acknowledge feelings, and apologise. This will help re-establish trust.

The skills of Stage Two are described in detail following the table below, which itemises them and relates the skills to their purpose. Using these skills, in conjunction with Stage One skills, enables the speaker to continue exploring her story, but at greater depth. In doing this you and the speaker will reach a better understanding about the nature of the difficulties she's facing. A clearer picture will also emerge of the speaker's strengths and what solutions she has tried in the past. When the speaker moves towards action, with your support, she will be better able to identify meaningful goals and ways of achieving them.

Table 10-1 The Three Stage Model: Stage Two – Understanding

The Listener Uses Exploring and Clarifying Skills to:	This Helps the Speaker to:
Deepen empathy	Talk and explore
Identify and link themes and why	Understand more about how he or she feels
Identify and fill gaps	Consider options and examine alternatives
Create immediacy: *here-and-now* and *you-me* talk	Choose an alternative
Make specific	
Specify	
Challenge	
Confront	
Focus	
Problem-solve	

Responding with deeper levels of empathy

Empathy comes in several levels:

- ✔ Basic empathic responses help as part of a repertoire of empathic responses, but are subtractive: Emotional intensity is lower in the response than the speaker's expression of feeling.

- ✔ A level of empathy more in tune with the speaker's obvious and expressed experience comes closer to recognising the force of feeling and is important for relationship-building.

✔ Deeper empathic responding not only contains a good approximation to the expressed feeling but goes beyond to identify feelings not yet voiced. You will have picked these feelings up through careful and sensitive observation, drawing on your experience of your own emotional world and that of others and your hunches or intuition. If a feeling is already recognised but not declared, perhaps for fear it will not be accepted, or even be ridiculed, the speaker will feel anxiety, so this communication of deeper empathy is challenging. If the help-seeker believes that she's accepted and you're trustworthy, she's likely to feel relieved.

✔ Even deeper are feelings on the edge of the speaker's awareness. If the speaker does not recognise the feelings but the listener pinpoints them then they become potentially more challenging to hear. A help-seeker may feel that you can read her mind, which is disturbing. By the same token these insights can be very powerful and lead to profound change.

Empathy can deepen as the relationship deepens, and deeper responses lead to greater disclosure and trust. Handled ineptly the opposite can happen. Under threat the help-seeker may withdraw into herself, become very defensive or, even worse, withdraw from the helping encounter itself.

Because the deeper levels of empathic responding are more challenging and should not be used too early, before a reasonable level of trust has been established, they form part of Stage Two, but rest on the relationship-building skills of Stage One, which continue throughout the helping process.

In the later part of a helping conversation deeper levels of empathy also need to be restricted. They can lead to a connection with deeper emotion, which should be avoided when the speaker is soon returning to the outside world.

Noticing themes

A helpful aspect of the listener's role is being able to identify recurring themes and making links between different parts of the speaker's story or experiences. Here's an example:

The help-seeker seems puzzled at her own feelings about a desired change. The listening helper says:

'As you were talking about how scared you are about the changes facing you, even though you really want these changes, I remembered that you talked last time we met about a previous time you had some big changes. You told me they weren't of your choosing and you suffered a lot of stress and anxiety. I am wondering if there is a connection?'

Levels of empathy in action

Here is an example of increasing levels of empathy at different stages of the helping process with a young man who lacks self-esteem.

Help-seeker: 'I'm finding it really hard at college. I'm sure everyone thinks I'm stupid. I dread going, so I get up late, miss the bus, wonder if it's worth going. I get really panicky and sick. I daren't tell Mum, she'd kill me for not going, especially 'cos I was the one who wanted to go – they wanted me to do my A levels at school.'

✔ **So, you're finding it difficult at the moment?** A basic empathic response which might help the person open up if it is accompanied by non-verbal communication of empathy. It is subtractive because it does not fully acknowledge the feelings being expressed by the student.

✔ **It sounds like you're finding this very hard, to the point where you feel sick and panicky and worried about what everyone will think about you, especially your parents.** This attempts to pick up the key feelings. It is a little wordy (always strive for economy), but you would usually have heard more from the help-seeker than the quote above before intervening.

✔ **You sound as though you're really worried about several things and it is making you feel an awful panic and dread.** You have several possible responses so you need to make a choice – do you pick up on the

dread and what it is about or the feelings about not being able to talk to parents? You have to strike a balance between accurately reflecting and being economical so that the attention returns to the speaker fairly quickly. Using your voice to emphasise key words can turn a basic empathic response into something more meaningful.

✔ **You sound as though you're worried so much it is making you have awful feelings of panic and dread. I also sense you're very scared of admitting it to your Mum, that you believe you've let them down . . . again?** Here the listener highlights the help-seeker's strong feelings and his fear of admitting them to his parents, but also draws on prior knowledge from the student of issues related to guilt and feelings of inadequacy. Without a sound relationship this could seem like a judgement.

Using this last level of empathy prematurely could damage the helping relationship. Helping relationships are not an exact science but depend on your sensitivity and judgement about the way the encounter is going and what level of empathic responding is appropriate. With good rapport and trust the student will realise, from this response, why he feels so strongly, which may have been inexplicable to him before. Often people are troubled by the strength of their emotions when they don't understand the source fully, so this can be an important factor in the help you offer.

The hypothesis that the listening helper is suggesting is that the previous experience of change, which was painful, is affecting reactions now so that this change is perceived, or experienced, as frightening.

Using language: metaphor and imagery

Language is powerful. Using the help-seeker's language, in a general sense, is part of getting on her wavelength and promotes rapport. The same idea applies to the use of metaphor and imagery – but metaphors, analogies, and similes are also useful because they're image- and emotion-laden, symbolic, and often convey richer meaning than more straightforward description.

People often use metaphors to express feelings that are too frightening or confusing to express directly. By tuning in to the speaker's metaphors the listening helper can convey empathy and extend the metaphor to deepen exploration or challenge the client's frame of reference in a less threatening way.

A client talked about feeling fragile, 'like a reed in the wind'. I asked him what a reed was like and he began by talking about how frail it was and couldn't stand up to things. After he spoke a little more in this vein, it gave me a good understanding of how he felt weak and lacking in confidence. I asked him if reeds had any positive qualities and he went on to talk about reeds as things that bent rather than broke, which helped him see himself in a more positive light.

Next time you're able to listen to someone else's conversation (for example, in a TV programme) notice how often metaphors and images are used. We frequently refer to all sorts of emotions and experiences as though they are other sensations, objects, or images. When we want to describe strong feelings vivid images are routinely used: 'He was a real pain in the neck' (body imagery is common), 'I thought I was going to die, it was so embarrassing, I wanted the earth to swallow me up.' When someone is depressed she may describe it as if she's in a deep, dark pit feeling like she cannot get out.

In this example, the depressed person might be encouraged to further describe her experience by telling you how deep the pit is, what the sides are like (texture, colour, material, and so on). This describing of an imaginary pit enables you to vividly enter her experience. In exploring her imagery, the possibility exists that the person will recognise and release more emotion, which is therapeutic, and discover something helpful to her recovery.

Challenging and Confronting

To reach an understanding of the true nature of whatever the help-seeker's difficulty is, notice and highlight discrepancies, gaps, and contradictions. What is left out of what the help-seeker reveals can be as significant as what she says. These gaps may be within:

> ✔ **The story.** For example, missing information (refer to Chapter 9 on gaps).
>
> ✔ **The speaker.** Hidden feelings; contradictions between words and demeanour; faulty thinking patterns.
>
> ✔ **You.** Conflicting feelings or feelings at odds with the speaker's.

Look for small gaps in the narrative and note any contradictions. Bring them to the help-seeker's attention at an appropriate moment, such as when you summarise, being careful not to sound judging. You can also explore these discrepancies in the help-seeker's story in various ways, as described in the following sections.

Using immediacy

Immediacy refers to the ability to comment on what is happening here and now in the relationship between the helper and the help-seeker. A key skill for deepening exploration, immediacy is arguably the most difficult to develop.

This skill has a number of variations, some being easier than others, but always involving risk because you make yourself vulnerable and challenge the speaker, who may not welcome what she hears. You need to develop empathy, a foundation of trust with the speaker, and confidence in yourself.

These variations of immediacy are at different levels which can help or hinder the relationship:

> ✔ The most basic and easiest form of immediacy is to comment on what you notice in the speaker – for example that she looks sad (refer to Chapter 9 for information on reflection).
>
> ✔ A slightly more challenging form of immediacy is to comment on how the speaker's story affects you, for example that hearing the story has left you feeling angry at the injustice that she has experienced. This variation is a form of self-disclosure and can enable the speaker to identify repressed emotions, so it is most useful for you to do when the help-seeker is not expressing feelings.
>
> ✔ Another aspect of immediacy is what is sometimes called *then-and-now immediacy*. Here a link is made between how the speaker describes a relationship with another person (for example her parent) and how you experience the relationship between the speaker and yourself. Sometimes patterns of behaviour are repeated: A person's relationship with authority figures (of which you may be one) often reflects power

relationships from much earlier in her life. An example is, 'You have just been speaking about how you were unable to speak honestly with your mother, and I sometimes get the feeling you're not quite open with me.' Again, self-disclosure of feelings evoked in you is required, of a more risky kind than in the previous level of immediacy. The intention in the helper must be in the help-seeker's best interests – in other words with the purpose of helping the speaker to make useful connections between her behaviour in the present and older patterns of reaction.

✔ *Here-and-now immediacy* probably feels the most risky form of *you-me talk* (another way of referring to immediacy). Here you reveal your true feelings about the help-seeker and how they affect you. This last version of immediacy is less likely to be used in a counselling skills situation than in a formal counselling relationship because it is most useful when a person is working in depth on deep concerns.

Being specific and concrete

Many people talk in generalisations. For example, they may say something like, 'Everyone looks at me,' or 'I'm always getting things wrong.' This kind of generalisation is not always, or even often, upheld by reality. Asking for specific examples with concrete details ('nuts and bolts') helps the speaker

✔ Realise that she's generalising from one or two incidents.

✔ Recognise that she's making unfounded assumptions about the attitudes of others.

✔ Understand the difficulty more clearly and thereby suggest possibilities to challenge generalisation and assumptions.

An example of being specific is, in response to 'I'm always getting it wrong', to say something like, 'You say you're *always* getting it wrong. Could you tell me about a time when you feel you got it wrong?' Another possibility is, 'How do you know when you're getting it wrong?' This kind of exploration enables you and the help-seeker to gain a fuller picture, but also to find exceptions (examples of when the problem is absent, she behaves differently, or others behave differently towards her, and so on). Exceptions can assist the help-seeker to gain insight into the problem and how she might become more like she'd like to be.

Being specific and concrete also ties in with filling the gaps and noticing contradictions.

Thinking about thinking and beliefs

Many people are unaware of their thinking and belief patterns. Recognising and pointing out self-defeating and illogical patterns of thinking, which is part of challenging and confronting, can be very helpful. This includes pointing out *automatic thoughts* – the conclusions you jump to without evidence.

One way of dealing with self-defeating thinking is *positive reframing*. People often focus on the one bad instance out of several good ones. In positive reframing you redress the balance. People who lack confidence tend to see anything short of full success as failure. However, you need to celebrate achieving a few steps towards success and look upon it as positive. Another aspect of positive reframing is to support the speaker to think about experiences as *learning opportunities* – in other words, rather than thinking, 'that's terrible', blaming herself, and taking it no further, you encourage her to discover what she can learn from it to guide her future choices and actions.

Other aspects of challenging thinking and beliefs include:

- ✔ **Reformulating attributions.** Some people attribute their problem to other people or circumstances, giving away their power. Sometimes there may be reasons for relative powerlessness – don't ignore these, and it's also true that many people are unaware of their own power and ability to bring about change.

- ✔ **Identifying unrealistic beliefs, especially self-beliefs, and helping to find more realistic ones.** You will draw on the other skills in this chapter, as well as Stage One skills such as summarising, to gain the understanding that a self-belief is unrealistic.

- ✔ **Challenging negative inner self-defeating dialogue.** Everyone has internal conversations, some of which can be disheartening rather than encouraging. These voices are often from earlier experience. Enabling the speaker to recognise that the inner voice is not her own but more like a tape recording from the past can help her let go of it, or at least realise when it's happening and make a more conscious choice about whether or not to listen. Changing these habits of thinking takes time.

- ✔ **Working together on coping self-talk (such as, 'I *am* OK').** This follows on from the previous point. Sometimes people find it helps to write reminders and stick them in strategic places to reinforce their messages to self.

All these ways of challenging beliefs encourage the individual to have more control over her own life. To do this kind of challenging you use the Stage One and Stage Two skills of reflecting back and noticing the themes in feeling and thinking patterns, using immediacy and what you know about the help-seeker from your conversation so far to challenge her helplessness and habitual patterns of self-destructive thinking.

Focusing and prioritising

When you meet someone in a helping encounter that is relatively brief and perhaps short-term, retaining a sense of purpose is helpful both to you and the help-seeker. The help-seeker's situation may be muddled and complex, presenting a number of issues that you may be unable to deal with in the time. However, assisting the speaker to identify what the issues are, then to help *her* to decide priorities, can be very helpful. If she can choose a priority to focus on, you can support her to achieve something, thus increasing her sense of agency (power over her own life) and self-esteem.

A simple way of providing focus is to ensure you summarise from time to time. Summarising (discussed in more detail in Chapter 9) gives listener and speaker time to reflect and consider where to go next in the conversation. Trainee listening helpers often say, after a practice session, 'I didn't know where to take it.' Reflecting back key issues and feelings, inviting the speaker to prioritise, is particularly helpful at this point.

Deciding the direction or priorities is not your responsibility. If you find yourself having a conversation in your head about which direction to go, consider saying it out loud and inviting the speaker to decide. Always support the help-seeker to make her *own* choices and decisions.

Sharing your thoughts will be productive and also empowering to the help-seeker. An example would be admitting you don't know how best to help; another is telling the speaker you're struggling to keep up with what she's saying or you're feeling confused and need to go back over things. Obviously you need to use care and empathy as well, to avoid appearing attacking or seeming dismissive. These are examples of being *congruent* or *genuine*, one of the Core Conditions described in Chapter 8. Being transparent in this way is potentially useful at any stage in the helping process, but is particularly helpful during this middle stage when you're trying to develop a deeper understanding.

Chapter 11

Stage Three: Working with Action and Endings

- -

In This Chapter

▶ Making an assessment

▶ Working with problem-solving and obstacles to change

▶ Discovering your own attitude towards endings

▶ Dealing with endings

▶ Referring to other agencies

▶ Evaluating the results

- -

*A*s the helping conversation moves towards an ending, Stage Two (the *understanding* stage), segues into Stage Three, which is concerned with *action* and ending. The first part of this chapter focuses on making an assessment of how you can support the help-seeker in deciding on and then moving towards action. The later sections focus on endings.

Endings and partings are inevitably linked with transition and change, which I cover in Chapter 14. In this chapter I ask you to think about your own attitude towards endings because this can unconsciously colour your approach. I then prepare you for both individual session endings and the ending of a helping relationship.

Stage Three of the Three-Stage Model

Some people simply need a chance to offload, which your careful and supportive listening can give them the opportunity to do (using all the skills of Stage One and Stage Two as described in Chapters 8 to 10). Others need your support to work out and work on some achievable outcomes and then to end the helping relationship. Some of the skills described in Chapter 10 (noticing themes, being concrete and specific, challenging and confronting, thinking about thinking, and focusing) contribute to problem-solving and the move towards decision-making and action. In this chapter I suggest additional skills and activities to support the help-seeker's efforts to change. Following a collaborative assessment with the help-seeker, you use these problem-solving skills to support him through the process and your understanding of the meaning of endings to bring the work to a close.

Table 11-1 sums up the skills used to assist the help-seeker to move on.

Table 11-1	Skills Used in Stage Three
The Listener Uses Action and Closing Skills to:	**This Helps the Speaker to:**
Make an assessment	Develop clear, achievable objectives
Encourage active participation	Form specific action plans
Identify goals	Do what needs to be done, with support
Work with obstacles	Recognise what has been done
Maintain a positive outlook	Manage the ending
Monitor progress	
Support	
Evaluate	
End	

After the help-seeker has decided, in a general way, what he wants to work on you need to collaborate in deciding whether you can work together, so I begin with that assessment. The process of assessment starts early in your contact with the help-seeker, but by the time you reach the transition from Stage Two into Stage Three, you and the help-seeker usually (occasionally not) have a clearer idea whether you can help him.

Making an Assessment

In the context of a helping conversation, *making an assessment* means you and the help-seeker deciding on the way forward with the issues he needs help with. These are normally the options:

✔ The help-seeker simply needed an opportunity to talk, either to offload or to clarify things in his own mind and so the helping relationship comes to an end.

✔ The help-seeker needs a continuing opportunity to talk freely, which you either will or won't be able to provide, dependent on your circumstances and context.

✔ The help-seeker would benefit from a more specialist or in-depth counselling relationship, for example sex therapy or bereavement counselling.

✔ Another type of help is appropriate, either instead of or alongside what you can offer. This might be debt counselling or health advice from medical services.

If the opportunity to talk has released something or clarified the present scenario, no specific action may be necessary or appropriate. The chance to talk openly often enables people to regain their own sense of purpose and problem-solving capacities or simply to accept that they can't, or don't, wish to change (refer to the cycle of change in Chapter 8 for more on assessing people's readiness to change). The help-seeker and you may agree that on-going support from you would be helpful.

For others some action is desired or required. You and the help-seeker together need to assess how far you *can* help him. You may be able to support him to reach his desired outcome, in which case you'll be moving into the action skills of Stage Three, or maybe you realise that you can't, because you don't have the required skills or time. The outcome could be a referral to services that can offer more specialised or in-depth help.

The questions you need to ask yourself and the help-seeker in making an assessment are:

✔ Do we have a good enough relationship for it to be productive?

✔ What kind of help does the help-seeker want or need?

✔ Do I have the necessary skills and time to help adequately?

✔ Is the help-seeker sufficiently motivated to engage in change?

Assessment is not a task just for the beginning of a helping relationship, but continues throughout. In a first session you need to assess whether you can work with the help-seeker and this decision will take most of the session to arrive at. As the help-seeker trusts you more and reveals more you may come to realise in subsequent sessions that the help he needs is beyond your skills and experience. Assessment also encompasses evaluation which you always need to build into any task-orientated work you do with a help-seeker.

Problem-Solving

Many people have not learned problem-solving skills and some have acquired positively unhelpful methods of solving problems and making decisions. You may find yourself temporarily in the role of teacher at this point.

Identifying goals

People commonly have trouble identifying goals. Here's a list of obstacles they often face when attempting to do so:

- They're caught in an either/or dilemma.
- The goal is not the help-seeker's own so he isn't truly committed to it.
- The goal seems massive and unobtainable.
- Even if the goal is seen as potentially achievable, working out how to reach it seems impossible.
- They desire too many goals, which leads to discouragement, inertia, and disappointment.
- They can't decide between various options.
- A goal may have some negative consequences.
- Sticking to a goal can be a challenge.
- They lack support and encouragement to help them reach their goal.
- The goal may turn out to be the wrong one.

Some problem-solving techniques can help with anticipating these challenges. See the next section for ideas for working with each of the above obstacles.

Supporting problem-solving

During most conversations I'd normally discourage you from using writing materials – they can act as a barrier and tend to put you in the role of 'expert' – but working on problem-solving is a good time to use pen and paper in a collaborative way with the help-seeker. Large sheets such as flipchart paper, lining wallpaper, and A3 paper and big, coloured, felt-tip pens can be very helpful and liberating when dealing with problem-solving (although some people may be rather frightened of it because it reminds them of school and being useless at art and so on, so be sensitive to their reaction).

Obstacle 1: Creating more alternatives

Brainstorming is useful at various times in the process. Either/or thinking is very common: People often get stuck in polarised, limited thinking. You can assist the help-seeker to challenge his fixed either/or view by brainstorming as many reasonable and silly ideas as possible. Prompting with statements like:

- ✔ If money was no object . . .
- ✔ If you could wave a magic wand . . .
- ✔ If no obstacles of any sort existed . . .
- ✔ If nothing else mattered . . .
- ✔ If you had all the support you could possibly need . . .

These kinds of statements free the imagination – once alternatives appear, seeing possibilities becomes easier.

When someone is stuck with either/or alternatives, another way to reach a different perspective is to make sure *both* of the alternatives are explored – often only one of the two is seriously considered. I find this particularly helpful when couples are considering splitting up – by fully exploring the implications of parting, as well as how to stay together, they can discover how committed they are to the relationship (or not, of course).

Another approach to creating alternatives is a technique called the Miracle Question. The suggestion does not generate goals but leads to more ideas. These in turn open up potential goals. The help-seeker is asked the Miracle Question:

> If you went to bed tonight and during the night a miracle happened and everything was as you'd like it to be as soon as you woke in the morning, what would be the very first thing you noticed?

Encourage the speaker to begin with the moment he becomes conscious and then to describe his day, in as much detail as possible, from when he opens her eyes.

Prompt the help-seeker further with, 'And what else would be different?' Continue through a typical day or at least a reasonable part of one. Once you both have identified how the help-seeker would like things to be different the next question could be, 'What needs to happen, what could you do, to bring about that change?' or 'What could you do differently that might help bring about that change?' Another possible question is, 'How would you like things to be in a year's time?' Even if you don't specifically ask these types of question remember that movement and change are more likely if the person has a sense of what's called a well-formed outcome.

Obstacle 2: Checking out who owns the goal

If the goal is not the idea of, or acceptable to, the help-seeker, he isn't going to be committed to following through, especially if the going gets tough. This statement probably sounds obvious, but it's definitely worth checking. Remember that the help-seeker will be influenced, even if subtly, by friends, family, and authority figures in his life – including you. Always encourage the help-seeker to develop and use his own judgement (sometimes referred to as his *internal locus of evaluation*). Some of the techniques discussed in this section on problem-solving can help to uncover whether the help-seeker is personally committed to the goal that he has identified.

Obstacle 3: Making achievement feasible

Breaking large goals down into smaller steps or sub-goals makes achieving the final goal more likely. Achieving small successive goals boosts confidence and self-esteem and supports the impetus and commitment to change. A useful acronym to remember is SMARTER, which stands for **S**pecific, **M**easurable, **A**chievable, **R**ealistic, **T**imed, **E**valuated, and **R**eviewed. To find an explanation of this acronym, check out Chapter 3, where it's used in relation to mapping your support network.

People are often rather vague about goals. Be sure to encourage the help-seeker to be clear and specific about the goal that he adopts. Once it's specific, then turn it into an activity that can be measured in some way. For example, if he wants to be more relaxed, first identify an activity that helps him relax and then help him decide how often he will do this activity. Taking it a step further to ensure that it definitely happens, consider what is both possible to achieve and what is realistic, given his lifestyle and demands on his time and so on. A good question to pose is, 'What is going to get in the way or stop you?' By giving himself a deadline or identifying specific days and times of day when he can do the activity he's more likely to make a contract with himself to carry out the plan. Finally, through reviewing and evaluating you check out together whether the goal was realistic after all, celebrate any achievement, however small, and rethink or add to the goal.

In the planning phase the help-seeker may be over-optimistic. Arranging a follow-up time is preferable unless the help-seeker is clearly very confident, realistic, and committed to the change and he has support in his environment or context. Recommend that he reviews and evaluates his progress at regular intervals. If you're working with someone over several sessions you can do the reviewing and evaluating together: This is an essential part of the learning approach and helps to avoid giving up on the goal if it doesn't immediately work out.

Obstacle 4: How to reach the goal

Sometimes a goal can feel quite inaccessible. One way to approach this problem is to think about things which surround the goal. For example, if an individual wants to become more confident, you could ask the Miracle Question (see 'Obstacle 1' earlier in this chapter) or talk about what being confident is like, using the five senses:

- What does it look like?
- What does it sound like?
- What does it feel like?
- What does it taste like?
- What does it smell like?

Those last two may sound silly, but laughter and silliness can foster creativity.

Breaking the goal into smaller parts, perhaps based on the ideas generated by the questions, makes the target seem much less remote (see also the role of support and hope in number 9 below).

Obstacles 5 and 6: Prioritising and deciding

Having too many goals is a sure way of not getting anything done. The help-seeker may have too high an expectation of what your help can help him do. If you list the possible goals on a large piece of paper you can then go through the pros and cons of each. After completing this exercise you can ask some questions about the goals:

- Are some more important than others?
- Are there any linked goals?
- Are any easier to achieve than others?
- Do resources, strengths and limitations differ between goals?
- Do one or more goals have a disproportionate impact?
- Could one or more goals enable others to be more easily achieved later?
- Can a short-list now be drawn up?
- Which ones feel right to tackle (gut instinct, best fit, values)?

These questions can help lead to decisions. Sometimes making the decision is hard, which leads to Obstacle 7.

Obstacle 7: Anticipating expected and unintended consequences

Whatever good reasons may exist for change, an element of loss is always involved: self-identity can be disturbed and some known and some unsuspected costs of change can occur (refer to Chapter 2 for more).

When discussing the pros and cons of a goal encourage the help-seeker to consider the ramifications of change. For example, if someone decides to lose weight and is successful then he'll need new clothes. New clothes mean additional cost but also highlight the new choices that are available. With new-found confidence, the person may choose more up-to-date, sexy, or expensive clothes. This new appearance and confident demeanour, and increased spending, can have unexpected consequences on relationships. An inability to make a choice about goals could be related to these kinds of issues. Watch out for colluding with endless debate and indecision.

Obstacle 8: Maintenance (sticking to the goal)

Maintaining a positive outlook towards change is difficult. In preparing for change ask the help-seeker how he approached changes in the past (see also Chapter 14 on transition, change, and loss for more on this). Maybe he hasn't found adapting easy but the thinking involved in Obstacle 7 (looking at consequences, including desired outcomes) and Obstacle 9 (checking out other supports) should help him to face changes. Building on earlier successes, however small, is affirming. Reminding the help-seeker of the reasons for the goal and its importance, and of how it is going to feel when he reaches the desired outcome, supports maintenance.

Obstacle 9: Encouraging support-seeking and hope

People seeking help often don't have much support, which is possibly why they seek help in the first place. Sometimes, however, the help-seeker hasn't sought support or hasn't recognised where support may be available. With encouragement he may be surprised at the amount of help and supportive assistance he can gain from unexpected quarters. Part of this obstacle is to do with lack of confidence and feeling silly about asking for help, as though it's a mark of failure. Asking who else might like to see the goal achieved can generate some ideas. It's also important for you, as a listening helper, to make yourself aware of sources of help in your community.

The help-seeker's environment may include people who don't want him to reach his goals. Check out if anyone might be obstructive and help the speaker think about how he can manage this situation. Whether this is the case or not, your role as supporter is very important. Our culture tends towards a lack of praise and encouragement and many people are starved of both. Help the help-seeker to acknowledge his own achievements by identifying them rather than have all the praise coming from you – this will boost his self-esteem more than your praise, which can be minimised or dismissed by an individual with low self-esteem.

At times you have to face the paradox of encouraging hope while acknowledging – and not dismissing or minimising – the despair and hopelessness that the help-seeker is experiencing.

Obstacle 10: Monitoring and evaluation

With all the best intentions and coping with all these obstacles, progress towards the goal can falter or even be abandoned altogether. This result may be because:

- ✔ The goal wasn't the right one after all.
- ✔ The steps were too great.
- ✔ The timing wasn't auspicious.
- ✔ Unforeseen ambivalence or other obstacles cropped up.

For these reasons plan to keep checking on direction, motivation, and progress. Listening helpers often make the mistake of encouraging the help-seeker to set himself a task and not following through by enquiring how things are going. If the task isn't going well, blaming the help-seeker is unhelpful. Remember all the points about encouraging active participation, and that taking some responsibility yourself can be helpful. I find it useful to suggest to my client that perhaps I didn't help him enough to anticipate obstacles. This signals to the help-seeker that making mistakes is normal. It is also possible that the help-seeker is trying to please you (or someone else important to him) by agreeing to tackle something, rather than it truly being his own aspiration.

If you set a task, always follow up by asking how it went, *in detail*. Here's a sample conversation to illustrate:

Helper: Tell me what happened about talking to your sister about the wedding.

Speaker: Well, it went partly okay and partly not. She listened to what I had to say to start with and then it went pear-shaped – she ended up cutting the call short with some excuse. So, as usual I made a mess of it and as usual she didn't listen.

Helper: Can you take me back to the beginning? What day did this happen? . . . And it sounds like you decided to phone rather than see her face to face? . . . I remember we talked about checking whether she had time for a discussion. Did you remember to do that? . . . So how did the conversation go, how did you start? . . . Then what happened?

Mapping and measuring as problem-solving techniques

People have developed many techniques to assist in problem-solving. One example is mind mapping, which was developed by Tony Buzan and involves using a paper 'map' to link ideas, thoughts, or images to a central concept (in this case, a problem). I'm sure that you'll come across other ideas or devise some of your own. Here are just two more ideas.

Assessing strengths and limitations

In a similar way to mind mapping you can also map the help-seeker's support system (refer to Chapter 3 for more information about support systems). This 'map' can be adapted to focus on the positives – strengths, resources, supports – on one hand, and the negatives – obstacles, limitations, weaknesses – on the other. This analysis is sometimes referred to as *force-field analysis*: opposing forces towards and against change are identified and their weight or strength estimated. This analysis gives an indication of how positives and negatives counterbalance each other and which positives need strengthening or complementing so that the help-seeker is supported in his aims as far as possible. You also need to use other skills, such as challenging general negativity and negative self-assessment. These activities remind you that the individual is part of a context, with the strengths and pressures that brings.

Scaling and measuring

When deciding on a goal, or working towards it, gauging where you are on a scale of 0–10 is useful. At the beginning of working on the goal you can ask these questions:

- On a scale of 0–10 where 0 is the worst you can think of and 10 the ideal, what is 10 like, what would you be doing differently?

- Where on the scale would you be happy to settle for and what is that like? (Typically people say around 8.)

- Where are you now? (People usually say around 3.)

- What will it take to get from, say, 3 to 4? What has to happen and what do you need to do?

If you return to the scale regularly you can gain a sense of movement and progress.

Whatever techniques you use it is always best to try them first on a willing volunteer, or at least on yourself. And always remember basic skills, empathic responding in particular. Some of these techniques can make you appear calculating, cool and a remote 'expert' if used in isolation from the other listening qualities and skills.

As this exchange develops it begins to come clear that the speaker didn't carry out the plan quite as discussed, and then when his sister was too busy to talk he interpreted his sister's impatience as a sign that she didn't want to listen to him ('as usual'), which may or may not have been true. By going through a blow-by-blow account, understanding why the plan didn't work out becomes easier. Encourage the help-seeker to view any failure as an opportunity to discover more about the problem.

Another aspect of monitoring and evaluation, which is also important in the closing stages of a listening-helper relationship, is what I term *future-proofing*. Future-proofing means taking time to consider what might happen in the future, the possible challenges or signs of things slipping backwards, what you and the help-seeker have discovered, and what he can do if problems arise again. One of the aims of problem-solving is developing transferable skills and confidence. Through review and evaluation the help-seeker recognises, with your prompting, the achievements and skills that he's gained that can be applied if he faces a similar, or new problem, in the future.

Looking at Your Own Endings and Transitions

The way in which you approach endings is often related to your earlier experiences of separation and ending – sometimes your very early experiences. Fears of being abandoned, of losing control, of never recovering, fantasies of damaging the one you leave, as well as more positive feelings like excitement and relief, are common experiences. You sometimes find your reactions painful or even shameful. People handle these feelings and defend themselves in different ways, influenced by personality, learned family patterns, particularly significant or memorable experiences, and so on.

The questions that follow are about your own experiences and tendencies in relation to endings and begin by focusing on significant endings you have experienced because these are most likely to continue to affect you, and therefore how you approach the ending of a helping relationship. 'Significant' doesn't necessarily mean major – what seems to an outsider to be a minor incident may have affected you deeply because of the particular meaning and/or vulnerability at the time. After that the questions move on to the way in which you manage your feelings about endings and the implications for your work with help-seekers.

Think about these questions, taking time and making notes to aid your reflection. Try not to censor yourself. You may find that this exercise stirs up uncomfortable feelings. Writing about uncomfortable feelings is very therapeutic. If you have anyone to share some of your experiences and insights with, that's helpful too.

- ✔ What is your earliest memory of being separated or experiencing an ending? Can you get in touch with the intensity of the feelings of being lost and thinking that you'll never be found, for example?

- ✔ Do any other particular memories stand out? Life is full of transitions and partings. As you reflect back over your life you may notice patterns in your experiences and your responses.

✔ Have you had different types of endings? For example, some endings may bring relief, others sadness, excitement, anticipation, dread, and so on. Sometimes people have mixed feelings or guilty thoughts about their true emotional reactions.

✔ Have you been able to share your true feelings about significant endings with anyone? What holds you back or encourages you to confide?

✔ Are you aware of significant partings or endings, but of having no memory of what happened and how you felt? This lack of memory can be the result of your feelings not being attended to or taken seriously at the time. People often presume that children are 'resilient' and 'bounce back' – they probably don't get an opportunity to do anything else. Often people, including children, suppress their own feelings in order to support, or avoid giving pain to, someone else.

✔ When faced with a parting, what kinds of feelings are dominant in you?

✔ Are you aware of having delayed reactions or unexpected feelings later?

✔ How are you at letting go?

You need to recognise that:

✔ Previous experiences colour how you approach endings with the people with whom you work.

✔ You need to be aware of the strength of emotion that those you aim to help may experience.

✔ The material that's brought to you as a helper also affects you – it may trigger unresolved feelings in you.

✔ When you work with someone – especially if the contact has been intense or over a long period, or you have invested in or identified strongly with the help-seeker – then you have emotions about the ending too.

How are you at saying goodbye in everyday life? Here are some questions to get you thinking:

✔ Do you like to end with some physical contact, such as shaking hands, a hug, or kisses, or is that your worst nightmare?

✔ Do you like to celebrate achievements, endings, and partings?

✔ Do you like to mark some occasions with a gift or other token?

✔ How do you react to receiving a gift or token as a mark of farewell? Is your reaction different depending on your role? If so, what is that about?

✔ Do you find it hard to leave or let others go? Do you prolong the good-bye or maybe leave things behind as an excuse to return or a way to leave a memento of yourself? Are you the last person waving on the platform as the train pulls away?

✔ Conversely, are you the person who makes an unnoticed exit, who doesn't like a fuss? Do you prefer to avoid goodbyes and protracted partings?

✔ Do you like to be the last to leave?

✔ Do you like to keep in touch with people you're unlikely to see again (in other words, never have to face saying goodbye permanently) or do you prefer to end and move on?

By your answers to these questions you can gain understanding of how you manage your own emotions around partings and endings. Your answers don't have any right or wrong. Understanding how you and others operate, and maybe function differently, is useful. In the helping relationship you need to be able to reflect on and understand your own predispositions in general, and how the work with this person in particular has impacted on you, so that you can manage the ending in the most helpful way for the help-seeker.

Managing the Ending of a Helping Session

Many people find dealing with the end of sessions tricky. You need to allow enough time so that you and the help-seeker don't feel rushed, but not so much time that you go well beyond the time you intended. Occasionally the ending draws to a close more quickly than anticipated, leaving you floundering. You can feel you need to fill the remaining time and so start asking questions, which unhelpfully opens things up again.

The suggestions in the following sections can help you end individual sessions. Some of them also apply to ending a helping relationship.

Being clear about what you're offering

You can avoid some of the potential difficulties about individual session endings, as well as endings in general, by taking care to be clear at the beginning about your role and what you can offer. You need to:

✔ Make sure that you don't seem to promise what you can't deliver.

✔ Be clear about the duration of individual sessions.

✔ Be clear about the nature and length of the overall contract.

Refer to Chapter 8 for more on the beginning, or *contracting* stage.

Setting a time

Having the idea of three stages in mind can help you manage the time (refer to Chapter 8 for more). Always make clear how much time is available for the conversation. If the conversation is spontaneous you may have to interrupt the session to inform the help-seeker of the time constraints. Doing this may not seem very respectful at that moment but on balance is more respectful; you're better off avoiding a situation in which you effectively stop listening because you're wondering how to get out of the session in order to get to a meeting on time.

Tell the speaker at the outset of a session that you'll let him know when the session is nearing the end so that you have time to check your progress and decide where you go from there. Move into the action stage in the last quarter of the time – you need to build in enough time to review the session and look ahead.

Using closing skills

Towards the end of a session you need to avoid using open questions that will lead the help-seeker to reopen issues or to open up new issues. Instead, use summarising to retain the focus on ending the session. You need to be fairly assertive with some people and make clear that the session is ended. Standing up and moving to the door, or using a gesture towards the exit helps. If you're seeing the help-seeker again, you can refer to the next session.

Sometimes a help-seeker reveals something important right at the end of a session, just as he's about to leave; this is referred to as a *doorknob disclosure*. This might be a completely new issue or another aspect of the problem already discussed. Don't be lured into sitting down again, unless an immediate and urgent safety issue arises (which is rare). The two major reasons for doorknob disclosures are:

- ✔ The help-seeker needs to gauge your reaction, because he fears rejection or judgement in relation to what may be the real issue.

- ✔ The help-seeker wants to prolong the helping relationship by producing new problems, out of fear of not being able to cope or not being ready to let go of the relationship.

Your immediate response needs to be to reassure the help-seeker that you'll discuss the disclosure at your next meeting. When such a disclosure reveals something that you would be competent to work with then you need to re-negotiate your contract with the help-seeker. If not, you need to discuss referral.

If the disclosure comes from a fear of coping alone or of ending the relationship then you need to spend a little time discussing this issue, rather than the
disclosure itself, perhaps reminding the help-seeker of his own and other
resources and allowing expression of sadness about letting go. The following
sections have more on working with the ending of a series of sessions.

Managing the Ending of a Helping Relationship

Even clarifying things at the start of your listening-helper relationship, as suggested in the previous section and in Chapter 8, won't enable you to avoid
every difficulty. Your empathy and sensitivity can help you imagine how the
help-seeker you're working with will deal with the end of a session or his contact with you. Understanding how you deal with endings yourself can also
help you avoid badly handled endings. The following sections explain other
strategies that can help you to prepare for and deal with ending a helping
relationship.

Reviewing and celebrating the work and the relationship

Help-seekers may experience the mention of review in an initial contract as
an imposed time limit. You may have intended to give the person the opportunity to consider, from time-to-time, whether the contact is helpful for him
but he often hears this as 'That's it, time to finish', so remember this aspect if
you intend to conduct reviews.

Generally, I recommend regular reviews, but the precise timing of these
depends on the overall length of the contract you have. If you're working
with someone on a long-term basis, reviewing at frequent intervals may be
a distraction. By contrast, in a short contract (say 4–6 sessions), and even
in a single session, it can be very beneficial to check whether the contact is
proving helpful around half to three-quarters of the way through. Reviewing
not only acts as psychological preparation for ending, it also contributes to
evaluation of your work (see the section 'Evaluation' later in this chapter for
more information).

When reviewing, not only is it important to acknowledge what you've worked
on together, but also to reinforce the learning that has taken place and

'future-proof', whether it's a one-off session or the end of a series of sessions. So, in the reviewing process include these questions (phrased appropriately to you, the help-seeker, and the situation):

✔ Looking back to the beginning of the contact and the presenting problem, can the help-seeker remember how he felt then?

✔ What progress and decisions have been made? Sometimes using scaling to gain a sense of the level of change is helpful (see Chapter 10 for more).

✔ Can you together identify what has been helpful and unhelpful?

✔ How do the help-seeker and you feel about difficulties that haven't been resolved?

✔ What may be future stress points?

✔ How will the help-seeker recognise indicators that show that he may need to take action?

✔ What has been learned through the helping relationship that will help?

✔ How can the work that has been done be acknowledged?

Part of the reviewing process that naturally follows from some of the preceding questions is acknowledging and celebrating any successes or growth. The answers to the following questions are worth thinking about:

✔ What is your own attitude to celebrating and praise?

✔ How does your attitude affect your approach to celebrating and praising the help-seeker?

✔ Is it appropriate to mark the occasion in any way? (See 'Saying Goodbye' later in this chapter for more about gifts, hugs, and handshakes).

When a help-seeker lacks self-esteem, he may find it hard to give himself praise and also to hear it from others. Maybe you find it difficult too. Sometimes you may need to slow the help-seeker down for him to recognise his own accomplishments. Symbolic ways of acknowledging progress can be very powerful, such as a symbol reflecting what the help-seeker feels he's gained from the helping process (he can use real or imaginary objects). Alternatively some people find drawing, poetry, or other writing exercises good to sum up their experience and progress (see Chapter 12 for more on how people operate more strongly in some domains than others). As you gain experience you'll become better able to work with both your own and the help-seeker's preferences.

Planning your endings

The reviewing process includes planning the end of the contract and of the helping relationship. Planned, mutually agreed, endings must include some or all of the following – in addition to reviewing, celebrating, and future-proofing (see preceding section). The precise level of concentration will vary:

✔ Preparation for ending

✔ Recognition of where the help-seeker is now (positive, neutral, and negative)

✔ A decision about the manner of the ending (immediate or phased)

✔ Goodbyes

In helping the help-seeker to end you need to draw upon what you know about his attitude and experience of endings. For many people it's a relatively small issue – if they are fairly self-supporting and motivated they probably move on with little regret. For others it's a much bigger event.

Be sure to flag that the end is drawing close and to give an opportunity for the help-seeker to comment on how he feels about the end. The longer the contact you've had, the more time you want to allow for this discussion and the earlier it needs to happen. Listening helpers tend to worry about the speaker being upset when the session finishes and this is considered under difficult endings below.

Although you need to make the time limit clear in the initial contract, both you and the help-seeker are sure to have feelings about the ending of even short-term work. The extent of feelings probably relate to the intensity of the work and the investment in it by each party. How will this be acknowledged? Are you comfortable with acknowledging and working with such feelings, which may surprise you if you don't expect them in short-term work?

When you engage with a help-seeker for a number of sessions you have a choice between an immediate end and a phased ending. A phased ending can take different forms:

✔ A planned 'weaning off' through graduated longer intervals between meetings.

✔ Ending with a follow-up: a follow-up meeting after an interval of, say, 2–3 weeks or a couple of months.

✔ An 'open-door' ending.

Immediate endings have advantages and disadvantages:

- ✔ A definite end can convey a sense of confidence in the help-seeker's ability to go on without you.
- ✔ You may be better able to 'let him go'.
- ✔ The help-seeker has the opportunity to face the ending.
- ✔ An immediate end has the potential to be abrupt and feel unfinished.

Phased endings also have advantages and disadvantages:

- ✔ The help-seeker has an opportunity to consolidate learning and changes with support but knows he can check in with you if any unforeseen difficulties arise.
- ✔ If you know in advance of any pressure points or difficult events, support at that time can help consolidate changes.
- ✔ An 'open-door' ending can enable the help-seeker to feel secure enough to leave the helping relationship – he may never need to make use of the open door.
- ✔ Continued success with specific changes can be celebrated.
- ✔ The issue of ending can be avoided.
- ✔ You have the potential to convey a lack of trust in the help-seeker's capacity to cope.
- ✔ Follow-up sessions could lack focus.

The important thing is to think about your work with each individual help-seeker. Discuss the pros and cons with him, as well as with your internal supervisor and a trusted colleague, especially while you're in the earlier stages of learning when you're likely to feel the least confident about managing endings.

Working with Difficult Endings

Endings can be problematic or challenging in a number of ways:

- ✔ The help-seeker being very upset at the end of a session
- ✔ Abrupt endings
- ✔ Unexpected endings
- ✔ Breaks leading to a cancelled contract
- ✔ Reluctance to end

The following sections describe what you can do it these situations.

Emotional upset at the end of a session

Here are some things you can do to avoid leaving the speaker in a difficult emotional state at the end of a session:

- ✔ Towards the end don't use open questions about emotions. These open up exploration inappropriately.

- ✔ During the session watch out for emotionally difficult areas and don't open these up again in the last ten minutes.

- ✔ If a new aspect of the story presents itself near the end, avoid going into it. You can say something like, 'I realise that might be an important topic which unfortunately we don't have time to do justice to at the moment. Do you think we could talk about that next time we meet?'

- ✔ Sometimes a bombshell is dropped towards the end of a session, or even as the help-seeker is leaving. It may be the real reason for him seeking help. Don't make the mistake of settling down again to explore this new issue. The reason the issue has been left to the end isn't chance. Use a similar tactic to the last point. If it has taken courage for the help-seeker to disclose a significant issue, make sure that you acknowledge his bravery.

- ✔ You cannot guarantee to leave someone in a state that makes him ready to face the outside world. If the help-seeker becomes very upset during a session make sure to manage the session to allow more than the usual time for the ending part, so that he has enough space to gather himself to leave safely. If you're in the fortunate position of having a waiting area or private room and a receptionist who can make a drink, take advantage of that. Trust the help-seeker to manage himself and let him have privacy to do that and leave when he's ready.

- ✔ If the help-seeker is upset with you for some reason you probably feel quite challenged. For example, the help-seeker may have unrealistic expectations about what you can do for him. No easy way around this situation exists. You must hear and acknowledge how the speaker is feeling. You could say something like, 'I can hear that you're disappointed and angry that I cannot do what you hoped for, and I'm sorry that you feel this way. This is what I *am* able to offer . . .' You need to be able not to take the criticism personally, stay calm, and stay with the speaker's feelings whilst being clear about your role.

Abrupt endings on either side

An abrupt ending of the helping relationship by the help-seeker usually leaves helpers with difficult feelings and decisions. You may feel rejected or that you have failed. You may feel angry or disappointed with the help-seeker or very let down. You need to consider:

- ✔ Will you have contact with him again?

- ✔ What form and content will that have (letter, phone call)?

- ✔ If you phone will the help-seeker feel obliged to say yes to further contact or will doing so make him feel cared for?

- ✔ Do you know if he has adequate privacy and literacy skills to receive a letter?

- ✔ You need to decide whether to use a standard letter or to send something more personalised to the individual.

- ✔ How much of yourself will you put into such a letter? How much comment will you make on the content of the contacts between you?

- ✔ Is it useful to discuss these issues with someone before acting, perhaps in supervision or with a trusted colleague?

A help-seeker sometimes ends the helping relationship abruptly because he can't face the sessions or the ending. When someone is suffering from depression or has other difficult issues he may simply feel unable to face dealing with anything. Also, his life moves on and the reason why he doesn't turn up for a planned meeting may have nothing whatever to do with his contact with you. Some of the people you help may live quite chaotic lives. If they've forgotten the appointment or something unexpected happens so that they can't let you know, they may feel too embarrassed to make contact. Many people need huge courage to make and maintain contact and face their issues. These are all factors to take into account when deciding on your course of action.

Service users sometimes complain that their helper abruptly terminated their contact. Some observations about this situation are:

- ✔ You may have unconscious reasons for finishing working with someone. Feelings of boredom (sometimes an unconscious cover for hostility in either party), confusion, inadequacy, fear related to endings, and so on, may go unrecognised and lead to premature ending.

- ✔ The help-seeker may feel inadequately prepared for ending, even if some time has been spent preparing to end. It can help to warn people that they may experience unexpected feelings of abandonment or loss (as may you, also).

So, take care to think through and plan your ending with each person as an individual. Remember that even with the best intentions you won't always get it right.

Unexpected endings

A help-seeker may tell you that the current meeting is going to be his last. You may or may not feel he's ready to end. This kind of unexpected ending can lead to some challenges and questions:

✔ Taken unawares you may not think to discuss his feelings – or your own – at that time, or think about how both of you will feel after the end. Do you have a duty of care to do this?

✔ What will you do about your own feelings?

✔ Is the help-seeker fearful of endings, perhaps related to his history?

✔ Has he picked up on your difficulty with ending?

✔ Is he ending because he feels he's let you down in some way or that someone else is more deserving of your help?

Unexpected endings generally leave some difficult feelings behind. You may benefit from exploring and expressing these feelings either through writing in a journal and/or discussing it with a trusted colleague or in supervision.

Dealing with breaks

Giving a help-seeker as much warning of a break as you possibly can is good practice. During a break (for example, when you or the help-seeker is on holiday), he may realise that he doesn't need you. Alternatively he may feel abandoned because you've taken a break and react by not turning up, cancelling, and so on. These sorts of reactions are more common than you might realise and you need to make a note of any patterns like this, particularly in a longer-term contract, as they indicate that the relationship is very significant for the help-seeker. Usually people deny that they're angry because their head tells them it's perfectly reasonable for you to have a holiday, attend a funeral, have a doctor's appointment, and so on. But when their heart speaks it's a different story and they may need permission to express their 'irrational' emotions.

Reluctance to end

Sometimes someone is reluctant to end the relationship. Is this you or the help-seeker? You need to consider ethical issues related to *non-maleficence* – the term used in ethical codes to describe not doing harm to someone you help. For example, avoid creating dependency, gaining financially, or working outside your competence. When the help-seeker is reluctant to end, the resulting state of affairs can be difficult to handle. The situation needs to be discussed openly, the help-seeker's feelings acknowledged, and if the appropriate decision is that the helping relationship should end, then a planned ending would probably be the most beneficial.

In some settings you may have pressure to finish working with the help-seeker for various reasons. How will you decide how to act in his best interests in these circumstances? Often such a situation raises issues of referral and other support. Make sure that you know what is available in your area and assist the help-seeker to make the necessary approaches. See the section 'Referral' later in this chapter for more information.

Saying Goodbye

You may now have an idea of whether the person you're helping avoids physical contact or is a tactile person. You need to work out what range of ending behaviours feel comfortable to you. You also need to consider what comes after the ending; for example will a follow-up session be appropriate?

No single correct way exists to end a helping session or relationship. You need to be sensitive to the help-seeker's style, your own preferences, and the nature of the contract and work you've done together.

Physical contact

Always be cautious about touching the help-seeker because you don't know what experiences, such as abuse, may have shaped his responses.

If you began the first session with a handshake, then ending each session, or the final session, with a handshake may be appropriate. Some people find this too formal and redolent of authority figures. You might feel like giving a hug at the end of a session – perhaps the session has been difficult and emotional. Perhaps you're normally a tactile person to whom touching is part of your approach to people in general and especially to those who you have more intimate relationships with, including as a helper.

My advice to you in a listening-helper role is to always talk with the help-seeker about how you feel and why, and invite the help-seeker's response before deciding whether physical contact is appropriate. It's unusual for hugging to be a regular part of a listening-helping relationship. If you find that hugging becomes a regular action with one or all of the people that you're a listening helper to, then discuss the situation with someone you trust and make sure that it really is in the help-seeker's interests and not just yours.

The role of gifts

What do you do if the help-seeker brings a gift? Here are some considerations:

- ✔ Is it okay to receive gifts at all – for example, what is agency policy?
- ✔ What kind of gift would it be all right to receive? Is that to do with the nature or the monetary value of the gift?
- ✔ How will the help-seeker react if you refuse the gift?
- ✔ Do you consider the gift personal to you or to the organisation you work for? How will the help-seeker feel if you accept it on behalf of your organisation rather than for yourself personally?
- ✔ Should you discuss the receipt of a gift with anyone (supervisor, manager)?
- ✔ If the gift is wrapped should you unwrap it there and then or open it later? Does it make a difference if the help-seeker gives it to you at the beginning or produces it at the end?
- ✔ What is your reaction to the help-seeker when you receive the gift? Do your reactions/emotions feel uncomfortable to you?

As with many other ethical issues, no single correct answer exists. You must make sure that you know any organisational policies around gifts and work out a form of words to explain this to the gift giver. If your organisation considers receiving gifts acceptable, usually this is a token or perishable gift, such as flowers.

Another aspect of gift giving is whether you may give people you help something to take away with them. Whilst giving a gift in this situation is perfectly legitimate, you do need to think your reasons through carefully. Sometimes helpers like to give a poem or picture or a self-help handout that has a meaning in the light of the work that has been done with the help-seeker.

> ## Accepting gifts with good grace
>
> When I was working for an organisation, some clients brought a large plastic bin-bag to the final session – I assumed that they had been shopping and asked if they wanted to leave it downstairs in reception to save lugging it upstairs, but they insisted on bringing it with them. At the end of the session they handed me the bag, which contained a lovely hand-made object that must have taken some time to make.
>
> After saying thank you, I said I was not able to accept such a large gift – could I accept it on behalf of the organisation? They were mortified and insistent that although they appreciated the work of the organisation, they felt how I had helped them was to do with me and our relationship.
>
> I could see that not receiving it was going to be hurtful and seem very ungracious, so I accepted the gift. I talked it over with my manager who said I should keep it, and I have it to this day. It can be hard in the moment to weigh all considerations; keep your eye on the relationship as well, and reach the right conclusion.

Referral

Quite often, as a listening helper, your role is to assess and refer help-seekers on to more appropriate help. Sometimes you continue to support the help-seeker until the other help starts, or alongside it. In the latter case you need to be clear about the difference between your role and the role of other helpers.

When you suggest referral the help-seeker needs to understand that this is not a rejection. Many help-seekers have been passed from pillar to post and despair of genuine help being available, so they may feel cynical and/or rejected. It's also possible that, having shown considerable courage to get this far, they feel daunted by approaching someone else and starting all over again.

On the other hand experience has shown that, in general, a referral is more likely to be taken up successfully if the help-seeker arranges the appointment for himself. If you think the help-seeker needs support with making the contact, you have several ways in which you can offer to assist:

- ✔ Contact the agency concerned and find out about referral and appointment procedures. Be clear in your own mind, possibly after conferring with the help-seeker, what information you will pass to the agency in any discussion that arises during a telephone call.

✔ Contact the agency by telephone whilst the help-seeker is with you so that you can hand over to him to make the appointment after you have made the initial enquiry.

✔ Write a referral letter to the agency. You could send a copy to the help-seeker so that he knows the letter has been sent to the agency. You might consider drafting the referral letter with the help-seeker so that he agrees the content.

At all times your goal is empowering the help-seeker rather than taking over and doing it for him. If you look at the cycle of change in Chapter 6 you will see the importance of the help-seeker's commitment to change.

Evaluation

Evaluating your work is important so that you can continuously improve your practice. It also gives the help-seeker the opportunity to provide truthful feedback. The review process enables you to gain useful feedback. You may want to consider whether a pro-forma evaluation form is appropriate. For most listening helpers who are part of an organisation the evaluation needs to be broader than the listening-helper relationship. Evaluations can include:

✔ Ratings of satisfaction with the overall service received.

✔ Statistical information, for example the average length of time people wait for appointments.

✔ Demographic information such as a record of disability, racial background, whether in receipt of benefits. These help to provide a picture of whether the organisation is meeting the needs of its area, target users, or funding bodies.

✔ Straightforward language, avoidance of black printing on white paper (which is bad for people with dyslexia and some visual problems, so consider using coloured paper), and provision of alternative formats – such as online, large-print, or audio cassette information – to enable people with different abilities to use them.

✔ Anonymous completion and return of proforma evaluation sheets to gain a valid evaluation.

Of course, in addition to these categories you want some kind of rating of satisfaction with the helping relationship and possibly some open-ended question opportunities for the help-seeker to make other comments.

Likert scales

Very often a Likert-type scale is used in questionnaires. A Likert scale allows the person completing the questionnaire to rate various items that you have selected for feedback. For example:

Please rate how satisfied you were with the service overall:

Not satisfied at all . . . 1 . . . 2 . . . 3 . . . 4 . . . Very satisfied.

Put an even number of rankings so that the person completing the form has to choose either side of the middle.

When devising questionnaires stick to the KISS principle: **keep it so simple** and if you can, allow some space for unstructured feedback (that is, not directed by you towards particular items you want feedback on).

Finally, consider whether a follow-up appointment would be helpful (see the section 'Planning your endings' earlier in this chapter where I discuss phased endings, which includes following up). If an action is planned (for example referral or a change of some kind) the help-seeker may find it useful to check in with you. Having a rationale for a follow-up is better than just drifting into suggesting it because you find it hard to say goodbye.

Part IV
Understanding People and Problems

In this part . . .

Understanding people and how they tick is important, and that's the focus of this part. You explore how social and psychological experiences shape people's lives. I explain how the *BEST-I BEST-R* model can help you to understand the whole person that you're helping, and the context of his or her life.

Chapter 12

Being Prepared for Common Personal Problems

*T*o say that everyone is different is an obvious truth. Every individual has their own particular experience of growing up, with their own mix of:

✔ Culture – in broad terms as in national culture, but also the particular regional or local culture

✔ Socio-political and economic influences

✔ Family background, family attitudes and values, place in the family, family rules and roles

✔ Educational experience

✔ Peer-group experiences, which are especially powerful in adolescence

✔ Biological predispositions

✔ Personality and attributes.

The last two items in the preceding list, biology and personality, affect how you react to all the other influences and events in your life. You begin life with differing strengths and susceptibilities. You then learn from your family (or substitute family) the habits, thinking patterns, expectations, roles, assumptions about yourself and others (such as whether you are loved and loveable) and so on, which you use to deal with the difficulties and challenges that life inevitably brings. Later experiences in school and in other relationships can have a profound effect, and life beyond school continues to influence your capacity to manage.

People seeking help often have failed to acquire helpful and healthy coping strategies, or sometimes they're temporarily unable to locate their own resources, within or outside of themselves, and need support to regain their resourcefulness. This chapter explains the BEST-I BEST-R model, which outlines those areas of a person's life expressed, or affected by, the issues for which she's seeking help.

Using the BEST-I BEST-R Model

The BEST-I BEST-R (body, emotion, sensation, thinking, imagery; behaviour, environment, spirit, time, relationships) model is one which draws on the work of many writers who have gone before me, including the eminent counselling theorists Gerard Egan and Arnold Lazarus.

Gerard Egan distinguishes between thoughts, feelings, and behaviour – he calls them *islands of experience*.

Egan suggests that these islands of experience should be linked up in the helping encounter to complete the picture. When people tell their stories they often neglect one (or even two) of these areas. You probably notice in everyday conversations that sometimes a person only talks in terms of her thinking, or she speaks mainly in terms of behaviour ('She said . . . then I said . . . and she did this . . . so I did that . . .') barely mentioning her emotional reactions. Conversely some people dwell solely on their feelings, not recognising that it's their thinking patterns or their behaviour which are causing them trouble.

As a listening helper you want to encourage people to fill in the gaps in their stories. With a more complete picture, understanding the situation is easier and helps the speaker to find some aspect that can be focused on to bring about change.

Broadening the categories of experience

Arnold Lazarus pointed out that people operate in different ways and that as helpers you need to be aware of these differences and be adaptable to the individual you're helping. You may have your own favoured modes of operating but those whom you help may work in a different way from you so you need to be flexible to meet their needs.

The model I use is wider than Egan's or Lazarus's. The reason for this is that I think it's important to recognise the potential influence of the help-seeker's environment, time factors, and spirit, which aren't emphasised in Egan's or Lazarus's models. My model aims to encourage you to consider the whole person in context, which gives you a deeper understanding of the issue that is brought to you for help and also assists the help-seeker in identifying what can support her or help her to feel better.

BEST-I BEST-R, in the tradition of acronyms, is designed to jog your memory and help you review what's important in any help-seeker's situation you encounter.

BEST-I BEST-R stands for:

Body	Behaviour
Emotion	Environment
Sensation	Spirit
Thinking	Time
Imagery	Relationships

The following sections describe each category. I encourage you to consider whether anything else that you think is important is missing from the list – no theory is complete.

Body

Various aspects of the physical body are pertinent to the helping relationship.

Very often body issues are entwined with the presenting issue, or may be the presenting issue itself; such things as body image, health worries, self-abusing behaviour (unhealthy use of alcohol, drugs, or other self-harm including eating disorders). Observing the body can give useful information about the person and how she experiences the world and her difficulties.

- ✔ **Substance misuse:** If you see signs that someone's drinking to excess or that other substance use is interfering in her functioning, recommend that she seeks appropriate help (from her GP or a specialist service). If her everyday life is affected then the help-seeker may be unrealistic about these effects precisely because of the mood-altering substance. In this case you may need to challenge the help-seeker. Issues of a breach of confidentiality may arise if someone else, particularly a child, is at significant risk (refer to Chapter 4 for more on confidentiality matters). You may be able to continue to offer support but not as a substitute for specialist help.

- ✔ **Physical presentation:** Observe the way in which a person presents herself physically. As a listening helper you may unconsciously or deliberately mirror the speaker's posture and notice bodily sensations as a result. These sensations give clues to what the speaker is feeling internally and may be reflected in ailments. Such bodily sensations can also be reflected in the metaphors used (see the section 'Imagery' later).

Physical presentation also reflects the emotional state. For example, the person who lacks confidence and self-esteem may compensate by being very well presented (never a hair out of place, perhaps reflecting anxiety about being judged) or poorly turned out (perhaps reflecting anxiety about being noticed or being too low in mood to be bothered). Self-esteem affects demeanour – lack of eye contact, slouched posture, and so on – although these can be misread as shiftiness or rudeness or given various other negative attributions.

Notice my use of 'perhaps' in the previous paragraph – always be slow to reach conclusions about what a certain behaviour means, suspend judgement, take time to understand, and be guided by what the speaker tells you about underlying issues.

✔ **Trauma and the body:** The body and senses often store memories of traumatic events, which may not be consciously remembered. Survivors of sexual and physical abuse, torture, and life-threatening events frequently have, often without realising, associations between physical/sense memory and other traumatic memories (emotions and images) which can be triggered by physical things in the present. As a trivial example, I haven't been able to eat marshmallows since the age of 7, when I was very sick after a trip to the circus where I was treated to a large bag of marshmallows.

A young woman that I worked with was terrified of visits to the dentist. It eventually emerged that the physical feelings associated with having fingers and implements in her mouth brought back, through physical similarities, the emotional memory (fear, panic, invasion) of the sexual abuse she experienced as a child, along with the physical reaction of sickness she had experienced then.

✔ **Encouraging healthy patterns:** Encouragement of healthy body care, such as exercise, sensible eating, and healthy sleep patterns, assists the individual to cope better with other problems she has. If you don't sleep well, have a poor diet, and so on, finding the energy and will to concentrate is difficult. Taking exercise leads to the release of natural substances in the body, called _endorphins_, which lift the mood. Making a mental note of these things as they emerge, checking them out if they don't (only if it seems appropriate), and encouraging a move towards healthy living as part of a holistic approach is beneficial. Explaining the benefits of healthy eating and exercise may encourage the speaker to visit her GP for advice or to take up exercise which is appropriate to her situation.

Excessive exercise is harmful, but may be hard to challenge. People can become addicted to the release of endorphins and the sense of control that over-exercising can bring; relationships can suffer (exercise may be a way of avoiding relationships or relationship issues); and over-exercisers are susceptible to using potentially harmful drugs and unbalanced diets as part of the regime. If you work in an exercise or medical environment you may be a key figure in noticing such unhealthy habits. These habits may give clues to other unbalanced areas of the person's life.

Emotion

Whatever issues bring someone to seek help, they always include an emotional element. With some people, the emotion is abundantly obvious. However, most people edit their feelings for public consumption and some won't identify their feelings without encouragement. Emotions are an overlooked and important part of our decision-making.

An iceberg typically has only about one ninth of its surface above the water and the rest is below. When people describe and/or display their emotions, what they show is only the tip of what lies hidden beneath; not unlike an iceberg.

Developing a vocabulary to describe feelings and emotions is very useful. You need a wide vocabulary to demonstrate empathy, encourage the other person to acknowledge feelings, and to promote deeper exploration (flip to Chapters 8 and 9 for more on empathy and emotional exploration). Emotions have a great impact on how we operate in the world but they are not always obvious to the listener or the speaker. When they are not fully taken into account you may find that you move the speaker too quickly towards solutions, with the result that your work becomes stuck or sabotaged.

On a piece of paper, using four columns, write the words *MAD, SAD, BAD,* and *GLAD* at the head of each column. Under each emotion, write as many synonyms and feelings as you can. For words like *jealousy* or *upset* think in more detail about what goes into these feelings – I call such words 'portmanteau' words because they're like Mary Poppins's big portmanteau bag, from which popped all sorts of surprising things. Don't assume that what you mean by these words is the same as another person's meaning – probe for detail.

Sensation

When people are in distress, however mild, the distress registers in the body in some way. Some people are more comfortable in believing that they have bodily symptoms rather than emotional ones. They would prefer to be plagued by back pain, stomach problems, or headaches sooner than know, or want to know, that they're in emotional pain. Either way, noting what is said about sensations that are experienced is useful. Unless you're medically trained, don't presume to 'diagnose' sensations as merely psychological. However, emotional relief is likely to bring a measure of physical relief also, even if symptoms are due to physical ailments.

If someone has persistent problematic physical symptoms, always advise that she checks with her GP.

Thinking

To some extent your feelings are moulded by your thoughts, especially the making-assumptions part of your thinking. If you think in terms of catastrophe and disaster possibilities when you approach a task, then you're likely to set about it with trepidation (*catastrophising*) and become stressed. These anticipations may even bring about the very thing that you fear (for example, over-anxiety leads to lack of concentration, which in turn leads to failure at the task).

People with depression, low self-esteem, and feelings of panic and anxiety tend to be subject to irrational or illogical thoughts and beliefs about themselves and their world. The pioneer of cognitive-behavioural therapy Albert Ellis identified the prevalence and importance of such underlying beliefs. Below their lack of self-worth are ideas such as: 'I'm useless,' 'I deserve it,' 'I should . . . (be perfect),' 'I must . . .,' (Ellis called this *musterbation*), and generalisations such as 'Everyone thinks I'm useless,' 'Everyone was looking at me,' and 'Everyone criticises me,' usually without evidence. Such thinking tends to be circular and self-fulfilling such as 'Everyone thinks I'm useless so I must be useless and I *am* useless so everyone thinks I'm useless.'

How you feel affects the way you think. When you're distressed, you're less able to focus and think coherently, which then compounds the problems. As a listening helper, you need a balance between acknowledging and giving space to the help-seeker's feelings and identifying and challenging any muddled thinking. If you pick up too swiftly on the latter, you can appear unfeeling and lacking in empathy.

ANECDOTE

Travelling not so light

I once worked with someone who had grown up in a family where travel was a nightmare of stress and anxiety. As a consequence this person avoided going anywhere new. The persistent and nagging thoughts, learned from her parents, ran along the lines of, 'What if I get on the wrong train?' 'What if the train is late?' 'What if I get off at the wrong station by mistake?' 'What if I can't find the bus stop?' and so on. All questions without any thought-out answers. The only identified consequence was that the trip would be a disaster.

The results of this mindset were physical and emotional feelings of panic, intense worry, and fear. When an important appointment came up for some much-needed and long-awaited treatment at a specialist hospital, the thought of having to get there was so appalling that the person was seriously contemplating not turning up. We took time to explore what was the worst that could happen in answer to each of the questions ('What if...?') and what could be done about each one to gain a more realistic approach. This story is an example of how thoughts can affect feelings, but also shows how as a child the person picked up the panicked feelings which were expressed in the 'What if . . .?' pattern of thinking.

Thinking affects feelings, and feelings affect thinking. You need to discover both sides of the equation.

Imagery

Imagery and metaphor are important aspects of almost every person's story, which may surprise you. Very often we describe things in terms of other things; just listen to some everyday conversation and notice how feelings and reactions are described. Imagery, metaphor, analogy, and simile are powerful. They're conveyed through language but all are laden with emotion and symbolism. They often convey richer meaning than more straightforward description.

Noticing figures of speech

People often use *metaphors* (figures of speech, or symbols) to express feelings that are too frightening or confusing to express directly, or they recount dreams which express something about their experience. Some symbols appear universal, such as light and dark, water, and fire, and are regularly drawn from nature. Often metaphors refer to the body in some way ('He was a pain in the neck', 'I was gutted'). When you hear such terminology, you need to look inside yourself for a reference point so that you can understand the metaphor. The danger is that you can make an assumption that the meanings and associations used by someone else are the same as your own.

My students use the common image/metaphor of a journey to describe their experience on the course. What does the word 'journey' conjure up for you?

By tuning in to a person's metaphors, you can convey empathy and you may even extend the metaphor to deepen exploration or to challenge her *frame of reference* (her way of looking at the world and her experience) in a less threatening way.

Images and symbols

In literature about the meanings of dreams and images, you frequently find particular meanings attached to certain symbolic representations. When you're in a helping relationship, you're better off to put such definitions away from you. Meanings of symbols are very personal. Although some symbols appear to have universal meaning within their cultural milieu, assuming that the person you're speaking to is using the symbol in the same way is dangerous.

The meaning behind an image or metaphor or dream is highly personal and often charged with emotion. The meanings you give to images and metaphors may not match the speaker's so always check out your understanding with her. If the speaker asks you what a symbol means, say something like, 'I wonder what it means to *you*?' or 'I think what's more important is what it means to you.'

Behaviour

When people have difficulties in their lives, these may be due to or result in (or both) problematic behaviour – behaviour that creates difficulties for them in everyday living. For example, a person may have a slightly obsessive-compulsive tendency which gets less manageable when under extra stress – the need to clean her home may become excessive and affect family relationships, which in turn may be the precipitating factor in her needing to talk to someone. As a listening helper you won't be able to treat her obsessive-compulsive tendencies (even if she's very motivated to overcome them) because that would be better attended to by specialist help. You can, though, help her reflect on how her behaviour is affecting her and those around her, what the underlying stress might be, whether anything can be done about that, and maybe identify some strategies that she normally finds helpful for dealing with stress, apart from the obsessive cleaning.

Some people tell you about their feelings and/or thoughts but neglect to mention how these affect how they live.

Environment

Try to avoid thinking about a person and her difficulties in purely psychological and individualistic terms. Instead, think of the person in context and the problem in context.

- ✔ You need to respect the values and beliefs of the help-seeker, even if open to question, as part of the helping process. Society today is individualistically orientated but many people within this society still follow more family/community-orientated lives and for them their role in the family – and the effects of their actions on the family – is more important than their own desires.

- ✔ Even individualistic people are part of a wider system that imposes constraints. And if the 'system' has a problem then making changes becomes difficult for the individual. For example, stress in family relationships can be due to each partner having different shift work, which doesn't easily allow for quality time together. Recognising the source of stress offers the possibility of increased choice, such as sacrificing something else to have quality time together, changing jobs, and so on. This type of issue is particularly relevant in workplace settings, but equally applies to the home and the wider environment.

- ✔ Sometimes, practical environmental issues have an effect on the problem that the help-seeker needs resolving. You can only seek higher-order needs such as relationships, self-esteem, and spiritual fulfilment after you meet the basic physiological needs such as food, shelter, clothing, and so on. If your own life is comfortable, you may find it difficult to recognise another person's lack of what you take for granted.

Spirit

In the counselling world, a growing interest in spirituality has taken place in work with clients. You can interpret spirituality as relating to a person's religious beliefs, but taken in its widest definition, spirituality encompasses the meaning and purpose of life, a sense of belonging, and the question of who we are. Many of life's bigger events can trigger a crisis or re-evaluation of beliefs and identity, and a reconfiguring of life priorities, with all the fall-out amongst family, friends, and colleagues that can ensue. Spirituality can also refer to a desire for creative and uplifting activity and being part of a bigger picture, such as being close to God, nature, or energy.

Sometimes this perspective can be a helpful challenge to the limited way of thinking that people can get into. Often when someone is in a dilemma, her thinking has become polarised to either/or (either I have to do this, or else I've got to do that), and the wider perspective and other alternatives are lost.

Because the subject of spirituality is not much discussed in society generally, or in counselling skills literature until recently, you may feel shyness or diffidence, or a lack of confidence, to engage in this kind of discussion in a helping relationship (or to admit that you do). If you, as listening helper, are uncomfortable talking about spiritual matters then whoever you are trying to help is likely to feel shy about it too.

Time

Time is important in a number of different ways. Always consider, 'Why now?' What spurs someone into seeking help now? Often people live with problems or issues for a long time before seeking help, so what precipitates that action? The cycle of change (refer to Chapter 6) is important in terms of a person's readiness or not to make changes in her life and what may help and hinder her. If the spur is a response to someone else pressuring the speaker to seek help, then she may not be motivated to engage in the helping process.

'Why now?' can also lead to identifying a life stage (see Chapter 14), which helps to normalise the experiences of the help-seeker as well as help you to understand some of the possible associated issues. For example, a young woman may talk to you about struggling with adjusting to her new baby, feeling helpless and lost. This stage of life also means that she has possibly given up (even if temporarily) a career and the associated positive self-worth from her working identity, and lost her social circle which is often based around work colleagues. She may not have considered these issues as part of the reasons for her emotional state.

Assessment

Time is also important in assessment of whether it is possible for you to work with someone on the issues she has brought. As a listening helper, the amount of time you have may be limited. Be cautious about how much you open up the issues a person brings to you because you may not be able to follow through, leaving her in a worse place than when you began. You may also be left feeling over-responsible (refer to Chapter 3 about the importance of self-care).

You can gain some indication of whether you can work with someone by paying attention to the history of the problem. If the problem has been long-standing then helping becomes more difficult. The speaker's previous efforts to help herself and her success or otherwise (even if temporarily successful) contribute to your sense of whether it is possible to work with her in a counselling skills way. The person may lack support in making the changes she hopes for, in which case you may be able to provide short-term support.

Be careful and clear about how much time you have when a helping situation arises. These situations can happen when you least expect them and sometimes you may feel that you have no alternative but to respond by engaging in a conversation. However, be clear about what you can offer at the outset – this will stand you in good stead when you realise that you're running out of time. It's easier to refer back to an earlier comment when you said that you would be able to offer, say, 20 minutes, or to arrange an alternative time, than suddenly look at your watch and announce that you have to leave, or continue listening whilst feeling impatient or anxious about other responsibilities.

Time as healer

Although it's is no doubt trite to say that time is a great healer, the statement is often true. I suggest, though, that you're cautious about how you phrase that if you voice it to a person seeking help – she may hear it as dismissal or belittling of her concerns. I've heard bereaved people speak of how angry they felt when someone said 'time is a great healer' to them. Someone who is bereaved doesn't want to forget her loved one in the way this saying might suggest. However, thinking of time as a healer is a way of putting things in perspective for yourself if you find you take on too much of the speaker's worries. Many people do get better in time and without help. I see this perspective, though, as similar to having a broken leg – it will probably heal without medical intervention, but you might end up lame. Understanding something about the effects of time (as reflected in 'stages' through which individuals pass following transitions) is potentially helpful for you and the help-seeker (see 'Dealing with life stages' later in this chapter).

Relationships

Problems with relationships and the problems for which a person is seeking help are often connected in some way. A person may be seeking help because she's experiencing problems in one or more relationships or perhaps other issues are having an impact on relationships. A good example is what happens in workplace settings where relationships at home affect the person's capacity and capability at work, and problems at work affect working and out-of-work relationships. Always question how any difficulty may be affecting relationships at home and at work, or how any relationship difficulty may be affecting other things.

A help-seeker's presenting issue may mask an underlying problem, and this is just as true for any issues you're facing (refer to Chapter 2 on understanding yourself).

The other important thing to remember about relationships is that when the speaker leaves you she may need to find other support. Encourage her to find support in her friendships, intimate relationships, and other affiliations if possible. She may be reluctant to divulge her concerns to others. The listening-helper may be able to challenge preconceptions, if they are unrealistic.

Research demonstrates that people who belong to a group (for example a faith-based group linked to a church, synagogue, or mosque, or a group that shares a common interest such as dancing, painting, or bird-watching) are more likely to have good mental health. In fact, a sense of belonging is important to most people's psychological well-being. Research also shows that pets are a benefit to positive mental and physical health. If a person doesn't have the kind of support offered by these sources, the lack of support may be the focus of the work you do with her.

Support networks are important to well-being.

Identifying Signs and Symptoms of Distress

Here's a signs-of-distress list, identified in terms of BEST-I and BEST-R.

- ✔ **Body:** People may experience disturbance in their patterns of sleep, eating, and ingestion of other substances. They may also experience symptoms of panic (see Sensation). Body patterns can become erratic or over-controlled (for example, facial or body tics and stiffness), as can their observed emotional expression.

✔ **Emotion:** Outward expressions may sometimes appear disturbed to others, but often the feelings are hidden but nonetheless painful and worrying to the person experiencing them. Feelings can be experienced as frightening, out of control, jumbled. Therefore, in order to maintain outward functioning the individual may have cut off from feeling (even to the extent of out-of-body experience or dissociation) and appear cold, withdrawn, or lifeless.

✔ **Sensation:** A person in distress may have body symptoms which she may or may not attribute to her mental state. Many people experience *panic attacks*, where breathing becomes very rapid, shallow or difficult, the heart feels like it will burst out of the chest or is beating abnormally (palpitations), and they have feelings of sickness and fear in the stomach, along with constipation or diarrhoea. More people experience these things than you may think. People feel ashamed or stupid, so they hide the symptoms or avoid certain situations, which hampers the person's life. Other body symptoms of stress include headaches, backache, neck problems, and digestive disorders (such as irritable bowel syndrome).

✔ **Thinking:** Disordered thinking is a by-product of distress. Until a person releases her emotions (called catharsis), the person may not be able to concentrate enough to think straight.

✔ **Imagery:** When people are worried, they often have strong negative imaginings. Sleep patterns may be disturbed by distressing dreams.

✔ **Behaviour:** A person's emotional state can be affected by behaviour. The person may act out of character and erratically, compared with how she normally is. If she has a tendency towards obsessive-compulsivity she may be more prone to obsessive behaviour, such as constantly checking ('Have I got my keys?' 'Did I lock the door?' and so on). She may be snappy and negative in her responses.

✔ **Environment:** Distress tends to push people towards the extremes, which can be reflected in the person's environment, appearing as obsessively tidy or very messy.

✔ **Spirit:** If you don't know the person who is seeking your help, it may be less easy to spot changes in her spirit. Someone who knows the person may observe that she's out of sorts and dispirited. Sometimes people lose faith if life has been tough, and this loss leaves a large gap in their lives.

✔ **Time:** Distress can lead to a sense of a lack of future, and meaninglessness. Day-to-day commitments may be hard to complete in the time allotted. People often miss appointments when they most need to keep them, not from ordinary carelessness but because they can't organise themselves when they feel all at sea.

✔ **Relationships:** Not surprisingly, relationships suffer when a person is distressed, making the situation even worse.

This is not an exhaustive list. I'm sure that you can add to it from your own experience. You can help to normalise, and show acceptance of, someone's experience by pointing out that many people respond to distress in these ways. Frequently, when people are in this state they think that they're abnormal or going mad or being stupid. Remember the tip-of-the-iceberg effect (explained in the previous 'Emotions' section); the true depth of feeling may be masked.

Having discovered fully what the person is experiencing, the next step is to help her prioritise what to work on. You can read more about prioritisation in Chapters 9, 10, and11.

Recognising Issues That Cause or Result in Distress

Events in the present may trigger earlier distressing experiences that people have managed to hide from others and sometimes themselves, such as childhood abuse. People's coping strategies sometimes cause more problems, such as the misuse of alcohol. The potential list here is very long, so I cover some categories in other chapters. Chapter 13 deals with oppression and prejudice which can lead to stress and distress. In Chapter 14 I discuss the psychological causes of distress in more detail, for example, the effects of childhood experience, which can emerge in the present.

Dealing with change

Many of the issues which present themselves to you as a listening helper are concerned in some way with change. People learn to manage change in different ways. Even those who are good at change can find transitions difficult if other things are working against them. Research suggests that people can manage a maximum of three major events in a year, including negative experiences such as death and divorce, as well as positively embraced change, like promotion, choosing to move house, or holidays. I've stopped being surprised at the number of people who come for help wondering why they're struggling with day-to-day life, and then tell me a story such as: they got a new job, moved house, their mother died, their best friend was diagnosed with cancer, and finally the boiler blew up and was going to cost more than expected to put right. Ill health, life events, and other accidents leave their mark.

Others may not have learned how to manage change. Part of coping with change involves managing anxiety. Some people become paralysed in the face of seemingly impossible decisions, often polarised into either/or choices. Another aspect is not having acquired techniques for problem-solving and making choices.

Working with loss

Loss is tied up with change and transition. Many, if not all, of life's changes involve some form of loss. Even when a change is for the better and wished for, it can be unsettling to lose familiar patterns, despite them having been difficult or painful. The losses we experience always involve change. Most people underestimate the effects of transition, change, and loss and hold unrealistic ideas about how they or others should be reacting. Self-imposed 'oughts' and 'shoulds', which can be reinforced by a person's social circle, lead to negative self-judgement, and lowered self-esteem and isolation, compounding the feelings of loss. Check out Chapter 14 to find out more about transition and loss.

Some people find the prospect of endings too difficult to face, which may be related to earlier experiences. These feelings may be deeper than can be dealt with in a counselling skills way and can affect the person's willingness to make changes and also to let go of the helping relationship. Have a look at Chapter 11 for more about dealing with this situation.

Dealing with life stages

Another aspect of change is the set of transitions which can be summed up as life stages. Childhood is full of milestones and transitions that sometimes have long-term effects on the adult. As a listening helper, you regularly come across people starting out on a new stage in their lives – people who have left home for independent living for the first time; those who have started living with their life partner; or some who have become any one of a number of things for the first time: student/employee/spouse/parent/pensioner. All these roles involve adaptation, which may be exciting but also potentially stressful.

Coping with sexual issues

Sexual difficulties are exceptionally common. The problem may be temporary (such as having problems getting an erection because of a stressful time in the person's life), or a longer-term issue (such as matters related to concerns about sexual identity or orientation). Chapter 14 is the place to go for more information. Finding someone open-minded and confident enough to talk about sexual issues is difficult. As a listening helper you must overcome any barriers you have to talking frankly. Many people in helping roles aren't comfortable about discussing sexual issues. As a sex therapist, I've had numerous clients who've had medical treatment that has affected their sexuality in some way, and very seldom have they been given appropriate information or an invitation to discuss the effects of their illness and treatment on their sex lives. This silence leaves people anxious and self-judging – thinking to themselves, for example: 'Am I abnormal for having these feelings?'.

To increase your comfort with the area of sexuality, you can watch television programmes that challenge your attitudes and broaden your experience, and you can read books and articles about sexuality.

Improving relationships

Anything which affects an individual is likely to have ramifications in her relationships: in couple and family dynamics, friendships, and work relationships. Many relationships are robust enough to withstand these difficulties and give support to the individual. However, people often seek help because the relationships cannot support, or are threatened by the same events. For example, when a family member is seriously ill, each person in the family is affected. It's common for relationships to feel under intense strain in such circumstances and for little energy to be left over to care for each other adequately. Perhaps one family member is the 'strong' one but will succumb to signs and symptoms of distress later.

By the same token, strained relationships can cause problems in other areas of people's lives. Sometimes teasing out which is the cause and which is effect proves difficult. Be aware that if someone is behaving uncharacteristically (snappy, reactive, moody, and so on) at work, she may be dealing with issues outside work.

Controlling unmanageable feelings

A common cause of seeking help is not being able to control certain feelings such as panic attacks, anger, uncontrollable tears, mood swings, low mood, and depression. To be in the grip of unmanageable feelings is disorientating, worrying, and extremely unpleasant. If the feelings are concealed, the person feels exhausted and isolated. The need for concealment indicates that she probably thinks that her feelings are abnormal and/or unacceptable. If the feelings spill out then, after a time, others lose sympathy and become irritated or distance themselves.

Some of these experiences can be alleviated by talking and receiving reassurance. Others require referral to a service or individual with specialist knowledge and skills. You can read more about this aspect in Chapter 14.

Chapter 13

Understanding People from a Social Perspective

. . . .

. . . .

*P*eople usually set out to be listening helpers with what seems like a simple wish to assist others to feel better or to improve their situation. Elsewhere in this book you're challenged to look at the underlying emotional drivers to being a listening helper – your hidden motivations. This chapter considers another area that is often hidden or not immediately obvious – the role of power and social influences in the helping relationship. Power differences affecting the helping relationship are evident at two levels:

⤳ In society

⤳ Between help-seeker and helper

Socio-cultural influences are obvious as they are reflected in clothes, speech, housing, lifestyle, skin colour, and so on. However, these outward signs are often misleading, as assumptions and prejudices can lead to inaccurate categorising and labelling. Assuming that everyone is the same is also dangerous. Such an attitude may seem to be an egalitarian one to adopt, but both neglects the richness of an individual's experiences and denies the reality of oppression and its effects. The help-seeker's life experiences are very pertinent to the presenting issue that he brings and also to the helping relationship.

Power in Society and in Helping Relationships

Power, as expressed in economic security, life chances, access to services, and the ability to control and direct your own life, isn't evenly distributed in society. Although our society has changed in many ways, these disparities continue and have an enduring impact on individuals, families, and certain social groupings. Particular groups can become *marginalised*: Not only are they disadvantaged by having low incomes or by being 'different' in some way, they are further deprived by being accorded lower status through prejudice and oppression.

The task of an aspiring listening helper is challenging because to work ethically you need to:

✔ Become more aware of the impact of the lack of personal power and the effects of prejudice and oppression on an individual's life experiences, including your own.

✔ Understand how seeking help is coloured by the help-seeker's previous experiences of authority, being labelled as 'different', and so on.

✔ Understand how oppression is internalised by both helper and help-seeker.

✔ Appreciate the way in which the helping relationship can perpetuate oppression.

✔ Make a commitment to anti-oppressive practices – finding ways of making help accessible and of empowering the help-seeker.

These activities involve thinking about what happens outside the helping conversation as well as within the helping relationship itself. Your responsibility isn't just for the conversation but also to consider the surrounding environment and what you can do to improve it.

Listening helpers frequently believe that they don't hold power in the helping relationship. Because most listening helpers are consciously altruistic and like to think of themselves as caring people, they think this makes them approachable and egalitarian. They can seriously underestimate both the difficulty for most, if not all, people in taking the step to seek help and the authority invested in them and their role by a help-seeker. These difficulties are compounded for any help-seeker who has previously been treated in discriminatory ways. Refer to Chapter 5 for more discussion of the role of power in the relationship.

ANECDOTE

Challenging assumptions

The counselling service Relate uses images of a range of people and relationships when advertising; black, white, gay, straight, and so on. Relate is deliberately trying to convey an invitation to all people. Relate believed itself to be open to all and not prejudiced, but came to recognise that they needed to convey a positive message to encourage members of minority groups to access their services. A client of mine told me that as a lesbian she'd assumed that Relate was only for straight relationships, but she'd made contact because she was desperate. An issue in our work together was her constant assumption that I'd judge her. She couldn't tell me the real reasons she was seeking help until she'd really checked me out. She feared I wouldn't want to hear certain things. I was concerned whether I would inadvertently convey non-accepting attitudes because, at that time, I had little experience of working with lesbian couples and their relationship issues. I didn't know how similar or different gay relationships would be from straight couple relationships and I hadn't received any relevant training during my basic couple counselling training. Part of her checking me out was asking if I was straight. I decided honesty was the best policy and was open with my client about my inexperience and my sexual orientation and this proved to be helpful.

Prejudice and Oppression

Discussing in great detail all the different forms of oppression and prejudice is impossible to do in one book so I encourage you to read texts that are more specialised on the topics (such as David Smail's *The Nature of Unhappiness* (Random House)). Two important themes linking oppression and the helping relationship are:

✔ **The absorption and perpetuation of prevailing attitudes in society:** People absorb prevailing views of social difference, which leads to assumptions, fears, and conscious and unconscious discriminatory attitudes and actions, whatever background they're from. Individuals from minority oppressed groups also internalise negative attitudes and hold expectations of themselves and others based on such negative self-beliefs. The listening helper must become more aware of the impact on himself and on those he helps of societal and internalised oppression. Helping theories have been mostly developed by Western theorists and reflect their time and social context. These theories may need to be adapted to take account of different cultural patterns – for example, the central importance of the family rather than the individual in some cultures.

✔ **The social construction of difference:** Listening-helping can be justly criticised for focusing on the individual rather than recognising the social construction of difficulties – and their consequences – that people face. Depression is a good example. Someone experiencing depression is usually treated as a person with an illness (this is the *medical model* at work and an example of *labelling*), and indeed he is suffering and may be helped by medical interventions. However, the root of the depression may be that the individual has experienced racial discrimination, sexual harassment, or poor social and economic circumstances due to the society in which he lives.

Whilst some people believe that everyone is middle-class now, this assumption isn't borne out by government and other statistics. People in lower socio-economic groupings tend to suffer higher rates of mental ill-health. Mental ill-health also *leads* to lower income and status, so those expected to cope with less easy economic circumstances are the least equipped to do so. This kind of cycle is replicated in other examples of difference and oppression.

Most people have prejudices. Prejudice is just an extension of a categorising system which everyone uses so that they can make sense of a potentially confusing world. As a listening helper your prejudices are likely to hamper the helping relationship. You need to begin to notice when you're making assumptions and stereotyping people and to challenge your own attitudes and your own internalised oppression. For example, if you're a woman, when you help another woman do you collude with her over gender stereotypes? If she talks about feeling stressed trying to manage child-care arrangements and household tasks as well as her work demands, do you sympathise with the difficulty of her position and attempt to help her organise herself better, or do you (at an appropriate time when the relationship between you is established) challenge her assumption that all these responsibilities are hers, rather than shared with her partner? Repeated evidence shows that women still bear the majority of the burden of child-care and household tasks even when they work full time.

Developing Your Understanding

You cannot possibly know about every single cultural permutation but you can expose yourself to different cultures and experiences of oppression through reading, watching television, and film documentaries, opening yourself to friendship, or being a volunteer with people from different ethnic backgrounds to yourself (for example, with refugees). In the helping relationship you can invite discussion about expectations, concerns, and the impact of cultural background on the individual's life and on the work you do together.

In the sections below I touch on some issues related to particular forms of prejudice as an introduction but I recommend you take your reading further. Remember that counselling theory has tended to be developed by white, middle-class men and can be justifiably criticised for having a Eurocentric, middle-class approach, so notice this in your reading. Always compare what you read to your own experience – just because something is written in a book or a professional journal doesn't make it correct.

Physical and mental disability

Next time you're walking in your town or village consider what being partially sighted or in a wheelchair would be like. How easy or challenging would it be? Talk to friends, family, colleagues who have any kind of disability to find out what impact their disability has on their daily lives.

The Disability Discrimination legislation may lead to changes in attitude, or at least facilitation for people with disabilities. However, in general, society has a negative attitude towards people with physical and mental disabilities and mental ill-health. Examples are:

- ✔ Disability is looked on as a medical problem and treated as something undesirable to be cured.

- ✔ Many of the physical barriers faced by people described as disabled are because the environment creates disability – for example, steps are everywhere, impeding access for many.

- ✔ Many organisations catering for these groups are run by non-disabled people and provide services *for* disabled people rather than *with* them.

- ✔ Many disabilities are invisible. For example, people with myalgic encephalopathy (ME) or multiple sclerosis (MS) may not noticeably be disabled, although they have to contend with many barriers – for example, services they need to access (such as clinics) are sometimes offered at times of the day when their illness is at its worst. Helping agencies may expect regular attendance which may be impossible.

- ✔ Some people hold socially formed views that disability is a tragedy, something to be pitied. Such views can cause you to inappropriately focus on loss when the issue could be something else entirely. Some people may also have a sense of disgust, helplessness or fear of contamination; these are commonly held feelings (whether consciously or unconsciously), and are communicated to the help-seeker.

- ✔ Because of negative attitudes people may be unwilling to be labelled as disabled and so not access support they'd be entitled to.

- ✔ People with mental ill-health or mental disabilities are often treated with fear, suspicion, and as if they're a potential danger. An example is sufferers of Tourette's (where the person makes involuntary vocalisations – sometimes grunts, often swear words – which people find alarming).

Negative attitudes and the experience of being treated differently can lead to groups opting for a separate culture. Some people who are deaf, for example, prefer to work and socialise with other deaf people because they share an understanding of their experience, have a shared culture and language, and for some, their shunning of the hearing world is a political statement.

Thinking about disability

When I was a trainee social worker my training group was sent out in pairs one afternoon with wheelchairs – one in the wheelchair and the other pushing (we swapped halfway through the afternoon). We went around the town centre to discover what it was like to negotiate the barriers and experience the attitudes we encountered, including those within ourselves. It was a salutary lesson. We found it was impossible to get into some shops, or to navigate around inside. When I was in the wheelchair I had my change counted out to my wheelchair-pusher at the checkout. When we went into a shop to look at underwear the assistant was clearly highly embarrassed that I wanted to look at pretty, sexy underwear, and she fled. I was aware of my own embarrassment at being a young disabled woman looking at nice underwear and what this implied about my sexuality.

Although this was three decades ago and some things have improved, much hasn't. For example, as a sex therapist I have worked in recent years with people who have disabilities or long-term illnesses who haven't been able to get help and advice from medical personnel about the impact on their sex lives. Sometimes their parents have wanted to protect them by keeping them sexless and ignorant. I know of people who've been employed specifically to work with disability issues whose own disability hasn't been allowed for before they arrive at work. They've had to start work in isolated and unsuitable office accommodation because no one thought to check that the office and facilities were suitable and accessible.

Different ethnic and cultural backgrounds

Racism is deeply rooted in society and cannot fail to affect everyone, whatever their background. Shocking examples of institutionalised racism in public bodies have come to light even in recent years. Black people have lived in the UK since at least the 17th century, so people who are assumed by some to be first or second generation immigrants may have a family history that goes back many generations in this country. The UK has had wave after wave of different groups from all over the world coming into the country and gradually becoming assimilated. As a consequence the picture is complex. When you meet someone you cannot make assumptions or generalise about them.

One assumption you *can* make is that if you're helping a person who is black, Asian, or of mixed racial identity then he's highly likely to have experienced discrimination. Black women are doubly discriminated against and low self-esteem or depression may be related to predominant white attitudes towards ideals of beauty and fantasies about black sexuality.

Class is still an issue

Many people in our society live in very poor circumstances, in some cases caused by disability or mental health problems. A number of research studies show that people from lower socio-economic groups are frequently judged by service providers as not capable of making use of listening help and are often met with a lack of empathy. Working-class people often carry an *internalised oppression* that they aren't as clever or articulate as the educated middle class; in other words, they've absorbed the attitudes of society and they anticipate negative judgements. Blind compliance or anger and unfulfilled potential are often the result. These attitudes can overlap with racism because black people and other ethnic groups are still discriminated against in the job market, as well as in mental health diagnosis and treatment.

Ageism across the spectrum

Ageism is discrimination that usually applies to older people. But, in fact, children and young people are also treated with prejudice and discrimination, which includes abuse. Abuse of children is easily hidden or disguised and children are at risk of sexual exploitation. Children are also taught to minimise their emotional reactions and frequently have no one who will listen and take their concerns seriously. Young people are depicted as trouble waiting to happen and services for them, such as youth groups, are haphazard. Many children live in single-parent families where sometimes poverty poses daily challenges, including discrimination due to not fitting in with the 'normal' expectations in the school environment. Adults often don't know how to talk to young people: Children and young people may need more help to express themselves, for example through non-verbal means, which requires training to do it well. For insight into the damaging emotional world of many children, pick up a book by the psychotherapist Alice Miller, who writes searing accounts.

At the other end of the spectrum older people are discriminated against in the job market and in provision of psychological services, and abuse of old people isn't uncommon. Such experiences can lead to loss of identity, feelings of uselessness, and depression. Because elderly people have a greater tendency to experience incapacitating or debilitating illness and major losses, they're more likely to be depressed but they often have poor economic or physical access to supportive services. Listening-helping services for the older adult are very limited for these reasons.

Gender inequality

Some people mistakenly believe that little gender inequality exists nowadays. However, surveys and statistics show that women are still economically disadvantaged in the workplace as well as in the home – where they tend to work more hours than their male partners even if they also work full time. Care of children isn't given due weight – women caring for children at home are seen to be 'not working'. Women are also at much greater risk of domestic violence, emotional abuse, and homicide from their male partners than vice versa. Generally they hide the abuse because of their attachment to the perpetrator, or out of fear, and the desire to protect their children. Emotional abuse can be hard to pinpoint but is highly damaging to women and their children who often witness or hear scenes.

Emotional abuse (which may or may not be accompanied by physical abuse) includes:

- ✔ **Isolation and control:** The partner forbids friendships, outings, seeing family, working outside the home, and controls finances, doesn't allow a mobile phone, takes away car keys, and so on.

- ✔ **Verbal abuse:** Accusations (of unfaithfulness, for example), and undermining or discounting which induce guilt and shame.

- ✔ **Inconsistent, unpredictable responses:** These may be very loving or apologetic at one time, and abusive at other times.

- ✔ **Abuse in private:** Outside the home the perpetrator is often seen as charming.

Women in abusive relationships usually find leaving their partners very hard and often meet with judging attitudes for not doing so. Don't be impatient, and recognise that women are often at greatest risk when and after leaving.

Sexuality issues

Despite the apparently open attitude towards sexual material in the media, my own practice as a sex therapist tells me that many people regard sex, or discussion of sexual matters, as shameful and embarrassing and sex education has been patchy or nonexistent for them. Many parents find it difficult to discuss these issues with their children. Added to these attitudes are the homophobia and sexism which exists in society.

The outcome of some of these sex-related issues is that, for a substantial number of people, they find adjusting to their sexuality a lonely and worrying process.

Write about the kind of person you want as your life partner – his or her personal qualities, character, personality, and values. Don't use any words that denote gender (such as he or she) – talk about 'my partner' or 'this person' – and don't describe any physical characteristics. If you're heterosexual, then imagine that you're gay, bisexual, or lesbian and think about telling family and friends about your partner. How might they react, how would you feel, how would you want them to be, how would it be different from a heterosexual person's experience? Consider, if you identify as non-heterosexual, whether your experience would be different if you were lesbian, a gay man, or bisexual (as appropriate).

Stretching your listening skills

As a listening helper you need to stretch your capacity to listen to a person who may have very different life experiences from your own. Even if you too have struggled with your sexual identity you may find it difficult dealing with someone else's experience. Could you listen to any of the following?:

- A man or a woman who tells you his/her marriage is unconsummated after 15 years

- A lesbian who is having sexual difficulties with her partner

- A younger (than you) man or woman who asks for sexual information/knowledge

- A much older (than you) man or woman who asks for sexual information/knowledge

- A woman who wants to tell you the details of a serious sexual abuse incident

- A man who wants to tell you about his rape experience

- A man whose cross-dressing has just been discovered by his wife

- A woman who is very attracted to another woman and doesn't know if this means she's lesbian

- A young person who wants to discuss whether he or she might be gay or bisexual

- A man who wants to discuss that he's hoping for a sex change and needs to live as a woman for the next year but he believes he's being discriminated against at work.

To be helpful to a help-seeker you need to be open and accepting. If you find listening to sexual problems embarrassing, then it might be best to admit it to the help-seeker so that you can either decide to work as best you can or refer the person on sensitively. You can desensitise yourself to hearing difficult things by exposing yourself to relevant literature and some of the many television programmes that focus on aspects of sexuality.

To help people become less embarrassed about sexual language, an exercise I do with students, which you can do privately, is to write down as many words for male and female sexual body parts and sexual activity that you can think of, both 'scientific' and everyday, including the rude ones. This exercise can be very liberating. You may never actually use most of these words with a help-seeker; the exercise is about becoming less inhibited generally.

Never make assumptions about how a person needs to be supported if he's going through the process of working out his sexuality or coming out as non-heterosexual. Many people find it helpful and supportive to talk to someone else who has been through the process and understands first-hand the pressures and worries, but this isn't true of all. Some help-lines and specialist services exist. If you support someone through this process, or, as a heterosexual, work with someone who is non-heterosexual on some other issue, you must offer the same acceptance and empathy – which means examining your own attitudes. Non-heterosexuals have sometimes found that when they seek help about an issue in their life, the helper tends to focus on their sexuality as the problem.

If you put 'homophobia questionnaire' into the Google search engine, for example, you get several questionnaires that can get you thinking about your own attitudes to homosexuality. One is a Heterosexual Questionnaire that turns the tables, asking questions about how you became a heterosexual, which is a clever way of challenging your assumptions about homosexuality.

The Influence of Your Setting

In a setting where you're an employee, or where the help-seeker is a child or young person, you may have constraints that influence your ability to be truly impartial or on the help-seeker's side. Your employer may expect you to return the help-seeker to work as soon as possible, for example, and this attitude could conflict with what you believe to be in the help-seeker's best longer-term interests. Whatever the nature of the working and helping environment, it's likely to seep into, and be reflected in, the helping relationship. In hierarchical environments, for example, you may be subtly or openly pressured to relate to the help-seeker in an authoritarian way.

Even in an environment which is in tune with the ethos of the listening-helper role described in this book, you're in much greater control of the setting and interaction than the help-seeker. The helping role can represent an unattainable ideal of someone in control of his life, problem-free, and therefore wise and authoritative and not to be challenged. You're offering a professionalised friendship which is criticised by some as influencing people to make less use of supportive friendship with others in similar situations, turning difference into an individual, pathologised problem, and increasing the power imbalance between those with problems and those (apparently) without. A potential for misunderstanding and misuse of power always exists when working across any social divide. As a listening helper you have a responsibility to reduce such possibilities and to meet the help-seeker more than halfway, for example by inviting and prompting the help-seeker to give honest feedback on the helping relationship and service.

Working Affirmatively

At all times, aim for an *affirmative approach*, which means consciously reaching out to people from groups who are normally oppressed. Working affirmatively includes:

- ✔ Taking a proactive stance to making any service you're involved in more accessible, including removing physical barriers, barriers due to perception of the service, and negative staff attitudes.

- ✔ Auditing premises, literature, and advertising to remove barriers and encourage uptake of services by specifically referring to particular groups, who may otherwise feel unwelcome.

- ✔ Challenging the prejudicial attitudes of others. This can be a tricky issue if the prejudiced individual is a help-seeker because it can divert attention away from the issues he's seeking help with, so needs sensitivity and appropriate timing. You may need discussion and the support of colleagues in your workplace to develop policies and skills in this area.

- ✔ Acknowledging difference and inviting discussion of expectations in one-to-one sessions.

- ✔ Acknowledging when mistakes have been made and apologising.

- ✔ Actively encouraging feedback, especially negative feedback, which most people are reluctant to give honestly.

- ✔ Helping service users to recognise when their difficulties may be influenced by social factors.

As a listening helper, you need to maintain a distinction between drawing attention to an individual's taken-for-granted self-expectations, which are moulded by oppressive attitudes in his environment, and pressurising him to change in ways that you believe to be desirable. The aim is empowerment, not brainwashing!

Chapter 14

Understanding Individuals from a Psychological Perspective

*T*he aim of this chapter isn't to equip you to 'diagnose' and categorise people's problems. I hope to sensitise you to the impact that life experiences can have on individuals and help you to recognise when a problem may be beyond your capacity to help. Because I can't cover every presenting difficulty you may be faced with, I recommend that you read additional books, take opportunities for further training, and discuss issues with colleagues.

Be aware of the limits of your competence and of your helping role in your particular context. Because everyone uses listening skills in a variety of different settings, I can't give comprehensive authoritative guidelines about your role or tell you when you need to refer a help-seeker. Consulting colleagues is advisable and ethically preferable if you have any question about whether you should work with a person. If you have concerns about a person's health, including mental health, be sure to suggest she talks to her GP.

Nature or Nurture?

Theories and debates abound about how people are shaped by *nature and nurture*, the dictates of biological or genetic inheritance, and the social and psychological effects of upbringing and experience. Suffice to say here that the impact on you of your environment and the people around you as you are growing up, and during adulthood, is huge. Even pre-birth and birth experiences, such as stress in pregnant women or post-natal depression, are believed to be significant for adult mental health and may be associated with ill-health later in a child's life.

As a listening helper you don't need in-depth knowledge of these influences to be helpful. However, having some understanding about possible links between an individual's earlier experiences and present difficulties and strengths in her life and relationships is useful.

Childhood development

Various developmental theories by psychologists such as Freud, Piaget, and Erikson attempt to define normal and abnormal development in particular areas – psychosexual, cognitive, psychosocial, and personality, for example. Although I can't summarise the complexity of human development here, I can say this:

- ✔ Early experiences can have profound effects on later development but negative effects are not inevitable.

- ✔ Risk and protective factors, most notably attachments, can have significant influences on individuals. Secure attachments in early life are likely to lead to positive adult attachments and self-esteem and a close, confiding relationship is protective against stress. Poor attachments and family discord are associated with poor social adjustment and self-esteem. Children of depressed mothers often experience adult depression (the emotional withdrawal affects self-esteem in the child). Peer attachments are key protectors or stressors.

- ✔ The age and maturity (physical and emotional) of a person when certain events are experienced influence how she understands and is affected by the events, including how she reflects on them as an adult. For example, adults who experienced trauma in childhood, such as the loss of a parent or sexual abuse, typically continue to blame themselves despite possibly knowing (intellectually) that they were not responsible.

- ✔ Negative experiences and their consequences can lead to a cycle of further reinforcing of negative experiences. For example, a child who is shy may be bullied or teased, which leads to further withdrawal and increased isolation. Gradually, the child may gain confidence through supportive experiences. However, a later traumatic occurrence may further reinforce the self-belief of being different and that 'something must be wrong with me', which influences friendships and partner choice in negative, reinforcing ways.

✔ Family patterns and systems may continue to reinforce strengths and vulnerabilities into adulthood. An individual can be locked into a role or pattern of behaviour, not only in relation to her original family but also in subsequent relationships.

✔ Exposure to, and successful management of, minor stresses during childhood and adolescence helps build coping strategies.

✔ Adolescence is a time of both vulnerability and opportunity because great physical and emotional changes take place. Peer relationships and pressures are particularly influential. Mental health problems such as schizophrenia and depression may emerge for the first time in this phase.

The meaning that an individual attaches to events and relationships is important to healthy emotional adjustment, so exploration of past experiences aims to enable the help-seeker make sense of her history. In my experience many, if not most, people aren't psychologically minded and don't realise the impact of earlier experiences on their development until someone draws attention to it.

Experiences and influences from childhood can be formative and long-lasting, but adult experiences continue to shape and influence. Be sure to explore current and recent experiences before delving into the past. The past is relevant only insofar as it connects to present patterns. The listening helper can assist the help-seeker to reach a new and more positive understanding of her current experiences.

Linking past and present

Some help-seekers are aware that childhood has an impact on present functioning and seek to explore their experiences with a non-judging listener. Listening help enables these individuals to make sense of experiences, connecting patterns from the past to patterns in the present. An important therapeutic, healing aspect lies in being able to express emotions that go with the story, bringing together thoughts, behaviours, and feelings.

A clue that may reveal a past-present connection is when emotions seem out of proportion with what's happening now. A good question to ask is whether the emotions remind her of similar feelings in the past. If so, she needs to explore her feelings about those past events in order to disentangle them from present experience. Emotions tend to 'leak' when they haven't been dealt with.

If someone has multiple traumatic experiences or finds containing emotions related to current life or history hard, enable her to access longer-term, or more in-depth, emotional help and support.

Coping with Transitions

Your previous experiences have an effect on how well you adapt to transitions. You can find various theories about change and bereavement, but whilst theory can be helpful in developing your own and a help-seeker's understanding, remember that individuals do not fit theories neatly. Be wary of using theories that explain loss in terms of stages. Loss is a process, not just an event, and has typical characteristics which change over time. Don't expect a help-seeker to move smoothly and predictably through a succession of identifiable stages. Both you, and more importantly the help-seeker, may be demoralised and frustrated if she doesn't fit the model.

Experiencing change

Change can be depicted as resembling the up and down curves of a roller-coaster; indeed change can sometimes feel like a roller-coaster ride, with wildly fluctuating emotions. Not all change is so vivid but similar emotions are likely, albeit at a reduced level of intensity. The change process may include

- **At the start, a wave of excitement, anticipation, euphoria:** 'This is exciting, just what I want.' Or negative anticipation, dread: 'I can't bear it.'

- **Denial or sense of unreality:** 'Can I be doing this? This can't happen.'

- **Minimisation (self-reassurance):** 'It can't be too bad.'

- **Uncertainty and loss of confidence – as you drop down the slope:** 'Why on earth did I start this? I'm no good at this. How will I manage?'

- **Depression or fear:** 'I don't think I can do this, I've made a big mistake.'

- **Crisis:** 'Oh dear, there's no turning back! It's awful.'

- **Acceptance:** 'Well I have to get on with it.'

- **Exploring and testing:** 'Maybe this is okay, perhaps I can do it, even enjoy it.'

- **Integration:** A new sense of identity and confidence.

The process doesn't proceed tidily, step by step. People cycle around or revisit stages, or even miss some. Some skip from beginning to end – perhaps they are change-lovers and/or people who suppress or deny some of their emotional experience. These are the people who sometimes find change catching up with them at a later stage.

Change and transition can be divided into two categories:

- Unplanned or unexpected change.
- Planned or chosen change.

Getting in touch with feelings around loss

This exercise focuses on a relatively minor loss; however, the feelings involved as you react to any kind of loss are similar – the difference is in the intensity and duration of the emotional reaction. Tuning into your own sequence of emotional reactions can give you some insight into the *process* a person experiences when faced with change, transition, and loss. You use your empathy to tune into the *depth* of her experience.

Close your eyes. Use your imagination to take yourself, as vividly as you can, to a time when you lost something fairly important (for example keys, wallet, rather than a major life loss) and preferably an item that you didn't retrieve. Tune in to immediate feelings (physical/emotional) as you realise it's missing. Scroll through your experience as you start searching, then realising it's lost, perhaps permanently, on to a week or two later and then a couple of months later. Note the succession of feelings.

When change is planned, you can prepare psychologically, giving time to rehearse reasons for the choice and let go of the pre-change situation: The process is visualised and rehearsed. However, many people don't anticipate or recognise the full impact; and even less do they realise the emotional consequences of unplanned changes. Positive life events can cause as much psychological disruption as negative ones. Planning for a holiday or wedding, for example, is highly stressful; a desired job change, house move, divorce, more so. I've worked with many people who begin by saying that they don't know why they're depressed or struggling and then go on to list a string of life events. Normalisation of reactions by drawing attention to cumulative pressure can be helpful. Managing more than three major changes in a year is very difficult to cope with, especially if they're unexpected. People experience more stress when events are outside their control and may need help to recognise that this isn't unusual and that their emotions need to catch up. You can help them to do this by encouraging them to explore what has happened, including expressing their feelings.

Significant life change adaptation tends to take much longer than most expect (typically 6–12 months, or longer) and you can experience a time lag between event and distress. Often crisis occurs about six months after a transition. Multiple transitions or stresses bring cumulative deterioration. Factors can help or hinder, such as preparation, economic and emotional security, health, a supportive (or not) environment at home and/or work and transition management skills. When several members of a family or team are affected by change, having sufficient emotional energy to support each other can be hard. Despite dangers though, transitions are an opportunity for growth.

Strategies for managing change

If you're helping someone with a planned change, you want to discuss and normalise the processes involved. You can assist the help-seeker to:

- ✔ Anticipate and plan for the emotional reactions.

- ✔ Anticipate and plan for practical consequences.

- ✔ Obtain emotional and other support.

- ✔ Monitor and look after herself: make time to eat, relax, sleep, exercise, socialise, and so on.

- ✔ Identify and prioritise other issues, including strengths and areas for development.

- ✔ Keep hope alive by planning something to look forward to every week and especially around the six-month stage following major transition.

- ✔ Symbolically mark major transition: If the change is leaving something bad behind, this symbolic action could be a ritual like burning a photograph of an abuser; If the loss is of a loved one a personal memorial can be created, for example a memory box. Positive changes can be celebrated.

- ✔ Postpone major decisions after major transitions.

When the change is unplanned, all but the first two items above also apply. In both planned and unplanned cases, remember that expressed emotion is probably only a fraction of the emotion that is experienced, and this emotion needs an outlet. This is where you can help by gently encouraging emotions to be felt, voiced, and accepted, using the active listening skills described in this book. People may experience shame attached to some feelings so you need to normalise and, as it were, give permission to speak the unspeakable. This also applies in bereavement.

Bereavement

Some of the previous information is equally relevant to the loss of someone significant through death. In my experience the impact of bereavement is underestimated by most people nowadays. However, grieving is a very individual experience and no rules exist.

In any significant loss you can expect the first year to be particularly difficult. Every birthday and anniversary is likely to bring distress; Grief can continue for years. Within this time you experience a variety and mixture of feelings:

✔ Initially you may feel numb, which often helps people get through the organising before the funeral and the period immediately after.

✔ Alongside numbness can go denial and disbelief – 'It can't have happened, it's a nightmare,' and 'I'll wake up soon,' and so on. Sometimes this feeling continues with people unable to let go of clothing, effects, or plans made together.

✔ Many experience anger, sometimes directed at doctors or other services – we need to blame someone for letting the person die. Or the anger is towards the departed – 'How can she leave us? Why didn't she take more care?' – or to the self (recrimination, guilt).

✔ Many yearn and search: Often a loved one will be 'seen'. Some think they're going mad, others are comforted by visions and 'visitations'.

✔ After this period of numbness, anger, and grief a number of emotions can be felt in succession or at different times, including loss of faith, depression (flatness and despair), desperate sadness, loss of role, loss of a sense of future, confusion, and loss of confidence. Relief and guilt may be more difficult to admit.

✔ Eventually acceptance and a letting go may come. For some this may involve a symbolic gesture, for example scattering ashes in a special place, creating a memorial, writing a letter, or revisiting the grave to say goodbye (sometimes these have happened too soon).

✔ Following acceptance, a reorganisation of life and self (in a new role) can take place more wholeheartedly.

✔ For some people, acceptance and renewed life seems impossible and they experience prolonged crisis.

Viewing the body of the lost loved one

I have been asked if a bereaved person should view the body of the deceased. I believe this must be the choice of the individual and no 'right way' exists. Enable the person to talk through what she hopes and fears from seeing and not seeing the body.

I know people who have found seeing the body of a departed loved (or hated) one comforting. Touching the body and say goodbye helps them.

Others are left with bad memories, perhaps feeling pushed into seeing or touching, which they experience as anything from empty or distasteful to horrific. I know others who have not been able to view the body, or who have chosen not to, and who have regrets. Parents of stillborn and other young children generally seem to find spending time with their dead child helpful, and some hospitals facilitate this.

Substance use and misuse

The misuse of alcohol and/or drugs can cause or accompany and exacerbate other difficulties and is common. You need to recognise that the extent of help you can offer is limited until the substance use is being dealt with (generally by a specialist service). A major challenge in working with this issue is minimisation and denial by substance abusers. (Refer to Chapter 8 for the cycle of change model, which highlights that a help-seeker must be ready to make changes, recognising and admitting that she has a problem.) Ongoing support alongside other specialist interventions may be possible, especially to partners and close relatives. Most agencies working with substance misuse have a policy of not engaging in a session when the person is 'under the influence' – little useful work can be done in this circumstance.

These 'stages' aren't fixed and mutually exclusive. A person may pass through one set of emotions, only to revisit those emotions at a later date. Over time feelings usually become less intense and grief is felt less constantly, but with patches of intense feeling at greater intervals. Quite often the second year of a bereavement can feel worse than the first, as the realisation finally hits home that the situation is permanent and the support of others has lessened while the person is trying to establish a life without the loved one. In my experience loss is often felt *more* acutely when the relationship with the person who has died has been unsatisfactory.

Some bereavements are harder to come to terms with:

- ✔ The death of someone with whom you had an unsatisfactory relationship. Death brings loss of hope that the relationship can be repaired or that things could be said. Abuse survivors sometimes find the abuser's death difficult for this reason.

- ✔ Sudden death. Although protracted dying is painful it gives an opportunity to say goodbye, and to resolve issues. Sudden death can leave feelings of guilt – 'Could I have prevented it?' 'If only I had/hadn't . . .'

- ✔ The death of a child, whatever the age but especially in childhood. Outliving your child violates the naturally expected order of events and can cause guilt and remorse. Sudden, unexpected death, for example cot death (sudden infant death) or a drug overdose, can be particularly hard to accept.

- ✔ Suicide leaves survivors with a very difficult set of feelings (anger, guilt, remorse). Parents of suicides are at high risk of suicide themselves.

- ✔ When there's no body, for example after a loss at sea, mourners find the death hard to believe and accept. People go to desperate lengths to find a body.

- ✔ When an individual has had to minimise her own grief in order to support others, especially (but not only) others affected by the death.

- ✔ When earlier unresolved grief is re-evoked by a present loss. The present loss (for example, the loss of a pet or ornament) may seem trivial to an outsider but evokes strong feelings which are related to the earlier unmourned loss.

- ✔ When someone has experienced a number of losses. The present loss is the 'last straw'.

- ✔ Survival, for example after a tragedy. This experience can leave 'survivor guilt'.

Helping people come to terms with loss involves encouragement to tell their story with appropriate emotions attached. Normalising emotions and identifying what interferes with expression of grief can help. If you recognise a complicated grief reaction – for example, that she seems unable to move past a particular emotion such as guilt or extreme sadness, or is depressed and unable to function – and this state persists over months (she feels 'stuck') you may need to refer her to a specialist agency such as Cruse.

Many bereaved people feel abnormal for continuing to experience grief. Often friends or family expect resumption of normal life in weeks. Some people married for thirty or more years take a long time (several years) to deal with their loss and parents of children who have died may never 'get over it', but only reach an acceptance. Grief becomes less painful over time but it endures and can return vividly and painfully with certain triggers, even years later.

My father survived two ships that went down during World War II. During the rest of his life he suffered from 'neurosis' (we would now call this PTSD – Post Traumatic Stress Disorder) and survivor guilt – how come so many brave young men died but he survived? Part of his distress was deep grief that never went away.

Generally we think of significant loss as a member of a person's family, a close friend, or a colleague. Occasionally significant loss can be felt by the death of a more distant person, for example the outpouring of grief following the death of Princess Diana. When someone identifies closely with another person her demise can trigger a deep sense of loss, often quite unexpectedly.

My hairdresser spoke of her very deep sadness at Princess Diana's death. She identified with Diana and her sons, herself and children being similar ages. Her marriage had also gone through difficulties and she followed stories about the princess in the media. She admired her land-mines work and her way with children. Diana's death was extremely shocking and personal to my hairdresser.

Disturbed Emotions

When people come for help they are usually in emotional distress. Some emotions are more difficult to deal with because of the listening helper's history, but most people struggle sometimes with how others express their feelings: Typically these are connected with extremes.

Anger

You may face someone who is very angry, perhaps about experiences elsewhere, or possibly about you. If you can't bear anger you won't allow the other to show it, least of all towards you, which is conveyed in subtle ways. Anger is healthy; aggressive behaviour is not. Anger is a potential motivating force for change because it has energy, which can be channelled, unlike depression. Seriously depressed people who begin to get in touch with their anger are arguably at greater risk of suicide because they have the energy to take their own lives.

The aggressive person is usually anxious, afraid, under stress, and may believe being aggressive is the only way to get her needs met. She's likely to have had bad experiences with authority before she gets to you.

Table 14-1 shares some thoughts about handling other people's anger.

Table 14-1	Some Do's and Don'ts for Handling Potential Aggression	
Do	*Don't*
Notice (anticipate): Appearance (without stereotyping). Body language: agitation and covert aggression such as staring, raised eyebrows, silence, icy calm, wagging finger. Your own feelings (especially 'gut' reactions – trust them). The environment including your safety and exit route; give personal space.	Neglect your own safety: If in doubt, get out.
Reduce overall level of arousal first, by: Acknowledging feelings and listening (especially to underlying issues). Giving personal space and offering privacy (but be safe). Ensuring appropriate timing of information, apologising for delays. Giving good-quality information Working in collaboration Improving the environment where possible e.g. using equal height seating	Take the aggression personally or overreact.

Do	Don't
Appear confident and concerned: Breathe. Relax your posture. Take time. Concentrate on listening. Be supportive and reassuring. Avoid her loss of face.	Invade the other's space.
Remember the Core Conditions: Be respectful and courteous, avoid 'pat' responses (be genuine). Use reflecting skills. Avoid argument. Negotiate (where appropriate). Be consistent. Normalise (where appropriate). Ask for help from a colleague. Monitor yourself and think: Accept your own feelings.	Justify or dismiss. Smile inappropriately or be insincere. Argue or try to persuade the other that she's wrong. Fall back on your own old defence mechanisms.
	Feel you have to deal with the situation alone.

Anxiety, panic, and avoidance

Situations that are very scary for some are unexceptional to others. The person experiencing panic and anxiety can experience a sense of abnormality and shame.

There are always reasons why a sense of fear has become attached to certain situations, and the resulting emotions and body sensations are real.

People plagued by anxiety and panic attacks are severely affected by:

- ✔ Disturbed breathing (hyperventilating) and light-headedness
- ✔ Sick feelings
- ✔ A pounding heart and a fear they are having a heart attack
- ✔ Profuse sweating
- ✔ A feeling of impending doom
- ✔ Avoidance of situations which might lead to anxiety

The listening helper can normalise experience and help just by listening. Acceptance, understanding, and reassurance may be enough, perhaps with some information about stress mechanisms, problem-solving, or step-by-step approaches to understanding and dealing with the source of anxiety (only once an attack is over!). However, if a person is experiencing panic attacks and severe anxiety, suggest that she seeks medical advice and specialist referral, to a cognitive-behavioural therapist or the local Mental Health Team, for example. Those who are considered for referral also include people with obsessive-compulsive traits that are interfering with their everyday life. Examples are compulsive checking and rituals, excessive washing of hands or cleaning, and so on.

Low mood and depression

Many people suffer fleeting or longer-lasting low moods. For most people, most of the time, the feelings pass in a day or two. Usually such feelings are brought on by life circumstances and may last longer if circumstances continue. An enduring flatness and emptiness which interferes with daily life may be diagnosed as depression. Depression is not the same as sadness, although a depressed person may also be sad. Anxiety can be misread as depression because it's so debilitating. To feel depressed is extremely bleak and hopeless. Often the feeling is worse at the beginning of the day. Generally a combination of appropriate drugs and counselling is helpful, so referral to a GP is advised. Low mood, including feelings of sadness and low self-esteem, can respond to listening help.

A popular misconception is that asking about suicide brings on the act, but no evidence supports this.

When someone is in a very low state, be sure to:

- Ask questions such as, 'How low do you feel?', 'Have you ever felt like you would rather not be here?', or 'Do you think about not waking up in the morning?' Follow these questions with a direct question about whether she has contemplated taking her own life.

- Ask about the way a person has thought about committing suicide. You will get a better idea of the seriousness of any intent if you do this.

- Check out when she most feels like taking her life.

- Be clear with yourself and the help-seeker about any responsibility you have to take action in the event that there's a suicide risk (know your agency's policy).

- Always check what supports and reasons for living she has.

- Offer The Samaritans' contact details.

People can feel enormous relief if they talk about just how awful they feel without their emotions being brushed off or minimised. You need to be resilient to stay with such feelings (refer to Chapter 3 for ideas about maintaining your resilience).

Post-trauma symptoms

When people go through a traumatic event they may be left with signs of distress. Symptoms of post-traumatic stress disorder (PTSD) include:

- Nightmares and flashbacks (daytime re-experiencing)
- Panic attacks
- Generalised anxiety and/or irritability (often severe); others notice 'personality' changes
- Poor self-esteem
- A sense of loss of future or impending doom
- Social anxiety or social phobia and isolation

Initially most people are helped by their normal support mechanisms and talking over what happened. Sometimes people don't recover well and after a few months, if they experience no improvement, they need to seek specialised help.

Difficulties related to life stages

As we progress through life, we encounter a number of transition points. These life stages are points of potential stress and vulnerability, involving identity re-evaluation. Within each stage listed here are intervening stages including:

- **Early years:** Beginning and changing school; becoming a sibling; adolescence; recognition of sexuality.
- **Young adulthood:** Leaving home; first job; first sexual relationship; first committed relationship; having a child and becoming a family.
- **Mid-life:** Recognition of potentially reaching and passing one's peak; children leaving home.
- **Older age:** Adjustment to older age; retirement; old age and adjustment to mortality; dwindling powers; death of friends and family.

This list is not exhaustive – perhaps you can add some from your own experiences. Individual adjustment is related to the experience of and adjustment to previous changes, social circumstances and supports, general health, and so on. Most people underestimate the significance and effects of transition points in their lives. They may seek help because they are unhappy, unsettled, or stressed without appreciating that these factors may be significant to their state, even when they are apparently happy events.

Mental ill-health

Mental ill-health spans a broad spectrum from mild to moderate depression and anxiety through to more severe disorders such as schizophrenia. It's impossible to do justice to the range here. In general, as a listening helper you won't be working with serious disorders, except when the individual is stabilised and can use befriending support. If you ever have doubts whether a person's behaviour could indicate a serious mental-health problem, seek advice and referral. Many agencies access specialist consultants for advice and support.

In the mild to moderate range you may well support someone with depression, anxiety, stabilised bipolar disorder (formerly known as manic depression), self-harming behaviour, and eating disorders. You need to know if someone is taking medication and what effects this may have – for example feeling 'spaced out' and therefore unable to engage in the helping process properly. Self-harm (including eating disorders) can be worrying to listening helpers, but it's quite commonplace. In such circumstances:

- ✔ Check the extent and frequency of the problem (the person may minimise or conceal the self-harm).
- ✔ Support the help-seeker to find specialist help.
- ✔ If self-harm is not life-threatening, shift focus to underlying or other issues, as the help-seeker wishes.
- ✔ If self-harm is the focus, explore the meaning of the self-harm to the person (which is very individual); how does it help her?

Relationship Problems and Sexual Issues

Typically people approach a listening helper when they can't talk to partner, friends, or family. The reason may be because of embarrassment, shame, fear, or just not knowing how to begin. The conversation with you acts as a rehearsal. You need to feel comfortable about discussing issues or else sensitively refer the person elsewhere. Sexual problems are extremely common in couples, especially with young families. Sex therapy is offered by Relate.(For some specific aspects of sexuality and relationships, refer to Chapters 12 and 13.)

Be alert to any suspicion of bullying, emotional abuse, or domestic violence and be ready to provide support: People minimise or learn to accept abuse. If a child is involved in any way ensure her safety: Being the subject of bullying is serious, as is being a witness to or overhearing domestic abuse/violence. Be aware of the agencies in your area that can offer help and support to couples, families, and children.

With relationship difficulties, whether in a couple, family, friendship, or work relationship, you need to strike a balance between respecting the person's perspective and realising that you're hearing just one side of the story. Be careful not to get drawn into taking sides. Remember that challenging is a Stage 2 skill, so if you believe a story should be challenged ensure you have a sound relationship first.

Working with more than one person, such as with a couple or family group, requires additional skills to manage successfully and is not recommended if you have no specialist training.

If you're supporting an individual who's going through separation or divorce, take particular note of the discussion of transition and loss in the earlier section 'Coping with Transitions'. Separation and divorce can be harder to come to terms with than bereavement because the partners have to continue a relationship if they have children and need to reach a point where they can co-operate as parents.

Any of the issues described in this chapter may have a personal resonance for you, trigger issues of your own, or be presented in ways that cause you distress and anxiety. Make sure you have supports in place and use them. Off-loading to a colleague, supervisor, or manager can help you to leave the feelings behind, as can writing up notes on the session. You can also check out any concerns you're left with so you don't take the burden of sole responsibility.

Part V
Handling Challenges

The 5th Wave   By Rich Tennant

"My hunch, Mr. Pesko, is that you're still making mountains out of mole hills."

In this part . . .

Here I look at different types of helping conversation and how to cope with difficulties. Sometimes – hopefully very rarely – you may have a negative experience, such as being taken advantage of, or someone formally complaining about you. This part can help you to anticipate potential difficulties and either avoid or cope with them.

Chapter 15

Coping with Different Types of Helping Conversations

- -

- -

*I*n the diverse settings where you use counselling skills in a helping conversation, you encounter different experiences of being a listening helper. Roles vary in terms of responsibilities and the focus of the helping conversation, and so demand a slightly different balance of skills. Helping conversations can occur through other means than face-to-face conversations; these conversations feel different and tend to use certain skills more than others. Whatever the setting or medium, you're certain to face the unexpected and challenging from time to time. This chapter explores some of the challenging situations you may encounter.

The Influence of Your Role

Your role, with its primary purpose and expectations, influences the type of listening-helper relationship and conversation you enter into. Some counselling roles involve more support while others involve greater challenge; some are wide-ranging and others more focused.

Using counselling skills as part of your primary role

Whatever your job title, your listening-helper role has a slightly different emphasis in terms of skills and focus, based on:

- ✔ The help-seeker's needs
- ✔ Your own inclinations
- ✔ The mode of communication
- ✔ The expectations of your role

Different role types

Your role with any particular help-seeker can be identified as falling into several types. This list of role types is in approximately progressive order.

- ✔ **Healer:** You support and nurture the help-seeker.
- ✔ **Parent:** Rather like the healer, nurture will be involved, but also protection and authority.
- ✔ **Friend:** The help-seeker is supported and encouraged.
- ✔ **Priest:** The help-seeker reflects on the meaning of his life.
- ✔ **Detective:** You work with the help-seeker to understand and explain what is going on for him by making connections.
- ✔ **Teacher:** The help-seeker is looking for support, encouragement, and guidance to learn new patterns of behaviour and skills.
- ✔ **Mentor:** The help-seeker is assisted to appraise, focus, and work to specific goals.

Each role type tends to draw more upon some skills than others. However, all have a strong foundation in the skills of Stage One and especially the Core Conditions (refer to Chapters 8 and 9). The Healer, Parent, Friend, and Priest role types tend to use Stage One relationship-building skills predominantly; the Detective moves into Stage Two (understanding skills); and the Teacher and Mentor focus more on Stage Three problem-solving and action skills.

The names I use for the role types suggest authority and power. The help-seeker may well see you in this light. As a listening-helper you want to work to minimise power differentials and to encourage the help-seeker towards autonomy and empowerment. (Refer to Chapters 5 and 6 for more on this.)

The help-seeker's needs

Your adoption of any of these types need to be the result of mutually agreed expectations. By mutually agreed I don't mean that you ask the speaker, 'Would you like me to be a detective (or parent, or . . .)?', but that you get a sense of what kind of help the speaker is looking for from the conversation and his emotional state. It may only be after the end of a session that you recognise what role you were taking with a particular help-seeker: It's a combination of your attunement to the individual's needs and what you are comfortable with. If a help-seeker is in great distress he won't be able to engage in detective work, making decisions, or taking action. Conversely, a person who isn't distressed and who wants to work out what to do will be very frustrated if you insist on digging for emotional responses. However, you need to remember that Stage One skills continue throughout because they support a positive collaborative relationship.

Your own inclinations

Each of the listening-helper types previously mentioned involves a different kind of conversation. The types are not mutually exclusive (and not exhaustive either) and a helping relationship will usually touch on more than one. You may find yourself more comfortable with one type than another. For your personal and professional development, notice which types you favour over others and extend your capacity to adopt others so that you can be more responsive to the individual help-seeker.

Expectation of your role

In some situations the most appropriate helping conversation is a supportive one – a befriending-type role is one example. In settings where the work is with young or vulnerable people, the emphasis may again be mostly more supportive and parental – because of the nature of your responsibility the listening-helper role may need to be secondary to a more authoritative position. In this instance you need to be aware of the influence of your authority (refer to Chapter 13 for more on the role of power in the helping relationship). In other environments, for example as mentor to a colleague, especially when a trusting relationship is established and the help-seeker is emotionally stable, a more robust working alliance could be more effective and desirable – a combination of teacher and mentor will use more challenging skills for an action focus. This kind of conversation works best if the agreed contract is for you to be challenging and focused.

If your role and the help-seeker's expectations don't sit happily together, and this cannot be resolved through review and discussion, he's best referred elsewhere. You can find more discussion about referral in Chapter 11.

Using counselling skills with friends and family

Perhaps you would like to develop your counselling skills but don't have a specific role that gives you the opportunity to use what is covered in this book. You may want to practise on family and friends – your relationships may even improve as a result. You have two ways of practising – one where you introduce your developing skills into everyday conversations at home and work, without advertising the fact, and another way where you ask friends or family to act as guinea pigs for a deliberate helping conversation. The second option gives you the opportunity to get some feedback. On the whole any kind of practising is benign and will help your relationships, but you need to be aware of some potential difficulties and side-effects.

Here are some cautionary notes:

- ✔ If your family and friends aren't reading this book they won't understand the changes you're making in how you approach everyday conversations.

- ✔ They may get fed up, and accuse you of playing counsellor and not being yourself.

- ✔ Your developing awareness may make you dissatisfied with the way some of your relationships work.

- ✔ Active listening skills are more powerful than you may realise, leading you to open up things you don't yet feel competent enough to deal with or don't really want to know.

- ✔ Suspending all your preconceptions about those you are close to is impossible, so you cannot be adequately impartial with friends and family. They will also find it hard to be impartial with you, so inviting feedback poses some risks to your feelings.

- ✔ Stage Two challenging skills can be misunderstood as an attack because of family preconceptions about you in your usual role.

Take care of yourself and find someone you trust to talk over issues with.

Despite the dangers I've just warned you about, all the active listening skills of Stage One can be very helpful and sometimes Stage Three skills as well.

Working through Different Mediums

Working with a help-seeker when you're unable to see each other poses some challenges but also some opportunities, compared with face-to-face conversations. Telephone help-lines have been in existence for some time now and e-mail and chat-room support is becoming more common.

An interesting phenomenon of communication that isn't face –to face is the freedom many people feel to speak without restraint. When that communication is also anonymous or conceals the individual's identity the barriers are even fewer.

My experience of working on a telephone-counselling help-line (which offered 20-minute sessions) is that most callers go far deeper into their issues, and more quickly, than would happen in a face-to-face session. I believe this is because:

✔ The caller has the ability to conceal his identity by being anonymous or using a pseudonym.

✔ He is free to end the call at any time.

✔ The sense of intimacy is greater. The telephone conversation suggests a very close and intimate space. Someone coming into the room (at either end of the conversation) breaks the sense of intimacy. Callers are very sensitive to background noises at the listening-helper's end.

✔ The lack of visual contact means the listener's reactions are a little less likely to be interpreted as judging.

✔ Without visual cues the listening-helper concentrates more closely on the non-visual cues, imparting an intensity of attention to the caller.

Similar comments apply to other forms of communication as to the telephone, although written communication has some significant differences. Even without visual cues much is communicated through tone of voice, silences, speed of speech, and so on, and a telephone conversation is interactive. In written communication, with the exception of instant messaging and texting, the communication is by alternate long monologues. Instant messaging tends to use abbreviations. These constraints can, as with the telephone, lead to greater disclosure by the writer, but you also have a greater risk of misunderstanding.

The set of skills you use if you work in other ways rather than face –to face isn't really different, but the configuration or application needs to be adapted to the particular situation. The nature of the contract that is made with the help-seeker needs to be framed slightly differently.

A contracting script for telephone work

As a listening helper, you may want to get some practice in counselling skills by volunteering for a help-line.

Here is an example of a scripted introduction for use in telephone work. You need to adapt it to your own situation. Keeping a clock in view is helpful. Calls that last a long time (more than 30–50 minutes) can be draining for both parties and become counterproductive.

'Hello, you're through to xxxx help-line. My name is xxxx (you may wish to use a pseudonym). Would you like to tell me *your* name?' Some people won't want to be identified in any way, in which case reassure them that's fine – but a name makes the call more personal.

'Before we start talking I just need to tell you that we have (up to) xx minutes – I'll keep an eye on the time and let you know when we're coming towards the end – and what we talk about is confidential.' (Your organisation may want you to make a statement about limits to confidentiality, but as the caller can remain anonymous, you may not have any meaningful information that you could pass on about, say, child abuse.)

Contracting

Careful contracting is important in all counselling skills work (refer to Chapter 8). When working on the telephone it's useful to have a script to remind and guide you through the essentials in a succinct statement (see the sidebar 'A contracting script for telephone work' for an example). You need to point out as soon as possible if the call has a limited duration so that the caller can pace himself. Offering to remind him a few minutes before the end is helpful.

If you're offering a text-based service you need to be clear about:

- How long you spend in communication. If this is e-mail, that means the length of time between you receiving an e-mail and then replying to it.

- When you are available for communication (for example, is it a regular time each week?)

- What you do if you receive communications in between arranged times.

- What action (if any) you take if you don't hear from the help-seeker as arranged (for example, with suicide risk or other safety issue).

These issues can be formalised in a written contract, or agreed, then confirmed in writing.

A different kind of situation that can crop up is if you take a phone call from a colleague or a member of your staff. In this situation you need to clarify your role and the expectations of the person who is calling to speak to you, as well as the time you have available for the conversation.

Adapting your skills

You may find that the intimacy leads to using the challenging skills of Stage Two more readily, which is both a potential benefit and a danger (refer to Chapter 10 for more information about Stage Two skills). You need to pay far more attention to the aural cues in telephone work, such as breathing, silences, pace, and tone, to gauge the caller's reactions. When writing you need to anticipate the possible reactions of the help-seeker to any written challenge and even mention your anticipations before or immediately after the section of text where the challenge lies.

Using text alone creates great scope for misunderstandings. People using writing in electronic formats are developing ways of communicating emotions and background thoughts to minimise misunderstandings, such as using punctuation marks and emoticons to indicate smiley or sad faces (for example, :-) :-(), or putting emotions in square brackets, such as [while I wrote that, I imagined how you might be feeling and I felt sad]. In a face-to-face situation your face and body language can be read by the help-seeker and you can more easily pick up on his responses to you. So when communication isn't face to face it's helpful to reveal your emotional reactions more openly. If you work for an organisation which offers text-based help, ask for specialised training.

If you work on a telephone –help-line you may receive calls from someone who is deaf via the operator or, if you have one, via a text telephone. Where the operator is involved, the operator receives text from the help-seeker, he then reads it to you, and you tell the operator what to write back. This kind of conversation is a rather disjointed experience and it may help to make notes as you go. You need to work harder at conveying empathy and understanding through the words you choose and the whole process may take longer.

Unplanned, Unexpected, and Difficult Conversations

The best way to manage the unexpected is to think about how you'd cope with potential situations. If you have been in your primary role for a while you should have some ideas about likely scenarios. But, however much you think ahead and prepare, you're bound to have experiences that take you unawares on occasion. Don't be afraid to take your time in responding – find ways of giving yourself breathing and thinking space. For example:

✔ Be honest with the help-seeker and tell him that you've been taken unawares or that now is not a good time for you to discuss the issue.

✔ Rather than commit yourself to action that you aren't sure about or feel rushed into, say something like, 'I need a little time to think this through to make sure that I'm giving you the right advice and correct information,' or 'I need to consult a colleague on this.'

Here are four other challenging areas:

✔ Challenges to privacy and confidentiality when working from home

✔ Dealing with abusive calls

✔ Breaking bad news

✔ Working with disclosures

The following sections can help you deal with each type of challenge.

Challenges to privacy and confidentiality

Some organisations use volunteers and staff who work from their own homes. This arrangement can be convenient but also causes some difficulties. Telephone and computer-based communications need to be private and confidential, which requires some forethought. If your house telephone is in your hall or living room you may find it hard to control background noise and provide a sense of confidentiality and quiet concentration. Preferably, arrange a quiet corner with any materials you need at hand (writing materials, information, and so on) and an extension phone. It's better for your personal and family life to have a separation of your work from home life.

Similarly, if calls and other communications are dealt with in a restricted time frame, it's easier to manage and to make arrangements for uninterrupted conversations that don't take you unawares and with the 'wrong head' on. Identify a specific period of time when you can take or return calls. Modern technology allows you to screen calls, have different ring tones for family and friends, and record outgoing and incoming messages. All these enable you to decide whether to answer immediately or within your identified time slot.

The same considerations apply to computer-based communication from home, but to ensure confidentiality you must password-protect your documents and use dedicated messaging accounts separate from your private e-mail.

Dealing with abusive calls

Occasionally the intimacy of a telephone call is abused by a caller (rarely in my experience, but that may depend on the particular type of help-line) who gains satisfaction from being verbally abusive or trying to shock (for example, telephone masturbators). Whatever the policies of your organisation, you shouldn't have to listen to abusive calls. If no policy exists, you can discuss ways of handling such things and create a policy. For example:

✔ You can end the phone call, with or without warning from you.

✔ You can put down the receiver without disconnecting the caller.

Some calls seem as if they're abusive, or developing that way, when in fact the caller is struggling with an aspect of his sexual identity or desires, or he may suffer from a disorder, such as Tourette's syndrome where a person makes involuntary noises, stutterings, and movements, sometimes including swear words and profanities. Although you may find this personally difficult, imagine how hard it is for someone in this situation to find help. Your organisation can help you to find ways of working with such issues, but you could reflect on what worries you about such calls.

Breaking bad news

I hear many complaints about how people have been given bad news, such as their illness diagnosis or about the death of a loved one. Three things in particular can have an impact on how the individual feels when given bad news:

✔ Initially the hearer of bad news goes into shock, which prevents him really 'hearing' what he's being told. Afterwards he may believe information has been withheld or not been given in a straightforward way.

✔ Another reaction to loss is to feel angry and maybe even out of control. Being angry with someone who has died because he died and left his friends and relations behind is considered unacceptable; being angry with God or fate is also difficult for many people. So, blame and anger are often directed at the bringer of the bad news or those who have been responsible for, or involved in, events surrounding the bad news.

✔ Sometimes the bearer of bad news is inept at communicating it. He may be embarrassed and awkward, uncomfortable with grief reactions in others, may have his own losses triggered by that of others, and be more tied up with his own emotions. He has no energy left to pay attention to the process being experienced by the recipient of the news.

Chapter 14 describes the processes involved in transition, loss, and grief as well as dealing with anger and other distress reactions, which apply to the first two points above. The final point highlights the need to develop your personal awareness, as described in Chapter 2. Chapter 7, which looks at barriers to listening and our defences, is also pertinent.

You need to be sufficiently comfortable with yourself to be able to pay attention to the other person's reactions as you deliver bad news. Pacing is very important and, if possible, give the recipient of the news the opportunity to come back to you to ask further questions at a later date. Sometimes a decision needs to be made quickly, such as urgent treatment decisions after a diagnosis. However, in these situations a relatively small amount of time spent in silence (most people overestimate how long silences last) or giving space to absorb and question the information and implications pays dividends.

Working with disclosures

At times, people will make disclosures that you'll find challenging. Often these are 'door-knob' revelations – in other words, made when a session is about to end. Inexperienced listening helpers may panic, thinking they have to discuss the disclosure fully then and there. If there's a suggestion of serious risk you may need to prolong the session, but often the disclosure has, consciously or unconsciously, been made late in the session for a reason. The help-seeker may want to gauge your reaction before committing himself further; it may have taken most of the session to get up the courage to disclose, and further exploration may feel too risky.

Rather than extend the session, acknowledge that the disclosure is important and was difficult to reveal, and commit to discussing the issue at the next meeting if the help-seeker wants to. You can ask if he'd like you to bring up the disclosure next time, in case he finds it hard to mention.

Chapter 16

Dealing with Difficulties

● ●

In This Chapter

▶ Managing demands on your time and abilities

▶ Defining the boundaries of your role

▶ Preventing harm to the help-seeker

▶ Dealing with complaints

● ●

*I*f you take reasonable care and ensure that you understand any guidelines offered by your organisation, you can probably avoid many potential difficulties. However, you can't realistically avoid all risk and mistakes. In this chapter, I cover some potential challenges, and show how you can manage them to bring about the best outcome.

If you encounter one of the challenges described in this chapter, you may want also to refer to Chapters 4, 8, 11, and 15, which cover the topics of risks, ethics, good practices, contracts, and referrals.

You're Being Taken Advantage Of

You can find yourself being taken advantage of in several ways, and they're not necessarily the help-seeker's fault. The role and qualities of a listening helper and the helping relationship are seductive for someone who is unused to being cared for. Naturally, she might want more support, and listening helpers can easily fall into the following traps in their desire to help:

✔ Wanting to rescue people

✔ Finding saying 'No' hard

✔ Doing things for the help-seeker instead of enabling her

✔ Being too nice

✔ Wanting to be liked

✔ Wanting to avoid upsetting a help-seeker

✔ Lacking assertiveness skills

Being assertive

Whenever you think you're being taken advantage of, you need to practise assertiveness skills. In this particular context a key aspect of assertiveness is being very clear in defining your role and what you can offer so that you can make unambiguous statements about these things. Writing down and rehearsing typical statements (in front of a mirror, into an audio-recorder, to a colleague) can help.

Note: You need more than just assertiveness skills to become assertive, however. In addition to the relevant skills discussed throughout this book, you also need to have self-awareness – so think about what prevents you from being assertive and refer to Chapters 2 and 3 for some ideas about how to develop your confidence to be assertive.

In addition, some help-seekers, recognising that you're a caring person, assume that you can be manipulated.

Certain professional trainings exacerbate some traits. For example, nurses are trained to assess and diagnose and are in situations where they have to do things for their patients or tell them what to do, which is very different from the listening role, even though nursing can include being emotionally supportive. Work with vulnerable groups can involve similar ways of dealing with people because the worker has a duty to protect, which can become over-protection.

You're Being Messed About

Perhaps you're in a position where you can offer flexibility, such as when you schedule appointments. While responding to individual needs is good, sometimes you may find yourself bending over backwards to accommodate someone who then, for example, doesn't turn up for the arranged session. Fortunately this manipulation doesn't apply to the majority of help-seekers.

If you recognise this pattern, be prepared and absolutely clear about what you can offer (without making special arrangements) and stick to it. Keep to a small set of options and say that you're not able to offer anything outside these. You aren't obliged to give a reason, and don't show your diary – once you go into explanations you potentially invite manipulation.

If you're the kind of person who tends to get messed about (not uncommon in listening helpers) perhaps you need to do some self-development work to understand what happens for you in these situations, and acquire assertiveness skills (see the sidebar 'Being Assertive').

Recognising that people may have reasons for messing you about is also important:

- ✔ People in distress are often in a state of chaos.

- ✔ Seeking help takes a great deal of courage and a help-seeker can run scared at the last minute.

You're Asked to Give More than You Can Give

Sometimes listening helpers are drawn into doing more for the people they help than is expected or appropriate in their role. Sometimes you deal with heart-breaking situations where you can see the extent of the help that a person needs but that it falls outside your remit. Or perhaps the help-seeker is panicking, infecting you with her panic.

You have a moral dilemma here. In general, you don't want to step outside your role limitations. Being calm and exploring the reality of the situation helps to contain the help-seeker's feelings and reduce the panic.

Here are a few reasons to stick within the boundaries of your role as a listening helper:

- ✔ You may set up expectations that you cannot fulfil.

- ✔ You may put the help-seeker into a position where she feels obliged to you which isn't good for the helping relationship or the individual's self-esteem.

- ✔ If the additional help means meeting outside the normal helping environment you may cross other boundaries such as those of privacy and confidentiality.

- ✔ You may become resentful or burned out.

- ✔ Your organisation may have rules about such situations.

However, in certain circumstances – in a crisis, for example – a person may need more frequent support than normal for a limited period and crossing a boundary may be justified. Always think carefully about your aims and rationale and consult with a colleague. At all times you need to consider what's really in the best interest of the help-seeker and what supports the help-seeker to maintain as much autonomy as possible. If you feel uncomfortable discussing the situation with a colleague, then you have a fair indicator that the action may be unwise.

I supervised someone whose client was in desperate financial straits, having been left with huge debts by her partner. The client mentioned that she didn't know how she was going to scrape together enough money to buy school clothes for the children. My supervisee had some appropriate outgrown clothes from her own slightly older children and wished she could give them to her client, but she recognised that this wouldn't be helpful to their relationship. In the end she decided to put a notice in the reception area offering them. Because the charity she worked for had other items available free and for sale this didn't seem unusual, and she was able to point the notice out to her client.

You're Being Too Nice

Many listening helpers are hampered by their fear of not being liked or of hurting the people they help. Although I don't advocate you become hard or unfeeling and insensitive, you do need to think about the purpose of the helping relationship and what it's aiming to achieve. Being too nice can get in the way of the help-seeker moving on and becoming more self-sufficient, because you don't challenge when challenge is needed. This tendency has more to do with your own fears than with the help-seeker.

When I was a trainee social worker, I did a short placement in a hospital social work department. At the end of the placement one of my colleagues complained that I had got more gifts from patients in six weeks than she had had in a year. I realised that the reason for this was, unlike in my other placements, I was being too nice. I found the vulnerability of ill people prevented me from being honest and genuine and brought out a rescuing tendency which I didn't experience in other situations. If I had remained in that placement I might have become burned out, giving more than I could sustain. The realisation came through a combination of personal reflection and discussion in supervision (refer to Chapters 2 and 7, which focus on developing your self-understanding, and Chapter 3 for more on support, supervision, and taking care of yourself).

You're Making Friends with Your 'Client'

You may encounter occasions when you feel the help-seeker would like to turn the helping relationship into a friendship. She may even be treating your relationship as if it were a friendship, talking about everyday things that aren't particularly relevant to the issues that have brought her for help or being very interested in your life ('Did you have a nice weekend?' 'Where did you go on holiday?' 'Where do your children go to school?' and so on).

A certain amount of 'chat' is usual: You'll probably recognise when it's more than usual, however. With some people, avoiding such conversations or deflecting them after a minimal answer is enough. With other people you may need to confront the situation, perhaps saying something like:

- ✔ 'We are here to focus on you, rather than me.'
- ✔ 'You seem to want to know more about me.'
- ✔ 'I get the feeling that you would like this to be a friendship, but if I was your friend I wouldn't be able to carry on offering you this helping relationship.'

Obviously you need to deliver these statements carefully so that they don't seem abrupt and rejecting. You may also need to have a continued conversation which explores and explains more and which may lead to recognising that the help-seeker is avoiding something. Perhaps she's worried about being judged by you. You can tease out the reasons using your listening skills.

You may feel guilty about not offering friendship, especially if you know this person lacks friends, but the aim of the work you do with her could be to support her in increasing her confidence to make social connections. This will increase her self-esteem and be more empowering. If you did change the relationship out of misplaced responsibility or guilt, then the friendship could never work, partly because of the power difference between you (the help-seeker will see you as an authority figure). The helping relationship would also prove more difficult. You need to consider all such dual relationships very carefully, as ethical guidelines for counsellors usually point out.

On the other hand, you may be the one who wants to be friends with your client. Sometimes the motivation for changing the nature of the relationship may come from you – if you met this person in other circumstances you could imagine being friends. This is one of the downsides of being a listening helper. Becoming friends with someone who seeks your help (although time can play a part in this) isn't advisable for the following reasons:

- ✔ The helping relationship is very one-way – you know quite a lot about the help-seeker, but only in certain dimensions, and she knows little about you. You don't know each other as well as you both may think, which isn't a good basis for starting a friendship.

- ✔ The helping relationship has a power differential which isn't easily left behind when moving into a different type of relationship.

- ✔ Once the relationship has been changed you cannot easily change it back, so the help-seeker loses the opportunity to approach you again should she need to seek listening help.

In general, turning the helping relationship into a friendship isn't a good idea. Becoming friends with a client, assuming the feeling is mutual, isn't banned but you need to discuss any change in the nature of the relationship with a colleague or supervisor to think through the implications. A cooling-off period and a frank discussion with the ex-help-seeker is advisable so that you can help her to understand the possible consequences. Such boundary crossings have led to abuse of help-seekers and while I'm not suggesting that you're likely to become an abuser by crossing the boundary, you need to be cautious and responsible. You can find out more about becoming friends with a client in the British Association for Counselling and Psychotherapy (BACP) Ethical Framework (available online at www.bacp.co.uk/ethical_framework).

Someone Is Being Harmed

When a person who's sought help from you comes to harm, it's very distressing. Examples I have encountered range from individuals self-harming – for example, cutting themselves or taking an overdose, domestic violence, child abuse, through to people successfully committing suicide, being murdered by their partner, or dying through illness or accident. These kinds of situations, which aren't everyday occurrences but are more common than you may expect, can cause you stress, worry, feelings of guilt, and anxiety, which is why being supported in your work and outside is important (refer to Chapter 3 in particular).

You also need to consider the harm that happens through the help itself – for example, a help-seeker being taken advantage of by her helper (hopefully not by you, but maybe by a colleague or other professional). If this is confided to you as a listening helper you need to think through the ethical issues around such disclosure. (Refer to Chapter 4 for an ethical decision-making model.)

Sometimes the helper makes a mistake that causes harm – for example, inadvertently or carelessly revealing a help-seeker's identity inappropriately. You may also make minor mistakes, which don't necessarily cause harm, such as muddling appointment times. If you recognise you've made a mistake, you're better off to acknowledge it and apologise, which is usually all the help-seeker wants and which normally defuses the situation. With more serious mistakes you may find that your organisation or insurers prefer you not to admit liability. If you're fortunate enough to have good supervision (preferably non-managerial), talk over any mistakes you think you've made with your supervisor and discuss what, if any, action you need to take.

You're the Subject of a Complaint

Being the subject of a complaint is a very stressful event, as you can probably imagine. If you're a manager responsible for handling the complaint process, pay attention to the support needs of each person involved, including yourself. Check now what policies, procedures, and supports are in place to help you and the complainant, as well as the person complained about, through the process. Ensuring you follow procedures correctly can reduce potential stress. If you're the person who is being complained about, make sure that you ask what support will be made available to you and also put personal supports together.

Relaying a complaint

I've been a supervisor to several people, and known others, who've been the subject of complaints. In every instance, when the individual was told a complaint had been made, he or she immediately experienced shock, feelings of sickness, panic, and disbelief, usually followed by intense consideration of all his or her actions and records. If you're informing someone that a complaint has been made against her, be sure to:

✔ Speak personally to the individual.

✔ Avoid leaving a message, especially at the end of the working day or week when the person will worry until she can speak to you.

✔ Understand that the person is probably in a state of shock and so may not be able to take in what she is told immediately.

✔ Give clear information about the nature of the complaint.

✔ Understand that the individual will probably not be able to answer the complaint during this first conversation.

✔ Give time for the individual to take in the information.

✔ Follow up with clear written information about the complaint.

✔ Ensure that the individual understands and has a copy of the procedure and any requirements, for example to produce records.

✔ Ensure the individual understands any rights she has, for example to legal advice via professional indemnity insurance.

✔ Check what support the individual has, if possible offering a specified support person who is not involved as an investigator of the complaint.

Complaints procedures usually begin with an informal stage where the complainant discusses her concern with a designated person within an organisation. Most often complaints are made reluctantly with the complainant not wanting to get anyone into trouble. What she does want is to be heard and for her dissatisfaction to be understood and acknowledged. An apology is often the only outcome that is looked for. Obviously the allegation must be investigated, and this needs to happen quickly with a clear understanding of what the complaint is about. Organisations need to tread a tricky line between taking a complaint seriously and launching too rapidly into a full-blown formal procedure. Professional bodies may be able to offer advice when such situations occur.

The next stage, if the informal process hasn't enabled a satisfactory outcome for the complainant, is a formal complaint, which is usually asked for in writing. Following the submission of the complaint a formal investigation takes place, where evidence (such as records/notes, and information from others, such as a supervisor) might be requested. The investigation of the complaint normally culminates in a meeting where the complainant, perhaps accompanied by a supportive person of her choice, attends and discusses the issues with a panel appointed to investigate. The subject of the complaint has an opportunity to respond to allegations and may also be able to have a supportive person present. Finally the panel will decide what the outcome should be.

As you can see, this process is reminiscent of a court-room proceeding. Although such procedures are normally intended to be less intimidating than a court-room, I'm sure that both parties do feel intimidated and benefit from support while going through the process.

Part VI
The Part of Tens

The 5th Wave   By Rich Tennant

"I'm tired of letting everyone pull my strings."

In this part . . .

Every *For Dummies* book has a nifty collection of mini chapters that provide instant inspiration and information. In this part you get a ready-reference to individual listening skills and some ideas of how to take your development further.

Chapter 17

Ten or So Key Counselling Skills

*C*ounselling skills often overlap and are sometimes difficult to distinguish clearly. However, certain skills are key to your counselling success. You need to use the skills described in this chapter within a helping relationship of trust, and they work together. Practise each skill to become more economical and proficient at it but remember, if you use the skills in a clinical way, without empathy and respect, you're not likely to be trusted and confided in.

Confronting

Confronting means drawing attention to discrepancies, gaps, or inconsistencies, and is another challenging skill. Be sure to base confronting in a sound, trusting relationship for best effect.

The purpose of confronting is to complete the story or picture, by helping the speaker, in a supportive way, recognise aspects that may by unrealised or denied and which need to be understood as part of the problem or solution. Because confronting may be uncomfortable, a trusting relationship needs to be in place, and timing and careful phrasing are important to prevent confronting being viewed as an attack.

You can find more about confronting in Chapter 10.

Elaboration

Elaboration is the use of skills, such as open questions, reflection, summarising, and paraphrasing, that encourage greater detail and depth of storytelling by the speaker. A key aspect of the helping relationship is to enable the person to tell his story. If the helping encounter is going to be fruitful then the story needs to be complete or, in other words, elaborated. Only then can the help-seeker and helper, by gaining a fuller understanding, work towards a resolution or solution.

Most speakers tell stories that have gaps. Often aspects of their own reactions and feelings (and perhaps those of others) are described superficially or missed altogether. While being clever and showing that you've filled in those gaps with your imagination is tempting, you can be far more helpful to the speaker by probing for the missing information, which just as powerfully shows your keenness to understand.

You can find more information about the skills involved in elaboration in Chapter 9.

Empathy

Empathy is a foundational part of the helping relationship. *Empathy* means conveying (through non-verbal and verbal responses) acceptance and understanding of what being in the other person's predicament is like. By showing empathy, you enable the other to feel understood and able to speak increasingly openly. Empathy also models acceptance.

Various levels of empathic responding are appropriate at different times. Deeper levels of empathy which uncover and identify hidden feelings lead to greater self-understanding for the speaker and deepen the helping relationship, but are also risky and only to be used at an appropriate time.

You can find information about empathy in several chapters because of its importance. See especially Chapters 5, 6, 8, and 9.

Immediacy

Immediacy is talking about what is going on in the room *in the present moment*, related to the listener's experience. In other words, it's a comment on, or description of, what is happening between speaker and listener or within the listener. Immediacy is an expression of congruence, one of the core conditions. Immediacy can include reactions in the listener to the speaker's story or to the demeanour of the speaker.

Immediacy is a more challenging skill, both for the listening helper and for the help-seeker because self-disclosing in this way can feel risky for you, and the help-seeker may hear something from you that's hard for him to digest.

Immediacy can clarify and deepen understanding of the speaker's experience, model being in touch with feelings, and convey a commitment to honesty. Turn to Chapter 10 for more about immediacy.

Non-Verbal Encouragement

Non-verbal communication, such as mirroring, nodding, facial expression, attentiveness, and so on, encourages the speaker to continue, by showing your attention and interest.

Non-verbal encouragement conveys acceptance and willingness to hear without judgement. An example is *mirroring*, a subtle copying (often unconscious) of the speaker's body posture, which helps create rapport and demonstrates empathy.

You can employ non-verbal encouragement to keep the story moving, showing you're tracking the meaning of the speaker, and conveying empathy. You can find information about non-verbal communication in Chapters 8 and 9.

Open Questioning

Questioning can put a help-seeker into a dependent and subordinate role, and can lead to the listening helper taking more responsibility than is helpful – so use with care! When you do need to ask questions, use open questions.

Open questioning means asking questions that encourage elaboration. Such questions tend to begin with how, when, what, where, who. Avoid questions beginning with 'why?' because they tend to sound accusative and demanding.

You can ask open questions to fill out the story to gain a more complete understanding for both speaker and listener. Questions also demonstrate to the speaker that the listener is attempting to make sense of the help-seeker's circumstances. The type of questions vary according to when they come up during the person's story and where you are in the helping relationship. I consider questioning in Chapter 9.

Paraphrasing

Paraphrasing is the art of taking a small piece of conversation and reflecting it back to the speaker using different words than he used. Paraphrasing is a skill that enables the help-seeker to elaborate on his story.

The purposes of paraphrasing are:

- ✔ **Tracking:** Showing the speaker you're following what he's saying and trying to understand (provided you add a tentative, questioning tone to your voice).
- ✔ **Clarifying:** Checking out through repeating back what the speaker has said and inviting clarification.
- ✔ **Opening exploration:** By using additional feeling words.
- ✔ **Closing exploration:** By summarising the feelings into generalised words.

I discuss paraphrasing in Chapter 9.

Problem-solving

After you identify a specific issue, you may want to use problem-solving skills to assist the help-seeker to work towards a resolution. *Problem-solving* is a set of skills and techniques that support the approach to resolving specific issues. These skills include focusing, prioritising, identifying pros and cons, and planning towards problem resolution using helpful techniques. Problem-solving involves a thorough understanding of what the real problem is and appropriate timing, if it's going to be effective. Problem-solving assists the speaker to move towards realistic, planned action.

I introduce techniques and skills associated with problem-solving in Chapter 11.

Reflecting

Reflecting is similar to paraphrasing, but here key words or phrases are repeated back to the speaker (usually in the speaker's own words or idiom), particularly emotion-laden words. Reflecting can also include observations on the tone and demeanour of the speaker, insofar as these indicate the speaker's feelings.

Reflecting is another key skill to assist in elaboration but also to demonstrate empathy and deepen exploration of feelings.

The purpose of reflecting is to give weight and recognition to the emotions. Emotions are important because they're key to understanding for both speaker and listener. I cover reflecting in Chapter 9.

Respect

Respect is not strictly speaking a skill, but is crucial. Respect is an *attitude* of acceptance that is conveyed through your use of other skills such as attending and listening carefully. You convey respect through non-verbal encouragement, paraphrasing, reflecting, and summarising, and by demonstrating empathy and genuineness.

Summarising

An under-used and underestimated skill in most beginning listening helpers, summarising provides a point for demonstrating that you have been listening and for both help-seeker and helper to reflect on what has been said. *Summarising* means summing up key points, especially emotional issues.

Short summaries show the speaker you are keeping on track and checking your understanding. They give the speaker time to think over what they have said and invite elaboration. Longer summaries help to locate a focus.

Summaries slow the conversation and give speaker and listener a chance to reflect on what is being said. Summaries are preferable to questioning – if in doubt, summarise. I discuss summarising in Chapter 9.

Chapter 18

Ten Resources for Improving Your Counselling Skills

*T*his chapter contains a collection of diverse resources to discover more about counselling skills. Many of these resources are most easily available via the Internet. If you don't have easy access to the Internet at home or work, then your local library can assist you.

If you want to pursue any training in counselling skills, most institutions nowadays expect you to use online information and word processing. You need to consider gaining some basic familiarity with the computer and the Internet, perhaps through your local college where good introductory courses are usually available.

Professional Bodies

Professional bodies are aimed at counsellors, psychotherapists, and the public. Their purpose is to promote counselling and psychotherapy and to provide protection for the public, through accreditation schemes, codes of ethics and practice, complaints procedures, and so on. These bodies are good sources of information about developing a career in the field of counselling. They also contain useful information for people who are not counsellors, including lists of therapists who are members and accredited members.

Professional bodies include:

- ✔ **UK Council for Psychotherapy (UKCP),** 2nd Floor Edward House, 2 Wakley Street, London, EC1V 7LT. Tel: 020 7014 9955. E-mail: info@ psychotherapy.org.uk. Web site: www.psychotherapy.org.uk.

- ✔ **British Association for Counselling and Psychotherapy (BACP),** BACP House, 15 St John's Business Park, Lutterworth, Leicestershire, LE17 4HB. Tel: 0870 443 5252 (General Enquiries). E-mail: bacp@bacp.co.uk. Web site: www.bacp.co.uk.

- ✔ **The Counselling Directory.** This is an online database of counsellors. The Counselling Directory has a code of ethics and lists counsellors who are willing to offer low-cost counselling. Web site: www.counselling-directory.org.uk.

UKCP and BACP are the two foremost and respected bodies for counselling and psychotherapy in the UK and both have rigorous accreditation schemes.

National Organisations with Volunteering Opportunities

Many national organisations offer opportunities for voluntary work with clients of the organisation, in your local area as well as overseas. The following list describes a few organisations that are often chosen by people who are considering a career in counselling or psychotherapy because they offer competent counselling skills training and/or good support and the chance to practise your active listening skills. They all have very helpful Web sites.

- ✔ **Cruse:** Like MIND, Cruse offers interesting volunteering opportunities across the UK, with training and support, and including a helpline in Richmond, Surrey. They support people who are bereaved, including children. They also provide information online about bereavement, trauma, and crisis at www.crusebereavementcare.org.uk. You can find them listed in your local telephone directory, as well.

- ✔ **MIND (National Association for Mental Health):** Apart from being a well-supported volunteering opportunity (offering training and supervision), MIND also offers excellent resources to inform you about mental health issues. Mental illness is a very wide spectrum affecting a substantial proportion of the population, not just the extremes of media portrayals that hit the headlines. See MIND's Web site for information, including leaflets about mental health, www.mind.org.uk or find them listed in your local telephone directory.

✔ **Relate:** Relate has a long-established reputation as a good training provider for people wanting to work with couple relationships. They have a new training centre at Doncaster College, and all courses are certificated. Relate Centres around the country may be able to offer training placements to complete the necessary client work that forms part of the training. Contact www.relate.org.uk or your local Relate Centre via the local phone directory.

✔ **Samaritans:** Samaritans offers a 24/7 service in all areas of the UK, mainly by telephone, to people in distress (not all suicidal, although that is what Samaritans is known for). The organisation offers good training and support and many centres offer face-to-face services also. Visit www.samaritans.org.uk or look in your local phone directory.

Other Volunteering Opportunities

You can find many sources for voluntary work where you can use your listening-helper skills. Check your local telephone directory for a Voluntary Action centre. The Yellow Pages directory has sections on Counselling and Advice, Youth and Community Work, and Social Service and Welfare Organisations. These organisations include advice for people suffering from alcohol abuse, drug dependency, sexual abuse, bereavement (in addition to Cruse, discussed in preceding section), and includes telephone helplines such as Childline and Parentline. Your local hospital and hospice welcome volunteers. Your religious centre may point you in the direction of faith-based community services. Several Web sites can locate volunteering opportunities for you, one example being www.do-it.org.uk, which locates by type of activity and by proximity, using your postcode.

Books and Journals

Here are some suggestions for where you can find relevant and useful hard-copy reading material:

✔ Relate recommends titles suitable for relationship issues (see www.relate.org.uk).

✔ You can download the UKCP's journal, *The Psychotherapist*, from their Web site (www.psychotherapy.org.uk).

✔ BACP publishes two journals. *Therapy Today* contains readable articles and information whilst *CPR (Counselling and Psychotherapy Research)* is just what it says, including a lot of practitioner research that is, again, very readable and informative for the non-expert.

You can find self-help books in many places. However, some books are of dubious quality and veracity. One source of dependable self-help books is the Books on Prescription service (see next section).

Check out Chapter 20 for suggested counselling books.

Books on Prescription

Many Primary Care Trusts operate a service where they recommend self-help books from an approved list. The GP can prescribe an appropriate self-help book from the range on offer from the public library. The list is a good resource for you to consult to expand your knowledge of common problems (including your own!) and some ideas of what might help people to overcome them. The list is also found on many relevant Web sites (type **books on prescription** into a search engine).

Self-help books can be very useful but they don't help everyone. Get to know the person seeking help and understand his difficulties and strengths first to ascertain whether he's drawn to this method of self-help. Also before recommending a book, be sure to read it yourself, or offer to work through it with the person, who may find the contents overwhelming. A self-help book that you liked may not suit someone else, and he may find a book you didn't personally take to more helpful.

Internet Resources

A vast amount of relevant information is available on the Internet for the listening helper. Keep in mind, however, that you may have a difficult time assessing whether the information is accurate because the content isn't restricted or vetted ahead of time. Unless you know the source or can judge whether a source is trustworthy, be cautious about what you find and always use other sources to compare and appraise what you read. This applies, for example, to the online encyclopaedia Wikipedia (www.wikipedia.co.uk), which has information compiled by its participants.

You can also find *blogs* (Internet 'diaries' or Web logs) and chat rooms focused on particular topics. Chat rooms can provide much-needed support but treat them with caution since you have no way of verifying the people you're chatting with. Abusers find this route gives easy access to vulnerable people.

Be very cautious about meeting in person anyone you meet through the Internet. Be aware that what feels like an apparent intimacy online doesn't mean you know the whole story about the other person.

Here are some Internet resources:

- **The Newcastle, North Tyneside, and Northumberland Mental Health NHS Trust:** www.nnt.nhs.uk/mh/content.asp?PageName=selfhelp
- **The BBC:** www.bbc.co.uk/health/conditions/mental_health
- **BUPA:** hcd2.bupa.co.uk/fact_sheets
- **SANE:** www.sane.org.uk

University Counselling Services

If you have access to the Internet, then you have access to university counselling service Web sites, which are good sources of information about common personal problems including links that they provide to other Web sites. BACP provides a link to these at www.student.counselling.co.uk/guide.html.

Further and Higher Education

A very good way of furthering your understanding of counselling skills is to take a course that gives you safe opportunities to practise skills with tutor support and feedback. Local further education colleges and universities usually offer introductory courses, typically 10 weeks in duration, 2–3 hours per session. The WEA (Workers' Educational Association) operates in many areas and may also have relevant courses. Check out their Web site (www.wea.org.uk) for your nearest regional office. As well as counselling skills, taking other self-development courses such as assertiveness training can be helpful.

Jobs

Jobs involving listening-helper roles are diverse. Many jobs in the voluntary sector include interacting with people seeking help. Acquiring counselling skills can enhance your employability in such roles and is likely to increase your self-confidence for job-seeking. Your local job centre, local newspaper, and Voluntary Action centre can provide information about organisations and possible job opportunities.

If you want to pursue a career in counselling, which entails lengthy training and time to gain experience, you can find out the requirements for becoming a counsellor and for accreditation. Visit BACP's Web site to obtain more information. To gain an idea of the kinds of jobs available, this part of BACP's Web site is helpful: www.bacp.co.uk/education/careersincounselling.html.

Your Local Library

The library can be a daunting place if you're not a regular visitor. However, your local library is a fount of information and usually has friendly and helpful staff who can assist you to navigate through the catalogues, shelves, and services available.

Amongst the information you can find are:

- ✔ Directories of charitable trusts that can fund education.
- ✔ Directories of local voluntary organisations.
- ✔ Books and videos relevant to counselling and counselling skills, including Books on Prescription.

Chapter 19

Ten Great Counselling Books

*T*he books I list in this chapter complement the topics in this book. The authors have useful and interesting things to say and write in an accessible style. If you can't find these particular books on the shelves of your library or bookshop, you may find others by the same authors. If a particular book doesn't connect with you, or is difficult to understand, try another one.

The Skilled Helper

Gerard Egan's *The Skilled Helper* (Wadsworth) explains his three-stage model in detail. The book is in a seventh edition, so has been revisited and revised by him over the years. If you respond best to diagrams and a detailed step-by-step model to guide you, then Egan is for you. He uses some ideas of Carl Rogers, the key figure in the person-centred approach, but Egan combines these with a more directive, goal-orientated approach. A companion workbook has exercises you can do.

Person Centred Counselling in Action

Dave Mearns and Brian Thorne are arguably the best known person-centred writers in the UK. Their *Person Centred Counselling in Action*, second edition (SAGE), is a good introduction to the theory first developed by Carl Rogers. *Developing Person Centred Counselling*, second edition (SAGE), is a follow-on title written by Dave Mearns. The approach is different from writers like

Egan; the Core Conditions (refer to Chapter 8 in this book) are explored in depth rather than taking a skills approach. Exercises and examples are supplied to help you think (and feel) through concepts, taking your personal development further.

Counselling Skills and Theory

Margaret Hough, the author of *Counselling Skills and Theory*, second edition (Hodder Arnold), has written several introductory texts that are easy to read and introduce the reader to the three main theoretical traditions in the counselling field. Other titles by her are *A Practical Approach to Counselling* and *Counselling Skills* (both Longman).

The Sage Handbook of Counselling and Psychotherapy

Colin Feltham has authored and edited many books on counselling, including introductory-level books with Windy Dryden. His style is straightforward. *The Sage Handbook of Counselling and Psychotherapy*, second edition (Sage), co-edited with Ian Horton, gives a valuable overview of counselling, with chapters on most topics you'd encounter on a counselling or counselling skills course. Each chapter has a bibliography which can guide your further reading on that topic.

An Incomplete Guide to Using Counselling Skills on the Telephone

Pete Sanders has written a number of helpful introductory texts on counselling skills, including *An Incomplete Guide to Using Counselling Skills on the Telephone*, second edition (PCCS Books), on using counselling skills on the telephone. The book is a very clear guide to adapting listening skills to the situation where you do not have any visual cues. It takes you through the process in a step-by-step fashion and includes helpful checklists. It's part of the *Incomplete Guide* series – the title doesn't do justice to the book!

Supervision in the Helping Professions

Peter Hawkins and Robert Shohet's book, *Supervision in the Helping Professions*, second edition (Open University Press), is intended for people seeking supervision as well as those offering it. The book encourages you to think about your role as a helper and the support you need to continue to work effectively, including avoiding overload and burnout. It suggests a model for the supervision process and how you can get the right kind of supervision for you as well as exploring what becoming a supervisor means.

Reflective Practice: Writing and Professional Development

Gillie Bolton has written several books on writing as therapy and writing to develop reflective practice and personal growth, including *Reflective Practice: Writing and Professional Development*, second edition (SAGE), which explains the principles of reflective practice and why it's important. Bolton explores ways of helping and encouraging you to write if you find starting to write difficult. This help and encouragement is especially true in another of her books, *The Therapeutic Potential of Creative Writing: Writing Myself* (Jessica Kingsley Publishers).

Referral and Termination Issues for Counsellors

Referral and Termination Issues for Counsellors by Anne Leigh (SAGE) has several chapters of relevance to listening-helpers other than counsellors, in particular the chapter about referring to specialised counselling. She describes different types of counselling – both theoretical approaches and client issues. One chapter covers ethical considerations when referring people on for other help and includes a sample referral letter to a GP and an assessment form, which you can adapt to your own needs and situation.

This title is one of a useful series from Sage, including *Medical and Psychiatric Issues for Counsellors*, second edition, a very helpful companion reference text for people in helping professions. The authors, Brian Daines, Linda Gask, and Tim Usherwood, cover situations that can arise in relation to assessment, referral, ethics and law, as well as medical and psychiatric conditions that you may come across.

On Training to be a Therapist: The Long and Winding Road to Qualification

If you think you'd like to go on to train as a counsellor then *On Training to be a Therapist: The Long and Winding Road to Qualification* is a 'must-read'. Written by John Karter and published by the Open University Press, it was highly recommended to me by a student who wished she'd been aware of the book before she started counselling training. Karter explains and normalises some of the experiences you're likely to have as a trainee, pointing out that each student tends to think they're the only one feeling stupid, isolated, weird, incompetent, and so on, and keeps it to themselves. Result? Every other student thinks they're the only one with those thoughts and anxieties.

Counselling for Toads: A Psychological Adventure

Counselling for Toads: A Psychological Adventure (Routledge) is a lovely little book by Robert de Board and uses the story from *The Wind in the Willows* as the basis for a tale of Toad's experience of counselling by Heron, at the insistence of his friends, Badger, Ratty, and Mole. Toad begins to understand why he has repeating patterns in his life and the reader gains some insight into the counselling process.

Part VII
Appendixes

The 5th Wave   By Rich Tennant

"I don't know if we have irreconcilable
differences or not. We never talk."

In this part . . .

Last but by no means least, here's a vital part of *Counselling Skills For Dummies.* Case studies in Appendix A can enable you to explore different problems that people may come to you with, and shows BEST-I BEST-R in action.

If you really enjoy using counselling skills and want to become qualified, Appendix B explains the steps you need to take on your way to becoming a professional counsellor.

Appendix A

Case Studies and Discussion

• •

*T*his Appendix brings together many aspects covered in this book through the use of case examples. These case examples raise ethical issues, and I include some other ethical dilemmas to get you thinking.

Limits of Listening

The nature of the listening offered by a listening helper is qualitatively different from the average, everyday conversation. The intensity of attention and accuracy of listening, when active listening skills are used well, enables people to open up. Speaking more openly, disclosing experiences, revealing more of the self in an accepting and empathic helping relationship, and making connections with different parts of experience, provides a powerful situation for the speaker. This experience of being attended to and accepted enables the speaker to listen to and accept himself, which puts him in a better position to use his own resources to resolve the issues he brings. The listening helper is also placed in a responsible position. You need to know your limits and the limits of your role, when to use closing skills and when to refer the help-seeker elsewhere. Your aim as a listening helper is to be an enabler – either simply supporting or moving the individual towards action.

As a listening helper your role is to enable a help-seeker to manage the everyday challenges he faces in life, to live life more constructively. The character of problems encountered in family, work, and social life is varied in type and intensity. To some extent what you can offer depends on the amount of time you have and the nature of your primary role in relation to the person who seeks your help (see Chapter 16), in addition to your own comfort and knowledge with different issues (refer to Chapter 5). In some situations you may be able to offer a long-term, open-ended contact whereas in other situations with very clear time limits, you may be limited to just a single contact and this affects the kind of work you can do with a help-seeker. In limited timeframes you need to be more focused and possibly aiming to refer the help-seeker to more appropriate help. In certain situations it's unwise to go into depth and I discuss these situations in Chapter 4.

Always consider whether working with someone in the following situations is appropriate:

✔ When you have a dual relationship with someone, a potential conflict of interest exists between the roles. For example, when you know someone socially, or work with their spouse, who approaches you at work for help.

✔ When you sense (or experience) that the issues cannot be contained in the relatively short time-span you have to offer.

✔ When you recognise that you'd be working outside your knowledge and competence. For example, a person with a specific sexual difficulty would be better consulting his GP and a sexual therapist; someone with OCD (obsessive compulsive disorder) would possibly benefit more from intensive cognitive behavioural therapy.

✔ When the help-seeker has unexplained physical symptoms. Often help-seekers experience physical symptoms. These may be brought on by their state of mind but as a listening helper it is wise to suggest they get checked out by their GP.

✔ When there are child protection concerns. You may be able to offer supportive contact whilst other agencies are involved, but you need to consider the best interests of the child first and then the help-seeker.

✔ When you have concerns about the help-seeker's mental health or suicidal thoughts. Again, it may be possible to offer support alongside other professionals. The help-seeker can find it exhausting to undergo two episodes of listening help in one week, for example, from a community psychiatric nurse and from you. However, many other professionals don't necessarily see their client on a weekly basis and the help-seeker may feel cut adrift without your continued support.

In most of these situations you may feel that offering continued support while the help-seeker approaches specialised help is appropriate. Being in a supportive role means using a more limited range of skills (see Chapter 16 for more on different role types and what they involve). You can find further discussion about limits of competence issues in Chapter 4, which focuses on good practice.

BEST-I BEST-R in Action

The BEST-I BEST-R model is intended to help you think about the whole person of the help-seeker. The initials are an acronym referring to different aspects of a person's experience, namely: *Body, Emotion, Sensation, Thinking,*

Imagery, *Behaviour*, *Environment*, *Spirituality*, *Time*, and *Relationships*. (For more about the BEST-I BEST-R model, refer to Chapter 12.)

To illustrate how the BEST-I BEST-R model can aid your thinking and application of skills using the *three-stage model* (refer to Chapter 6), here are two case studies, each laid out as follows:

1. **The Presenting Problem** is an outline of the presenting issue(s) brought by the help-seeker, which typically emerges in the first part of the initial helping conversation. The Presenting Problem may turn out not to be the key issue.

2. **BEST-I BEST-R** expands on presenting information.

3. A discussion of **Stages One, Two, and Three** of a three-stage model of the listening-help process follows, encouraging you to consider the whole person and how information would emerge from careful listening and prompting offered by the counselling skills attached to each stage:

   • **Stage One:** Mainly focused on establishing the relationship and *exploration* (refer to Chapters 8 and 9).

   • **Stage Two:** Deepens the relationship and increases *understanding*. This is the stage at which the underlying, and possibly key, issues may emerge if you use your skills well (covered in Chapter 10).

   • **Stage Three:** Focused on *action*, evaluation, and ending (refer to Chapter 11).

4. **Discussion** and **Outcome** add other thoughts, possible implications, and conclusions.

Case Study No. 1: Dean, a Struggling Student

Imagine you are Dean's college tutor, seeing him for a routine progress tutorial. You know he hasn't turned some work in on time.

The presenting problem

Dean, age 19, is struggling at college and he confides that he feels he's chosen the wrong direction – he wanted to please his parents but now he's finding concentrating hard and is very unhappy. Use the BEST-I BEST-R model to put Dean's experiences into context.

Body

Dean is lethargic, has stopped exercising and eating properly, and is using cannabis to self-medicate/self-sooth.

This last piece of information about using cannabis will only emerge if you are seen to be trustworthy through the Core Conditions and Stage One skills. You need to be clear about any responsibilities you have to disclose information and break confidentiality (part of Stage One contracting skills, and covered in Chapter 8).

Emotion

Flat, low mood, guilt, disinterest.

Dean may need encouragement to disclose his full range of feelings and for him to recognise their depth (often people bury emotion, being only semi-aware of it themselves). All the levels of empathic responding (see Chapter 9) come into play with increasing trust, so that defences can be lowered (see Chapter 7).

Sensation

Numb, spaced out.

These feelings become evident from what Dean tells you as you use Stage One skills to help him tell his story. You also use your observation of Deans' body language, tone of voice, speed of speech, and so on as well as noticing how your body feels if you have been mirroring his posture and gestures, to gauge his mood.

Thinking

'I'm useless, as a boyfriend, son, and student.' 'My parents will be furious if I change course or drop out of college to do something else.' Tending towards either/or thinking, generalised negative self-evaluations, and making a catastrophe out of events that might not be catastrophic.

Stage One skills help Dean to fill in the gaps in his story – linking thinking, feeling, and behaviour, probing with open questions to understand more about how he thinks. As the conversation moves into Stage Two skills you may be able to challenge Dean's thinking by highlighting gaps, inconsistencies, and contradictions; for example he may indicate that normally he has a close and supportive relationship with his parents.

Imagery

Seeing himself as failing, unlovable, without a future, especially when imagining his parents' responses.

As with Dean's thinking patterns, these images may emerge spontaneously as he responds to Stage One and Two skills, or you may probe with open questions, such as 'I wonder how you see yourself?' He may well respond by referring to imagined parental judgements. A Stage Two challenge could be to prompt him to make his own judgement. As tutor you may have evidence that contradicts his negative self-image, such as work he's handed in, and seeing him with his friends in class or the canteen.

Behaviour

Isolating himself, withdrawing.

If Dean doesn't volunteer information about his behaviour and social contacts, prompting him, using questions like 'How much time do you spend with friends?' is useful. As tutor you may be aware of Dean's attendance, which is a point of challenge to his feelings of uselessness ('So, you're still getting up in the morning and getting to classes, despite feeling down' – a Stage Two challenge).

Environment

Dean's family values are an important influence. He's part of an achieving family (second generation immigrant). He has friendships, even though he's somewhat withdrawn from them. He's been involved in activities outside classes until recently, attends classes, and has a part-time job. He lives in a shared house and goes home every few weeks. He texts his Mum a couple of times a week but avoids speaking to her.

Chapter 14 highlights the importance of life stages. Dean is at a stage of still having some dependence on his family but would be expected to be developing his independence.

Be aware of the danger of letting your own values and life stages influence Dean leading you to move too quickly into Stage Three skills of encouraging *action* in certain directions. For example, you may identify with, and want, Dean to please his parents or conversely want him to break free (see Chapter 6 on the *cycle of change* and Stage Three skills).

Instead, you need to encourage autonomy whilst respecting his values. These values are likely to emerge as you use Stage One and Stage Two skills to get to know him better. His family's values are influenced by their culture, which may be different from your own.

Spirituality

Dean's identity, enjoyment, and sense of the meaning of his life (using 'spirit' in the broadest sense) are in negative flux.

Stage Two of deepening *understanding* might include some questions related to Dean's future – 'If you think of yourself in five years time, how would you like yourself and your life to be?' (notice this isn't about what he wants to be doing but is about him as an individual). This aspect also links to the previous comments about *environment* influences.

Time

An important life stage where Dean is moving into adulthood, choosing a life path. He has only been away from home a few months. A positive sign is that he has taken action early, recognising his need for help now.

A good question to ask yourself, and the help-seeker, is 'why now?' and forms part of your assessment of whether he is able to engage in the helping process and be motivated towards change. What has prompted Dean to open up to you at this particular point?

Time is also an issue in relation to Dean's age: he may have a short-term perspective which could contribute to his sense of catastrophe about his choices and which might be challenged during Stage Two.

Relationships

Keeping away from family and friends. Avoids flat-mates and socialising at college. Has had a relationship break-up.

Dean may be experiencing an acute, unacknowledged and unexpressed, sense of loss in terms of the transitional point of his life and in changed relationships with family and a relationship break-up. Refer to Chapter 14 for more about transition and loss. These revelations are likely to emerge in Stage Two as you demonstrate your empathy at a deeper level. Beware of making assumptions or making an issue about the gender of his partner.

Isolation is linked to the *Behaviour* point above. Social support is very important and worth probing for. Dean does maintain some contacts but is prevented by low mood and shame from getting more support. Stage Two challenging skills might be appropriate to enable Dean to reality-check his shameful feelings, with a view to moving into Stage Three skills to encourage him to rehearse speaking to friends initially, and possibly family.

Discussion

Stage One: In this stage, you can enable Dean to speak openly about his worries and self-beliefs, his behaviour, assumptions, and aspirations. You can help him to express his feelings and thinking without the expectations and judgements he believes family and friends might have. The foundation of Stage One skills is vital here. As tutor you need to work to overcome authority issues so that you can discuss the issues of drug use and not handing in work in a collaborative way.

If Dean hasn't offered information about his family and activities spontaneously it's useful to probe; for example, 'Tell me about a typical day for you, from when you wake up . . .'. Pressing for detail is valuable in terms of information gathering and getting a vivid sense of Dean and his life, which helps the rest of the process, but also in showing interest in him and building the relationship.

Stage Two: With an established relationship of trust Dean may be open to having his assumptions challenged, for example:

- ✔ What evidence is there that his parents would be devastated that Dean isn't happy with his choice of course? An invitation like 'Tell me about your relationship with your parents' can enable Dean to reality-check his preconceptions.

- ✔ Dean is feeling very low in mood, but continues to get up, go to his job, attend classes: What enables him to do that and what does that say about him as a person?

- ✔ What would his friends really think if he told them how unhappy and unsettled he is feeling (perhaps they'd be more supportive)? How would he react if a friend turned to him in similar circumstances?

✔ You might disclose your own personal experience or what you know of other students' experiences about leaving home, or encourage him to ask his friends how they were adjusting to college life, to normalise Dean's experience, provided this didn't appear to minimise his feelings or be patronising.

✔ What effect has the ending of his relationship had on how he's feeling about his future?

✔ Has he considered how he's affected by leaving home (grief reaction and adjustment)?

You can use open questions to invite elaboration. The last two questions in the previous list may uncover unexpected emotion and hidden links for him, things that are on the edge of his awareness, and are an example of deep empathy if they result from your ability to enter his world and follow a hunch (as opposed to making a 'diagnosis'). These questions are framed tentatively, for example, 'You've told me how much finishing with your relationship has hurt you and left you feeling hopeless. I'm wondering if there might be a link with feeling hopeless about your future and this course . . . what do you think?' or, 'I notice that what your parents think is really important to you, and I wonder whether you're missing them, especially since you broke up with your girlfriend.'

After Dean has expressed and explored his concerns and emotions and the picture is more complete you may be able to move on to prioritising and choosing a course of action. You need to assess with Dean how motivated and ready he is to take action and how at risk he is. This assessment includes thinking about how far you can support Dean in your role and where else he can obtain support; also what action you need to take regarding non-submission of assignments.

Stage Three: Dean may rehearse with you the conversations he could have with his parents and with friends. You can encourage him to take more care of himself. Together you can agree any action required as a result of assessing how at risk Dean is of self-harm and mental health problems (just how depressed does he seem to be?).

Outcome

Dependent on how the conversation goes and how confident you feel about Dean's capacity to cope and your capacity to assess that, a variety of outcomes are possible. Several positive indicators show that he's continuing to work and attend classes. However, the conversation revealed some concerning features, so you could:

- ✔ Encourage Dean to see the doctor about his low mood
- ✔ Refer him to the college counselling service
- ✔ Refer him to the college guidance department for advice about courses and the options open to him
- ✔ Offer ongoing tutorial support

The relief Dean feels from taking some action, and discussing his feelings and situation, may be enough to enable him to move on. The result could be a renewed commitment to the course, or a decision to explore a change of direction. Alternatively, he may recognise that he's more severely affected by the losses he's experienced and would benefit from more time to share those with a counsellor. You may feel a personal emotional impact from hearing Dean's story, especially if you're concerned about his safety. Chapter 5 explains how being a listening helper could affect you, Chapter 3 covers taking care of yourself, and Chapter 4 is about good practice, all of which emphasise your need for support.

Case Study No. 2: Louise, a Case of Loss

You are a Personal and Social Education (PSE) teacher in a secondary school. The school secretary, Louise, age 45, buttonholes you one day when the office is empty and asks if she can speak privately to you.

The presenting problem

Louise's dog was stolen a month ago and she's bewildered by how hard she has been hit by it. Family and friends are urging her to get another dog but she feels too wracked by guilt and responsibility for the dog's loss to think about getting another. She feels silly to be so upset. What's worrying her even more is that she's usually quite quiet and mild-mannered, but now she's become very angry and is worried about it affecting her job. She wonders if you can give her any advice or know where she could get some help – she doesn't find it easy to talk to her GP.

Body

Louise gets a lot of headaches. She lacks exercise now she has no dog.

If the question of bodily feelings doesn't emerge spontaneously it's always worth asking about them (Stage One and Two questioning and probing skills). Mood is affected by eating and exercise patterns. If Louise shows signs of being committed to making changes (see Chapter 6 on the *cycle of change*) it may be possible to collaborate in a plan for exercise towards the end of the session (Stage Two and moving into Stage Three).

Emotion

Guilt, shame, grief (sadness), anger.

As with Dean (the first case study), some emotions will emerge as a result of using Stage One listening skills, but deeper levels of emotion may only be revealed when some trust has developed through all the foundation skills of Stage One and later the depth empathy of Stage Two (a more challenging skill).

Some reassurance and normalising of experience may help challenge Louise's shame and self-judgement (see Chapter 14 on loss) and enable her to reveal more of her experience and emotions to you. Many people experience strong feelings of loss when they lose something or someone precious to them, including pets. The feelings about the loss of the dog may stand for other unresolved emotions (see the later 'Discussion' section).

You can possibly move into Stage Three (*action*) which enables her to disclose her feelings to her family, especially her husband, perhaps rehearsing such a conversation with you. Like Dean, she may be ashamed of her 'weakness' and unable to express her full feelings. Louise may assume her husband and family would judge her or not listen.

Sensation

Empty feelings alternate with churning stomach. See also her dreams under 'Imagery' later.

Most people have physical symptoms that reflect their state of mind. Sometimes the physical symptoms are interpreted as signs of physical illness (which, of course, they may be, and you always need to take them seriously). Sensation includes feelings that are hard to distinguish from emotion and yet not always attributable to the body; for example, feeling heavy, distant, light-headed, as if disaster is looming, and so on.

Thinking

'I'm to blame,' 'I don't deserve a dog if I can't take care of one.' Worries and frets a lot, which is part of her normal pattern, but exaggerated at the moment.

These thoughts are likely to emerge as you listen attentively with Stage One active listening skills and the Core Conditions (see Chapters 8 and 9).

Later, when trust is established, it may be possible to challenge Louise's thinking patterns: Is she truly and solely responsible for what happened? What has she learned from the experience (if she did make a mistake)? What would she do differently if she did have another dog? A way of helping some-one to contemplate an action she is feeling averse to is to say something like, 'I'm not suggesting you should get another dog, but just supposing you did, how would you do things differently?' A cautionary note is that moving too quickly into this Second Stage skill without allowing adequate expression and exploration of emotions means that challenging and action-orientated inter-ventions fall flat and may alienate the help-seeker.

Imagery

Louise has dreams about the dog being badly treated or even killed. She wakes in a panic, feeling she should have prevented it happening.

These images are clearly related to Louise's sense of responsibility and feel-ings of guilt. Sometimes people's loss is exacerbated by unexpressed and shameful feelings. For example, maybe Louise was feeling fed up with having to walk the dog and was resentful of it eating into time for herself (although see 'Relationships', later). She may have wished other members of the family took more responsibility. After the dog's disappearance it may have felt as though she had willed it to happen, hence the guilt. People are often prey to magical thinking like this, usually only semiconscious. Continued empathy and close attention to body language, as well as continuing your self-exploration and per-sonal development, enhance your ability to tune in to such hidden ideas.

Behaviour

Angry outbursts with family and friends.

When people feel resentment and shame and don't express it, the feelings can 'leak'. Other trivial things become the outlet of tension and irritation, which is *displacement* (sometimes called 'kicking the cat': refer to Chapter 7). The *understanding* stage (Stage Two skills) can help links to be made between thoughts, emotions, and behaviour so that previously unexplained and puzzling behaviour becomes clearer.

Environment

Generally Louise's family and friends are supportive but they're impatient now. She has always loved her job but thinks she's jeopardising her future by her attitude to people at the moment.

The relationship between you and Louise may come to mirror her relationships with others. You too may find yourself becoming irritated or frustrated with Louise. Rather than suppress such feelings, find ways of being congruent (one of the Core Conditions). Such honesty can be daunting and challenging for both parties, so it needs to be conveyed carefully. For example, you could say, 'As you were saying that, I found myself reacting inside rather like you say your family do, so I wonder if it would help to slow things down and think about what's going on right now for us both.' This comment could lead to some exploration of Louise's feelings in the moment, tracing what they are and where they have come from and their impact on you. This is all Stage Two work of deepening *understanding*. Having someone you can talk with over this kind of exchange (preferably in supervision) is helpful.

Spirituality

Louise used to attend church and have a sustaining belief, but this has been rocked by the loss of her father in painful circumstances last year. She has a sense of lost identity as both daughter and mother (her youngest child has just left home for university).

Going to church used to be important for Louise so this may emerge naturally as she tells her story, supported by your use of Stage One skills. However, she may not have made links between the series of events and how she feels about her identity and faith. This is more likely to emerge as you use deeper empathy and with your awareness of the importance of these issues in people's lives.

Time

Louise is at a life stage transition in several areas – becoming responsible for her mother and an empty-nester simultaneously and possibly entering the menopause which may have implications for her self-esteem.

The issues highlighted under 'Time' and 'Spirituality' are all connected with other things going on in Louise's life over recent times. She may not think to tell you about these events if you don't probe. Ask what else has been going on recently, as part of the Stage One *exploration*. Stage Three, *action*, may include encouragement to speak to a spiritual adviser through her church (Chapter 12 has more on the role of belonging for positive mental health).

Relationships

Louise has to support her mother whilst suppressing her own grief over her father's death in order to help her mother cope. She was close to her father. She's resentful of friends whose children are still at home. The lost dog was an important listener on their solitary walks ('me time'). Louise's husband is at a loss to know how to deal with his much changed wife. She feels unable to confide her 'silly' feelings to him.

Often one event or issue can stand in for another, hence the sense that feelings related to the presenting issue may seem out of proportion. Whenever you have the feeling that a person's reaction is out of proportion, then that is usually a clue to some other important history which hasn't been disclosed. When a person has been supporting another person through loss and grief, her own loss and grief is often suppressed, with unhealthy consequences. The loss of the dog both triggers and, to some degree, allows the suppressed emotions to emerge in a kind of double-dose. You may be tempted to blame other people in Louise's life, such as her husband, but it isn't wise to inflame negativity towards significant people in the help-seeker's life – listen and encourage the expression of feeling, but look for ways to support the help-seeker's network of support and gently challenge isolationism and inwardness towards friends and family. She may be doing her best, but feeling quite baffled and helpless. Remember that you only hear one side of the story, and while you need to empathise with the help-seeker you need to keep some objectivity.

Discussion

Stage One: Because of Louise's guilt and shame you need to offer her plenty of empathy, non-judgemental support, and understanding for her feelings.

Stage Two: Louise doesn't seem to have made a connection between her current feelings and the loss of her father, let alone the other losses and stressors. Stage Two skills can enable Louise to tell her story more fully and begin to make connections. Some normalising of her experiences and reactions may help. You-me talk about the relationship between Louise and yourself may lead to Louise having greater understanding of her relationships with other significant people in her life. However, as a colleague you may decide this isn't appropriate to your situation and role.

Stage Three: Louise probably just needs an arena where she can express some of her feelings. After she realises that the reaction to losing the dog may be exacerbated by other losses and changes in her life she may be less prone to angry outbursts. You could encourage her to write a journal to help express her feelings about the events in her life. However, you could also suggest that on-going support can be valuable to replace some of the 'me –time' she's missing (see Chapter 11 on referral) and being more honest with her family. She may benefit from rehearsing a conversation with her husband.

Outcome

In your role as a colleague it may be inappropriate for you to do more than is involved in this one conversation, apart from an informal follow-up. The decision on what further action to take depends on your individual situation. You can discuss with Louise the possibilities for further support, for example from the charity Cruse who offer free, confidential help to bereaved people.

Thinking about the Ethical Dimension

The case studies in this chapter contain potential ethical issues, as with any person you work with. You need to sensitise yourself to the ethical dimensions of any work that you do because then you are less likely to be taken by surprise (see Chapter 15 on unexpected conversations and Chapter 16 on what can go wrong).

A number of potential ethical issues may arise when working with Dean. These include:

- If Dean were worryingly suicidal but wasn't prepared to seek other appropriate help or tell his parents, you'd have a decision to make about breaking confidentiality. Always consult in such an instance, but your own conscience is important too. Although parents in the USA have tried to sue colleges for not informing them of suicide risk, you aren't obliged, in the UK, to break confidentiality, but you may need to explain to a Coroner's court if he makes a successful suicide attempt. Make sure you know relevant policies and procedures in your organisation.

- Dean's use of cannabis could be subject to disclosure depending on your employer's guidelines. Always make sure you are clear for yourself and to the help-seeker about your responsibilities.

- If Dean agrees to be referred to another service the question arises of how this is to be done. In general it's best for people to make the approach themselves, but they may need support and assistance. If you're seriously worried you may wish to ensure an appointment is made by phoning and then handing the phone to Dean. If you feel you should follow up to make sure that Dean has attended, seek his agreement first.

- Referral may require a referral letter. Discuss with Dean what goes into the referral letter, maybe giving him a copy.

- You may want to challenge Dean's values. Whilst it can be helpful to do this, from a neutral questioning position, the listening helper can be a powerful influence, so this kind of discussion needs to be approached with caution.

Potential ethical issues when working with Louise include:

- Given that you are a colleague of Louise's you need to consider how appropriate it is to go into any depth. Much will depend on your role in the school and Louise's. Extra vigilance will be needed to ensure that there aren't any accidental disclosures to other colleagues, especially in any conversations about Louise's attitudes or performance.

- Louise mentions having headaches. These may be stress-related but you aren't a medical practitioner so encourage her to have a medical check.

- Louise has mentioned her angry feelings towards various people. Some caution is needed about encouraging her to express anger so that it isn't vented on family, friends, or colleagues in a destructive way. Encourage her to discriminate between feeling anger and expressing it and to find safe ways to express her feelings (see Chapter 14 for more on this).

- Louise expresses some doubts about her faith. Beware of taking sides in the internal argument that she is experiencing.

Chapter 4 raises some issues of good practice and introduces an ethical decision-making model. Some of the dilemmas coming up are mentioned in that chapter. I discuss them here in more detail.

- ✔ **A woman comes to talk about her relationship with her teenage son. She thinks that he might be taking drugs and you are beginning to realise her son may be one of your own teenage son's circle of friends at school. What are the issues and what do you do? Should you tell the help-seeker that your son and hers are friends?** Tell her that there may be a conflict of interest because you have a personal connection so it would be best for her to talk to one of your colleagues rather than you. Because you have a duty of confidentiality you cannot divulge this information at home or in school, although you could say without breaking confidence that it has come to your attention that some pupils may be taking drugs.

- ✔ **You have been speaking to someone about his relationship. Quite independently his partner contacts you and asks to speak to you (apparently not aware that her partner has also seen you). What are the issues and how will you respond?** You must not reveal to either party that you have contact with the other because this violates your agreement to confidentiality with each person. Try to avoid working with a person who is involved with someone you are already working with (including child, parent, sibling, and so on). In some situations avoiding seeing the second person is virtually impossible, but try to avoid her, because managing the maintenance of confidentiality is hard. You could find yourself the holder of secrets which are difficult to keep (just remembering what cannot be shared can be tricky). Explain that you aren't able to offer her an appointment and arrange for her to see a colleague wherever possible.

- ✔ **You work as a support worker in an organisation that also offers counselling. A client tells you he came for counselling before but didn't like the way his counsellor wanted to hug him every time they finished a session. They had also had to meet at the counsellor's home once (not usual in this agency) and he felt that the counsellor wanted them to become friends. The client doesn't want to get the counsellor into trouble. What do you do?** Encourage and support (but not press or bully) the client to make a complaint. You can explain that breaking the boundaries in the way this counsellor has done may not have been intentionally abusive but could do great harm to some individuals. You may wonder if the story is true. It's not your responsibility to decide but part of a complaints procedure for the complaint to be investigated by a complaints panel. If the client doesn't want to pursue the complaint you need to do so (see the BACP Ethical Framework which highlights duty to the profession and protection of clients). You may be able to do this whilst protecting the client's identity, but of course this cannot be guaranteed. The client is free to refuse to give you the counsellor's name. This situation will affect the relationship you have with the help-seeker and you need to approach him with great sensitivity. Make sure you get managerial or other support because you're likely to find the situation stressful.

✔ **A teenager comes for a first appointment, bringing a friend (or parent) and asks if the friend can come in with her. What do you do?** Ask for a few minutes alone to discuss whether it is appropriate for the friend to be present. Sometimes people feel they need this kind of support and sometimes they're under subtle pressure to include the person accompanying them. Encourage the accompanying person to wait outside. Check out if the help-seeker is happy to discuss whatever might come up if he insists the friend comes into the room. Suggest to both parties that it is generally best if the friend sits a little to the side and isn't included in the conversation unless specifically asked to take part at any time. Often the friend's presence is a transitional stage – once confidence and trust has been established the friend can usually be dispensed with. Sometimes the friend also has issues, which need to be dealt with separately.

✔ **A person arrives for his appointment with a child – the child-care arrangements have broken down. You know the issues to be discussed are traumatic. What do you do?** Ideally a child shouldn't be present when emotional issues are being discussed. Small children are disruptive to the process – even if they are quiet and well-behaved they usually cannot sustain quiet play for long enough. Even quite small children can absorb what's going on, which can be detrimental to them. Unfortunately the ideal isn't always possible and you may have a difficult choice between working with a child in the room or no help being offered. However, always explain that it's not ideal and ask if arrangements could be made to meet at another time without the child present. You need to be aware of subjects or emotions that the child needs to be protected from hearing or witnessing.

✔ **A journalist is writing an article about your organisation and has asked for contributions about work with certain issues. You have a particularly interesting example of some work you did with a help-seeker. What would you need to consider before submitting anything?** Clients have sometimes recognised themselves (or thought they were recognisable) even when a story about them has made them anonymous, and they have sued. Clients are sometimes willing to have their experiences used to help others, but need to give informed consent. Always get permission in writing.

✓ **You've enrolled on a personal awareness course and discover when you get there that one of the people you have been helping has also enrolled. What are the issues and what do you do?** At your earliest opportunity you need to think about what the issues are for you personally and to discuss with the other person what the issues might be for him. You may want to include the course facilitator in such a discussion. If the work with the help-seeker is ongoing it's best to drop out of the course. If you aren't currently working with him, but there's a likelihood of further work, the same applies.

Appendix B

Becoming a Counsellor

●●●

*H*aving worked with help-seekers and used counselling and listening skills, you may decide that you want to take the skills further. First, you need to be clear why you want to be a counsellor, after which come decisions about training and gaining experience – where and what type. This appendix gives suggestions about the issues you need to consider, such as the entry criteria for professional training, how to judge whether a course is right for you, how to gain experience, and professional accreditation.

Examining Your Motivations for Becoming a Counsellor

Usually people who want to be listening helpers don't initially recognise that they're not being entirely unselfish. For most, they just feel that they want to be helpful, give something to society, perhaps recognise they have been fortunate themselves, or lucky to have survived difficult times. I don't want to undervalue these important motivations but beneath these more obvious motives often lies the 'wounded healer'. This term refers to the fact that people entering helping professions frequently have their own emotional baggage, which is potentially a blessing and a hindrance. On one hand the emotional baggage motivates individuals to help and can enable them to empathise with help-seekers. On the other hand people sometimes, without initially recognising it, want to address their own problems by going through training and by helping others – as if they 'know' at some level that the training will also help them. If the helper avoids facing her own needs, seeing herself as 'fixed' and others as the ones with problems it's potentially harmful to help-seekers (and possibly the listening helper too).

So, on the positive side, if you've experienced emotional and other difficulties, you may be better able to empathise with the struggles of another person, her pain and confusion – understanding that 'pulling yourself together' isn't as straightforward or easy as it seems. You may be able to draw on your own experience to connect with the other person and understand her feelings. Clients often present for counselling because they don't receive this understanding from others.

On the downside, you may believe that because you managed, another person should be able to; or that the nature of her problem is the same as yours; or that what worked for you will work for her. If you manage your emotional difficulties by denying them, you may find unconscious gratification in working with people with emotional problems, and possibly from solving their problems for them. Solving someone else's problem gives you an altruistic buzz and makes you feel safer in an emotionally and physically unsafe, unfair world. However, whilst solving a person's immediate problem can be of some assistance to the client, doing so doesn't empower her or reach the heart of the issues. Chapter 2 discusses the need for personal development for these reasons, which apply even more for someone who offers herself as a counsellor.

A saying in counselling circles is that a client cannot go (emotionally) where the counsellor cannot go. Counselling tutors are aware that some people train in counselling as a way of dealing (or trying to avoid dealing) with unresolved and often unrecognised emotional difficulties and they'll have this in mind when considering your application for a training place.

Counselling is demanding, challenging, draining, and frustrating at times. Chapter 3 highlights the need for self-care for listening helpers. Counselling and the training can also affect your relationships.

Being Realistic about Job Opportunities

Counselling is still an emerging profession, which means that no career path exists. Opportunities for full-time work as a counsellor are limited and competition is strong. During the post-qualification period you need to continue to gain experience, possibly unpaid, before you're likely to be considered for a counselling post. Many posts are sessional and often counsellors have a *portfolio* career – in other words they have several sessional contracts, and possibly some self-employed work as a private practitioner and/or for Employee Assistance Programmes. Because counselling is an emotionally demanding activity there are recommended limits on the number of counselling hours that you should undertake in a week – 20 is generally accepted as an average. Not taking on too much is a matter of ethical and good practise: you'll do yourself and clients a disservice because they won't get the best from you and you may burn out.

Some people continue another career alongside counselling, particularly while they build up experience and reputation. Counselling as a career can be precarious if you depend on private practice (you may not get clients, you may become ill, and so on). Therefore, think wider about potential careers in which you can utilise your counselling skills, such as mental health support work and or being a learning mentor in a school. Many posts benefit from the sophisticated communication skills a counsellor has acquired and if you study at a college or university, you'll likely have a careers guidance service to help you. Some courses arrange careers guidance input during the course.

If you haven't been put off by all this negativity, the benefits of being a counsellor are that it *is* satisfying and rewarding, interesting, intriguing, and stretching: human beings are very complex so the learning has no end. Also, you can often fit your counselling work around other commitments.

Training and Education for Counselling

If you intend to become a professional counsellor and earn your living from counselling, you need to consider becoming accredited by a professional body, such as BACP (British Association for Counselling and Psychotherapy), one of the organisational members of UKCP (United Kingdom Council for Psychotherapy), or an alternative body such as the IPN (Independent Practitioner Network). Many employers now use BACP accreditation (or working towards accreditation, or equivalent) as an application requirement. BACP's accreditation requires applicants to have successfully completed courses that meet certain criteria, mostly at least at diploma level. UKCP accredits psychotherapy courses and requires a longer training period.

A Diploma in Counselling has become the benchmark of a professional qualification. However, you may find diploma courses that don't meet BACP requirements and courses at other levels, such as BA and MA, that do. Make yourself acquainted with professional body requirements and whether a particular course meets these. For simplicity, the information that follows refers to diploma courses.

Most courses at this level have some entry requirements and are likely to use a detailed application form and interview before offering a place. Interviews may be individual, with one or two tutors, and may include group activities under observation. Courses with a good reputation are likely to have more applicants than places and so may only offer places to applicants with more than the minimum criteria. The criteria for selection, outlined in the following sections, usually include:

- ✔ Counselling skills training
- ✔ Other qualifications
- ✔ Counselling skills experience
- ✔ Suitable personal qualities
- ✔ Maturity and life experience
- ✔ Ability to complete the course
- ✔ An understanding of the theoretical model that the course is based on (for some courses)
- ✔ Understanding of the commitment involved

No centralised register of counselling courses exists. For more on finding a course, refer to the later section 'Knowing which course is right for you'.

Counselling skills training

Some courses don't require any previous counselling skills training, but many do. If a course is popular and held in good regard, the institution can afford to be choosy and may require substantial previous counselling skills training, such as a Certificate in Counselling Skills of more than 100 taught hours. If possible, undertake some counselling skills training, even if such training isn't an entry requirement. Taking some counselling skills training is the best way to discover whether this is really the right direction for you – experience has no substitute. You can usually find reputable courses at your local further education college or at a university.

Other qualifications

Courses vary in what qualifications they require for entry. Within the further education sector you can take diploma courses at Level 4 (National Qualifications Framework). Such courses may not require any academic entry qualification.

At higher education level (university), diploma courses may be at undergraduate (Levels 4–6) or postgraduate level (Level 7). The amount of discretion for entry will vary from institution to institution: Some require formal qualifications at 'A' level or degree level, whilst others accredit relevant prior experiential and certificated learning. Some institutions provide courses that equip you for entry at the level required. When you apply make sure you give as much information as you can about courses you've done – their subject matter, level, and duration (for counselling skills courses give the number of hours of attendance). Don't assume the institutions will know details about any of the courses you have taken.

As well as looking at college and university Web sites, where you can find information about entry requirements, you may be able to talk to a course tutor informally or email her to check out whether your qualifications make you eligible for entry to the course. In the first instance, try contacting the administrator of the subject area, who may be able to send you additional information and answer some queries or tell you how to contact a tutor. The central enquiry telephone number or e-mail address usually directs you to the administrator of counselling courses. Open days or evenings are good opportunities for getting your questions answered.

Counselling skills experience

Most courses are likely to expect that you are using and developing your counselling skills studies in a people-related job on a paid or voluntary basis. Selectors will want to know how you have related your classroom learning to the real world. Typically, candidates are currently working, or have previously worked, in jobs such as nursing or teaching with particular responsibilities for emotional well-being – such as an oncology nurse or offering pastoral care – or are volunteering in organisations concerned with emotional welfare such as The Samaritans, Victim Support, and so on. Whatever you consider your experience to be, you're the one who needs to demonstrate that it's relevant.

Suitable personal qualities

Chapter 6 discusses the personal qualities expected of a listening helper. The selectors look for evidence of those qualities in your application and at interview. As part of your application you may be asked for a written personal statement about why you are applying and why you want to be a counsellor. You will be asked to supply references.

Maturity and life experience

Maturity and wisdom don't necessarily come with age or are absent in youth. Maturity means that you demonstrate certain personal qualities (see Chapter 6), and that you:

- ✔ Have a reasonable degree of self-knowledge, including your own prejudices
- ✔ Understand something about how you are perceived by others
- ✔ Have faced and learned from difficult experiences
- ✔ Have the ability to stand back and reflect
- ✔ Understand what motivates you to be a counsellor (both positive and less altruistic drivers, which everyone has)

Counselling courses often used to have a minimum age of 28. Although this age limit is no longer universal, many courses are cautious about offering places to people under the age of about 24. You need to demonstrate your maturity by being able to articulate what you have found out about yourself from your experiences. Age is not a bar. The average age of students on diploma training courses seems to have dropped over the past decade but the range remains wide, from early 20s to 60+.

Don't assume that age assures you of fulfilling the criteria of maturity and wisdom – like any other applicant you need to demonstrate what you've found out about yourself. Most course selectors are interested to know whether you have had personal therapy or what your attitude is to receiving personal therapy.

Ability to complete the course

A number of issues fall under this heading, all related to commitment and personal resources.

- ✔ **Time:** Diploma courses are usually demanding in terms of the time commitment:

  - **Attendance.** Normally part-time, around one full day per week (or equivalent) over 2 years. This may not sound a lot but fitting studying in with work and personal commitments can be challenging. Courses are likely to have an 80 per cent attendance requirement, especially if they are BACP accredited. This is because much of the training is *experiential*, in other words, it involves learning from experience through exercises and discussions with other students. Training involves personal disclosure, and that is risky and challenging, so it's vital that the group works together consistently to create a climate of trust which can facilitate such a learning environment.

- **Private study.** Normally twice as much private study as attendance is nominally expected. Most people probably don't achieve this, but you do need time to read and reflect, as well as to prepare assignments.

- **Personal therapy.** You may be required to undertake your own regular personal therapy as part of the commitment to personal development. Not all courses require this, but you would almost certainly find it beneficial in supporting and challenging you. Those institutions that do insist on personal therapy for students may ask for an ongoing commitment throughout the course, or maybe just a certain number of hours over the course period, 20 or 40 for example.

- **Counselling practice placement.** This may be from the start of the course or later. BACP requires a minimum of 100 completed hours of client work (no-shows and cancellations do not count) and some courses ask for more. To achieve this you need to set aside a half-day or evening every week for a year. Expect to attend relevant meetings and training at the organisation where the placement takes place.

- **Supervision.** Your placement practice will need to be supervised, normally at least 1½ hours per month. Supervision may be part of course attendance but could be extra. The placement may require you to have specialist supervision in addition to course requirements.

✔ **Finance:** The cost of diploma training is usually higher than other courses of similar level and length. This is due to small classes for certain parts of the course. Typically, personal development activities, in-class counselling/skills practice, and counselling supervision will have no more than 12 students with one tutor.

When enquiring about costs, be aware that some courses are 'all inclusive' and others have hidden extras. The extras are generally residential teaching costs (often a feature of counselling training), supervision, and personal therapy. Of course you also need to take into account the costs of travel, books, buying food and drink if you aren't able to supply yourself with packed meals and beverages (studying can make you hungry!), and child-care (some institutions have crèches).

Some applicants are lucky enough to have support from employers – either in terms of time to attend (make sure you are clear about the course attendance requirements) or financial support (again, make sure you know the full costs). Some institutions provide remission of fees for those on low incomes – contact the student support and guidance department of the institution. Ask at your local library for information about charitable trusts that support educational improvement. Local authorities rarely give financial support nowadays but it is always worth asking. With approaches for financial support from any source always make sure you have as much information about the course and course costs as possible.

✔ **Emotional strength and support:** Counselling training is tough. All further education and personal development tends to be unsettling because it leads to change, which has ripple effects on your life and others connected to you. Counselling courses expect you to explore yourself in depth and tend to lead to the uncovering and confronting of issues, some of which you may have thought were dealt with. You will almost certainly reconsider your life choices and change your behaviour in various ways.

In addition to self-discovery, you have to meet deadlines whilst coping with the normal ups and downs of life; for example your dependents become ill or troublesome, your work becomes more demanding, you get ill yourself. Are you sufficiently organised and able to manage stress and frustration? Universities have assessment regulations, which can be very strict, in the interests of fairness between students. They expect you to plan for normal life events and may refuse to grant extensions for the submission of assessed work unless you submit very good reasons, with evidence.

If you have recently undergone a major life event, such as bereavement, you may want to consider whether you need to take time to adjust before embarking on an unsettling period that such a course represents. Because counselling trainers understand how hard the course is they will be interested in whether and where you get support. See Chapter 3 for discussion of this issue.

One of the paradoxical aspects of any counselling course is the power of the group experience. On the one hand being in a diverse group can provide exciting and frightening challenges. On the other it can bring tremendous support and encouragement and firm friendships can develop. Some groupings continue to meet long after a course has finished. During the course you are in various group sizes, from pair and trio work through to medium-sized (6–12) groups, to larger ones (20+). If you find being in groups difficult you will feel challenged.

✔ **Study and academic ability:** Courses vary as to the academic level required. If you undertake a course at a higher academic level than you have previously experienced you may find that you struggle. Find out what support the institution has for helping you reach the necessary level during the course. Some colleges and universities have a commitment to widening participation – this means encouraging students who are educationally disadvantaged – by providing academic support. This support can take the form of tutorials, additional courses or workshops, drop-in study support, and the assessment of needs and facilities for students who have disabilities such as dyslexia or other impediments to learning. Don't be afraid or too proud to ask about, and take up, these supports. Don't rely on fellow students to support you – of course they'll help but expecting *regular* support from them isn't fair to their studies.

Course selectors may want to discover whether you have the capacity to complete the course successfully. You may be able to demonstrate ability through other means than academic qualifications. Some academic qualifications do not enable people to write well. One of the features of many counselling trainings is the development of the ability to write in a way that incorporates personal awareness into an academic style of writing, which is very different from what students have usually experienced in previous academic study. Most courses will require essays, presentations, audio- and video-recorded counselling with critical analysis, self- and tutor-assessed tasks, logs of counselling and/or skills activity, and reflective writing, such as keeping a journal.

Understanding of the commitment involved

A sense of commitment is important. You need to decide whether this is the right time in your life and whether counselling is something you really want to do. Think through all the factors that could erode your commitment over the next two years and what will sustain your motivation. See Chapter 9 about motivational interviewing which you can apply to yourself. Three factors that can help maintain your commitment are your respect for the teaching staff, the quality of the teaching delivery and content, and the peer relationships you develop.

You need to be aware that most people do not immediately move into paid work as a counsellor following qualification. Most jobs ask for BACP accreditation (or working towards accreditation). Accreditation requires 450 hours of client work experience. On the course you probably accrue between 100 and 150. It can take a year or two to amass enough further experience and gaining the initial 100+ hours can prove frustrating, as in some placements supply and throughput of clients can be unreliable for a variety of reasons. When applying for jobs remember that you have prior skills, knowledge, and experience that may be relevant for the job and make sure to highlight them.

Qualification doesn't mean the end of training and learning. If you want to become accredited, you need to continue with your professional development by undertaking further courses. The diploma is a starting point. Beyond this foundation you probably want to go on to develop specialised knowledge in particular areas. This additional knowledge could be substantial, such as provided in courses in couple counselling and sexual abuse. You could also study a course concentrating on in-depth development of a theoretical approach (perhaps an additional one to the one you trained in), or you could consider more focused and practical study, such as workshops on particular skills or topics like updating on legal issues.

Knowing which course is right for you

Several factors can influence your choice of course:

- **Practicality:** Most courses are part-time. If you want to pursue full-time study, you'll probably need to move area, with all that doing so entails. Institutions often provide assistance with finding accommodation. Courses are available in further education colleges and universities and some private training providers offer courses accredited by universities or other recognised accreditors.

  If you pursue part-time study, then the proximity and course calendar are more or less important, dependent on your personal circumstances. Remember that the course itself is demanding so consider whether you have the time and energy to travel long distances, perhaps struggling with public transport or parking. If you are in employment make sure that your employers recognise the demands of the course and are ready to make allowances or offer support. The pattern of the teaching (day, evening, weekend) is important, especially because courses usually have a minimum attendance requirement and expect punctuality.

  If you want to work within the voluntary sector and not undertake an independent Diploma in Counselling then you could consider an organisation such as Cruse or Mind or one of the many local organisations that offer specialised counselling and often provide their own training.

  The demands and support of your family will be crucial in helping or hindering your progress. Take time to plan carefully and make provision for contingencies. If you have holidays or a pregnancy planned that are going to impact on attendance, talk to the course tutors. They want you to be able to complete the course successfully so will give you sensible advice.

✔ **Academic level:** The choice of academic level is very personal. Given the practical considerations, your choice of institution and academic level may be limited or nonexistent. However, if you find a range of levels in your area, how are you going to choose?

First, the entry criteria may bring down the choice if you don't have the academic entry qualifications. Second, what level of academic challenge are you looking for? If you already have a degree or higher qualifications you may not be concerned about the academic challenge – some prefer not to place any greater demand on themselves than necessary. If you have ambitions to achieve a degree then it could be worth looking either for a degree course or a diploma that can be topped-up to degree level with additional study. If you have a psychology degree and want to pursue BPS registration, then you need Masters level study.

Finally, what are your future ambitions? At the moment the level of qualification is generally unimportant in the job field, but this could be changing. The government has been looking at the regulation of counselling through the Health Professions Council (HPC) and a suggestion has been made that those not meeting whatever criteria are set will not be able to use the title of counsellor. At the time of writing, the situation is still ambiguous. However, if your ambitions lie within medical settings (or settings funded through the public health sector) then you may need to be concerned about academic level. All but one of the professions currently regulated through the HPC are qualified to degree level. BACP is a good source of information on the up-to-date situation. In voluntary settings with their own training the academic level may be irrelevant. If you want to pursue a career in counselling my advice would be to achieve the highest level you can manage – you never know how useful that might be in the future.

✔ **Theoretical orientation:** Diploma courses, especially those that have achieved BACP course accreditation, have an identified theoretical model. This may be a 'pure' model, such as psychodynamic or cognitive behavioural, or may be 'integrative'. An integrative course uses an amalgamation of theories and may be a particular mix favoured by the course tutor team – you need to know what that mix is. See the discussion below on theoretical models and the choices you may have. Selectors may check your understanding of the model they offer to make sure that you are in sympathy with it.

One of the bewildering things about counselling for the novice is the proliferation of theoretical models (more than 400). My personal view is that none is superior to another or has the monopoly on wisdom. On occasion a client may benefit more from the techniques and approach of one particular theory, but mostly the client benefits from the relationship with the counsellor and the ability of the counsellor to adapt to the needs and expectations of the particular client. In view of this, you must choose, as a starting point, a theoretical approach that appeals to or makes sense to you and which you can believe in whilst maintaining a critical stance towards it.

✔ **Reputation:** Whichever institution you choose, first consider its reputation – both the whole institution and the counselling department. Here are some questions you can ask:

- What is their standing in the local area or region?

- Do they have rigorous entry criteria?

- What is the learning experience and standard of teaching like?

- Can you have an opportunity to meet the tutors and/or current and ex-students and form an opinion?

- Do they have many drop-outs from the course?

- How is the placement activity monitored?

- Are students from this course welcomed by placement providers?

- Is the course influenced by research into counselling and are course materials up to date?

- What do graduates of the course go on to do?

- What support does the institution offer students?

- Is the course accredited by a professional body such as BACP?

BACP has a list of courses accredited by them, available online at `www.bacp.co.uk/education/training.html` (click on accredited courses and then on your region).

You may find that some questions are difficult to get answers to but the attitude of tutors to answering questions may influence your feelings about the course. In the final analysis, if you don't feel confident and comfortable with the course ethos and tutor styles, then the course will be harder for you to complete.

Gaining Experience

You need to gain experience in applying your counselling skills before applying for counsellor training by working in some kind of supportive role with people. Face-to-face experience, with adults or children, is preferable, but telephone help-lines also give valuable experience. You have many possibilities for gaining this experience within the voluntary sector. Most towns have a volunteer bureau where you can find information about suitable volunteering opportunities. If you're a college or university student, volunteering schemes are probably available within your institution, as well as mentoring schemes or peer support activities. A number of national organisations such as The Samaritans and Cruse offer good training and support for the work they do. In addition local specialist organisations are well organised and offer training and support. You may have to try a couple of different types of voluntary work before you find your own niche and fulfilment, but you can narrow down your search by asking yourself if you're interested in a particular type of activity or client group (or if one definitely *doesn't* interest you).

You may be lucky enough to undertake your counselling placement (a normal diploma course requirement of 100 hours minimum of face-to-face counselling) within the same organisation. You're not normally expected, or encouraged, to begin counselling people before you start diploma training. However, begin thinking about your counselling placement early because good placements that offer support and training can be difficult to come by. Your diploma course will provide you with guidelines and some support in relation to placements.

If you're in employment, you may have opportunities to use your listening skills in some role there. This could be informal or as a result of speaking to your manager, perhaps during appraisal if your organisation has an appraisal system. If you take on a formal listening role then take care to discuss the boundaries of your roles so that you and management are clear about what is expected of you and can offer you the support you need (see Chapter 4 for more information about maintaining good practice).

Acquiring Accreditation

If you want to develop a career as a professional counsellor, you need to know about accreditation. The two major bodies in the counselling and psychotherapy field are BACP (British Association for Counselling and Psychotherapy) and UKCP (United Kingdom Council for Psychotherapy). Each has an accreditation scheme. Before you embark on counselling training, gain some understanding of these two bodies and what accreditation involves so that you have the required elements of training when it comes to accreditation. More information about accreditation and how to contact these professional bodies is in Chapter 18.

Index

FOR DUMMIES®

Do Anything. Just Add Dummies

UK editions

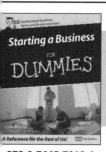

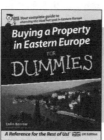

Buying and Selling a Home
978-0-7645-7027-8

Renting Out Your Property
978-0-470-02921-3

Buying a Property in Eastern Europe
978-0-7645-7047-6

PERSONAL FINANCE

Investing
978-0-7645-7023-0

Personal Finance & Investing All-in-One
978-0-470-51510-5

Bookkeeping
978-0-470-05815-2

BUSINESS

Starting a Business
978-0-7645-7018-6

Marketing
978-0-7645-7056-8

Business Plans
978-0-7645-7026-1

Answering Tough Interview
Questions For Dummies
(978-0-470-01903-0)

Arthritis For Dummies
(978-0-470-02582-6)

Being the Best Man
For Dummies
(978-0-470-02657-1)

British History
For Dummies
(978-0-470-03536-8)

Building Self-Confidence
For Dummies
(978-0-470-01669-5)

Buying a Home on a Budget
For Dummies
(978-0-7645-7035-3)

Children's Health
For Dummies
(978-0-470-02735-6)

Cognitive Behavioural Therapy
For Dummies
(978-0-470-01838-5)

Cricket For Dummies
(978-0-470-03454-5)

CVs For Dummies
(978-0-7645-7017-9)

Detox For Dummies
(978-0-470-01908-5)

Diabetes For Dummies
(978-0-470-05810-7)

Divorce For Dummies
(978-0-7645-7030-8)

DJing For Dummies
(978-0-470-03275-6)

eBay.co.uk For Dummies
(978-0-7645-7059-9)

English Grammar For Dummies
(978-0-470-05752-0)

Gardening For Dummies
(978-0-470-01843-9)

Genealogy Online
For Dummies
(978-0-7645-7061-2)

Green Living For Dummies
(978-0-470-06038-4)

Hypnotherapy For Dummies
(978-0-470-01930-6)

Life Coaching For Dummies
(978-0-470-03135-3)

Neuro-linguistic Programming
For Dummies
(978-0-7645-7028-5)

Nutrition For Dummies
(978-0-7645-7058-2)

Parenting For Dummies
(978-0-470-02714-1)

Pregnancy For Dummies
(978-0-7645-7042-1)

Rugby Union For Dummies
(978-0-470-03537-5)

Self Build and Renovation For
Dummies
(978-0-470-02586-4)

Starting a Business on
eBay.co.uk For Dummies
(978-0-470-02666-3)

Starting and Running an Online
Business For Dummies
(978-0-470-05768-1)

The GL Diet For Dummies
(978-0-470-02753-0)

The Romans For Dummies
(978-0-470-03077-6)

Thyroid For Dummies
(978-0-470-03172-8)

UK Law and Your Rights
For Dummies
(978-0-470-02796-7)

Writing a Novel and Getting
Published For Dummies
(978-0-470-05910-4)

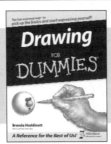

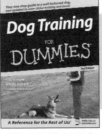

FOR DUMMIES®

The easy way to get more done and have more fun

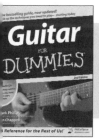

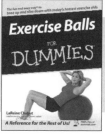
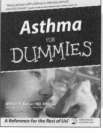

FOR DUMMIES®

Helping you expand your horizons and achieve your potential

INTERNET

978-0-470-12174-0

978-0-471-97998-2

978-0-470-08030-6

Also available:

Building a Web Site For Dummies, 2nd Edition (978-0-7645-7144-2)

Blogging For Dummies (978-0-471-77084-8)

Creating Web Pages All-in-One Desk Reference For Dummies, 3rd Edition (978-0-470-09629-1)

eBay.co.uk For Dummies (978-0-7645-7059-9)

Web Analysis For Dummies (978-0-470-09824-0)

Web Design For Dummies, 2nd Edition (978-0-471-78117-2)

DIGITAL MEDIA

978-0-7645-9802-9

978-0-470-04894-8

978-0-7645-9803-6

Also available:

BlackBerry For Dummies (978-0-471-75741-2)

Digital Photo Projects For Dummies (978-0-470-12101-6)

Digital Photography All-In-One Desk Reference For Dummies (978-0-470-03743-0)

Photoshop CS3 For Dummies (978-0-470-11193-2)

Podcasting For Dummies (978-0-471-74898-4)

Zune For Dummies (978-0-470-12045-3)

COMPUTER BASICS

978-0-7645-8958-4

978-0-470-05432-1

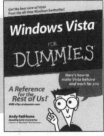

978-0-471-75421-3

Also available:

Macs For Dummies, 9th Edition (978-0-470-04849-8)

Office 2007 All-in-One Desk Reference For Dummies (978-0-471-78279-7)

PCs All-in-One Desk Reference For Dummies, 3rd Edition (978-0-471-77082-4)

Upgrading & Fixing PCs For Dummies, 7th Edition (978-0-470-12102-3)

Windows Vista All-in-One Desk Reference For Dummies (978-0-471-74941-7)

Windows XP For Dummies 2nd Edition (978-0-7645-7326-2)
